Mary Storrs Haynes

The crown of life

From the writings of Henry Ward Beecher

Marcus Lafayette Byrn

Useful Knowledge

ISBN/EAN: 9783337248703

Printed in Europe, USA, Canada, Australia, Japan

Cover: Foto ©Thomas Meinert / pixelio.de

More available books at **www.hansebooks.com**

USEFUL KNOWLEDGE

OR,

REPOSITORY OF VALUABLE INFORMATION.

BY

M. LAFAYETTE BYRN, M. D., Graduate of the University of the City of New York, Author of "Mystery of Medicine Explained," "Poisons in our Food," etc.

New York:

PUBLISHED BY M. LAFAYETTE BYRN, M. D.,

No. 80 Cedar Street.

1872.

PREFATORY.

Every one who reads this volume may well be led to say it is a "strange Book" in its combination, of many subjects of much value in a small space, and at a remarkably small price. Of the value of a good receipt book, none can tell until they have one and lose it and then not be able to get another; such a receipt book is the one now offered to the public. Besides its value as a receipt book, it contains information on a variety of other subjects of great importanee, which must be read to be fully appreciated. It is hoped that this little work may be the means of imparting knowledge which may be a blessing to those who read its pages.

M. L. B.

NEW YORK, 1870.

VALUABLE RECIPES.

——o——

Court Plaster.—Court Plaster is made by repeatedly brushing over stretched sarcenet with a solution of 1 part of isinglass in 8 of water mixed with 8 parts of proof spirit, and finishing with a coat of tincture of benzoin, or of balsam of Peru.

Eye Water.—Extract of lead 2 dr., wine of digitalis 2 dr., tincture of opium 2 dr., water a pint.

Godfrey's Cordial.—The Philadelphia College of Pharmacy, to prevent the mischief arising from the different strengths of this compound, directs it to be prepared as follows:—Dissolve 2½ oz. of carbonate of potash in 26 pints of water, add 16 pints of treacle, heat together over a gentle fire till they simmer, remove the scum, and, when sufficiently cool, add ½ oz. of oil of sassafras dissolved in two pints of rectified spirit, and 24 fluid ounces of tincture of opium previously mixed. The old wine measure is here intended. It contains about 16 minims of laudanum, or rather more than 1 gr. of opium in each fluid ounce.

Godfrey's Smelling Salts.—Dr. Paris says it is prepared by resubliming volatile salts with subcarbonate of potash and a little spirit of wine. It is usually scented with an alcoholic solution of essential oils.

Stoughton's Elixir.—Gentian 36 oz., serpentary 16 oz., dried orange peel 24 oz., calamus aromaticus 4 oz., rectified spirit, and water, of each 6 galls., old measure.

Swain's Vermifuge.—Worm seed 2 oz., valerian, rhubarb, pink root, white agaric, of each 1½ oz.; boil in sufficient water to yield 3 quarts of decoction, and add to it 30 drops of oil of tansy, and 45 drops of oil of cloves, dissolved in a quart of rectified spirit.

Dr. Latham's Cough Linctus.—Dover's powder ½ dr., compound powder of tragacanth 2 dr., syrup of tolu ½ oz., confection of hips, and simple oxymel, of each 1 oz.; a teaspoonful 3 or 4 times a day.

Cure for Piles.—Powdered nut-gall 2 dr., camphor 1 dr., melted wax 1 oz., tincture of opium 2 dr. Mix.

Morrison's Pills.—Consist of 2 parts of gamboge, 3 of aloes, 1 of colocynth, and 4 of cream of tartar; made into pills with syrup.

Calico Printers' Fast Dyes.

DYE STUFFS used by the Calico Printers for producing fast colors. The mordants are thickened with gum, or calcined starch, when applied with the block, roller, plates or pencil.

Black—The cloth is impregnated with acetate of iron, (iron liquor,) and dyed in a bath of madder and logwood.

Purple—The preceding mordant of iron, diluted; with the same dyeing bath.

Crimson—The mordant for purple, united with a portion of acetate of alumina, or red mordant, and the above bath.

Red—Acetate of alumina is the mordant, and madder is the dye-stuff.

Pale Red of different shades—The preceding mordant, diluted with water, and a weak madder bath.

Brown or Pompadour—A mixed mordant, containing a somewhat larger proportion of the red than of the black, and the dye of madder.

Orange—The red mordant; and a bath, first of madder, and then of quercitron.

Yellow—A strong red mordant; and the quercitron bath, whose temperature should be considerably under the boiling point of water.

Blue—Indigo, rendered soluble and greenish-yellow colored, by potash and orpiment. It recovers its blue color by exposure to air, and thereby also fixes firmly on the cloth. An indigo vat is also made, with that blue substance diffused in water with quick-lime and copperas. These substances are supposed to deoxidize indigo, and at the same time to render it soluble.

Golden-dye—The cloth is immersed alternately in a solution of copperas and lime-water. The protoxide of iron precipitated on the fibre, soon passes, by absorption of atmospherical oxygen, into the golden-colored deutoxide.

Buff—The preceding substances in a more dilute state.

Calico Printers' Fast Dyes Continued.

Blue Vat—In which white spots are left on a blue ground of cloth, is made by applying to those points a paste composed of a solution of sulphate of copper and pipe-clay ; and after they are dried, immersing it, stretched on frames, for a definite number of minutes, in the yellowish green vat, of 1 part of indigo, 2 of copperas, and 2 of lime, with water.

Green—Cloth dyed blue, and well washed, is imbued with the aluminous acetate, dried, and subjected to the quercitron bath.

In the above cases, the cloth, after receiving the mordant paste, is dried, and put through a mixture of cow-dung and warm water. It is then put into the dyeing vat or copper. [Ure Dict. Chem. &c.

Dyes for Bones and Ivory.—1. (Red.) Make an infusion of Cochineal in water of ammonia, then immerse the pieces therein, having previously soaked them for a few minutes in very weak acquafortis and water.

1. (Black.) Immerse the pieces in a weak solution of nitrate of silver, for a short time, then expose them to the sunlight.

2. (Green.) Steep in a solution of verdigris to which a little acquafortis has been added.

3. (Yellow.) Boil for 1 hour in a solution made with 1 pound of alum in 1 gallon of water, then take out the pieces and steep them in a decoction made with ½ lb. of turmeric in 2 quarts of water. lastly, mix the two liquors, and boil them therein for 1 hour.

4. (Blue.) Stain them green, then steep them in a hot and strong solution of pearlash.

Remarks.—The bones of living animals may be dyed by mixing madder with their food. The bones of young pigeons may thus be tinged of a rose color in 24 hours, and of a deep scarlet in 3 days ; but the bones of adult animals take a fortnight to acquire a rose color. The bones nearest the heart become tinged soonest. In the same way extract of logwood will tinge the bones of young pigeons purple.

Celebrated Washing Mixture.

Dissolve a half pound of soda in a gallon of boiling water and pour upon it a quarter pound of lime. After this has settled, cut up 10 ounces of common bar soap, and strain the solution upon it, and mix perfectly. Great care must be taken that no particles of lime are poured upon the soap. Prepare the mixture the evening before washing.

DIRECTIONS—To 10 gallons of water add the above preparation when the water is boiling, and put the clothes in while boiling. Each lot of linen must boil half an hour, and the same liquid will answer for three batches of clothes. The white clothes must be put in soak over night, and if the collars and wrist bands are soaped and rubbed slightly, so much the better. Clean cold water may be used for rinsing. Some prefer boiling them for a few moments in clean blueing water, and afterwards rinse in cold water. The clothes may not appear perfectly white while wet, but when dry will be clean white.

MUSK.—Artificial Musk is made by dropping 3½ ounces of nitric acid on one ounce of rectified oil of amber. In a day or two, a black substance is produced, which smells similar to genuine musk.

MAHOGANY FURNITURE.—Stains and spots may be taken out of mahogany furniture by the use of a little aquafortis, or oxalic acid and water, by rubbing the part with the liquid, by means of a cork, till the color is restored, observing afterwards to well wash the wood with water, and to dry and polish as usual.

PASTE, RAZOR.—Levigated oxide of tin [prepared putty powder] 1 ounce, powdered oxalic acid ¼ oz., powdered gum 20 grains, make it into a stiff paste with water, and evenly and thinly spread it over the strop. With very little friction, this paste gives a fine edge to the razor, and its efficiency is still further increased by moistening it.

PASTE, SHAVING.—White Wax, Spermaceti, and Almond Oil; melt, and while warm, beat in 2 squares of Windsor soap, previously reduced to a paste with rose water.

How to Make Artificial Honey.

To 10 lbs. of sugar add 3 lbs of water, 40 grains of Cream of Tartar, 10 drops of Essence of Peppermint, and 3 lbs. of Comb Honey.

Dissolve the sugar in the water, and take off the scum arising therefrom—then dissolve the Cream of Tartar in a little warm water, which you will add with some little stirring—then add the Honey, heat to a boiling point, and stir it for a few moments.

THE HUNTER'S SECRET—To Catch Game—such as Mink, Musk Rats, Weasels, Raccoons, Otter, &c.—Take one ounce of valerian, ¼ ounce of commercial musk, one pint of whiskey—Mix together, and let it stand for two weeks. Put a few drops of this on your bait.

PRESERVATION OF HAMS.—Most grocers, dealers in hams, and others, who are particular in their meat, usually take the precaution to case each one, after it is smoked, in canvass, for the purpose of defending it from the attacks of the little insect, the dermestes lardarius, which, by laying its eggs in it, soon fills it with its larvæ, or maggots. This troublesome and expensive process may be altogether superseded by the use of pyroligneous acid. With a painter's brush, dipped in the liquid, one man, in the course of a day, may effectually secure two hundred hams from all danger. Care should be taken to insinuate the liquid into all the cracks, &c., of the under surface. This method is especially adapted to the preservation of hams in hot climates.

INDIAN RUBBER BLACKING.—(BRYANT AND JAMES'S PASTE.)—Ivory black sixty lbs.; treacle forty-five lbs.; good vinegar and oil of vitriol, of each twelve lbs.; Indian rubber oil nine lbs.; mix.

II. LIQUID—Ivory Black 60 lbs., treacle 45 lbs., gum (dissolved) 1 lb., vinegar (No. 24) 20 gallons, oil of vitriol 24 lbs., Indian rubber oil 9 lbs. Mix.

Remarks.—The Indian rubber oil is made of caoutchouc eighteen ounces, dissolved in rape oil nine lbs. by means of heat. The ingredients are mixed together in the same order and manner as common blacking.

ALTERATIVE SYRUP.—American Sarsaparilla, Yellow Dock root, Black Alder bark. Prickly Ash bark. Burdock root, Sassafras bark, Wintergreen, of each one ounce, make four pints of syrup. Dose, a wine-glassful, 3 or 4 times a day. This syrup is useful in all diseases where the blood or general system needs purifying.

BITE OF A MAD DOG.—A writer in the NATIONAL INTELLIGENCER, says, that spirits of Hartshorn is a certain remedy for the bite of a mad dog. The wound, he adds, should be constantly bathed with it, and three or four doses, diluted, taken inwardly, during the day. The hartshorn decomposes chemically the virus insinuated into the wound, and immediately alters and destroys its deleteriousness. The writer, who resided in Brazil for sometime, first tried it for the bite of a scorpion, and found that it removed pain and inflammation almost instantly. Subsequently, he tried it for the bite of the rattlesnake, with similar success. At the suggestion of the writer, an old friend and physician tried it in cases of Hydrophobia, and always with success.

CANKER POWDER.—Powdered Golden Seal Blue Cohosh, of each one ounce. A superior remedy for Canker in the mouth and stomach. Steep one teaspoonful of this powder in a gill of hot water for one hour, then strain and sweeten with loaf sugar. Gargle the throat for 10 or 15 minutes at a time with this infusion ; likewise a table-spoonful may be held in the mouth for some minutes ; after which drink two table-spoonsful of it. Repeat it several times a day, until a cure is effected.

COUGH CANDY.—Cheap. Safe, and Excellent.—Take equal parts of Boneset, Spikenard, Elecampane, Comfrey, and Wild Cherry bark ; make a strong decoction ; to every pint of this decoction add molasses a pint ; extract of liquorice, four ounces, and honey four ounces. Boil down to a proper consistence for forming a candy, when add oil of tar, one drachm, essence of sassafras, two teaspoonfuls. Work it up into a candy form by hand in the usual way. It may be eaten freely.

BRONZING OF MEDALS—Ornaments of Copper, Electrotypes, &c.—Having thoroughly cleaned and polished the surface of the specimen, with a brush apply the common crocus powder, previously made into a paste with water. When dry, place it in an iron ladle, or on a common fire-shovel, over a clear fire for about 1 minute; and when sufficiently cool, polish with a plate brush. By this process a bronze similar to that on tea-urns is produced; the shade depending upon the duration of the exposure to the fire.

II. By substituting finely powdered plumbago for crocus powder in the above process, a beautiful, deep and permanent bronze appearance is produced.

III. Rub the medal with a solution of livers of sulphur, or sulphuret of potassium, then dry. This produces the appearance of Antique bronze very exactly.

BRONZING. SURFACE.—This term is applied to the process of imparting to the surfaces of figures of wood, plaster of Paris, &c., a metallic appearance. This is done by first giving them a coat of oil or size varnish, and when this is nearly dry, applying with a dabber of cotton or a camel-hair pencil, any of the metallic bronze powders; or the powder may be placed in a little bag of muslin, and dusted over the surface, and afterwards finished off with a wad of linen. The surface must be afterwards varnished.

Paper is bronzed by mixing the powders up with a little gum and water, and, afterwards, burnishing.

Iron Castings may be bronzed by thorough cleaning, and subsequent immersion in a solution of sulphate of copper, when they acquire a coat of the latter metal. They must be then washed in water.

BUTTER OR MILK—To Remove its Turnip Flavor This is said to be removed by either of the following methods: When the milk is strained into the pans, put to every six gallons one gallon of boiling water. Or dissolve one ounce of nitre in a pint of spring water, and put a ½ pint to every fifteen gallons of milk.

Silver Jelly.—Time to boil the feet, five hours and a half; to boil the jelly, twenty minutes. One set of calf's feet; one ounce of isinglass; one pint of the best gin; one pound of loaf sugar; juice of six lemons; peel of two; white of six eggs. Boil the calf's feet in four quarts of water, with the isinglass, until the feet are done to rags, and the water wasted to half the quantity; strain it, and when cold remove the feet, and the jelly from the sediment very carefully. Put the jelly into a stew-pan with the sugar, the juice of the lemons, and the peel of two; add the gin. When the flavor is thoroughly drawn from the lemon peel, put in the whites of the eggs well beaten, and their shells broken up, place the stew-pan over the fire, and let it boil for twenty minutes, but do not stir it after the egg has been added. Dip a jelly bag into hot water and squeeze it dry; run the jelly through it several times until quite clear, and then pour it into the mold. If calf's feet cannot be obtained, two ounces of gelatine and one ounce of isinglass will do as well.

Beaten Eggs.—One egg; one wineglass of sherry or one cup of tea; sugar to taste.

An egg beaten up in tea or wine will be found very strengthening for invalids. It is better to take the yolk only, as it is lighter.

Suet and Milk.—Time, ten to fifteen minutes. One teaspoonful of shredded beef suet; half a pint of fresh milk. Mix these ingredients and warm them sufficiently to melt the suet completely. Skim it. Warm the cup into which you pour it, and give it to the invalid to drink before it gets cool.

BRANDY, CHERRY—To every gallon of brandy put an equal measure of cherries, bruised between the fingers; steep for 3 days, then express the liquor; and add 2 lbs. of lump sugar, and strain for use.

To the above add 1 quart of raspberries, and ½ a pint of orange flower water. Quality very fine.

BRANDY, RASPBERRY.—I. Pour as much brandy over raspberries as will just cover them; let it stand for 24 hours, then drain it off, and replace it with a like quantity of fresh spirit; after 24 hours more, drain this off and replace it with water; lastly drain well, and press the raspberries quite dry. Next add sugar to the mixed liquors, in proportion of 2 lbs. to every gallon, along with a ¼ of a pint of orange-flower water.

II. Mix equal parts of mashed raspberries and brandy thogether, let them stand for 24 hours, then press out the liquor. Sweeten as above, and add a little cinnamon and cloves if agreeable; and lastly strain.

BRASS ORNAMENTS—When not gilt or lacquered, may be cleansed, and a fine color given to them by two simple processes. The first is to beat sal-ammoniac into a fine powder, then to moisten it with soft water, rubbing it on the ornaments, which must be afterwards rubbed dry with bran and whiting. The second is to wash the brass work with roche alum boiled to a strong lye, in the proportion of an ounce to a pint; when dry, it must be rubbed with fine tripoli. Either of these processes will give to brass the brilliancy of gold.

BRONZE POWDERS—Beautiful Red—Mix together sulphate of copper 100 parts; carbonate of soda 60 parts; apply heat until they unite into a mass—then cool, powder, and add copper filings 15 parts; well mix, and keep them at a white heat for 20 minutes; then cool, powder, and wash and dry.

II. Gold Colored—Verdigris 8 oz., tutty powder 4 oz., borax and nitre, of each, 2 oz., bichloride of mercury ¼ oz.—Make them into a fine paste with oil, and fuse them together. Used in japanning as a gold color.

CORDIAL ANISEED. I.—Aniseed (bruised) 1 lb.; proof spirit 6 gallons; macerate for a week; then distil 5 gallons; and add 2 gallons of clear soft water, and 1 gallon of clarified syrup. This will make 8 gallons of cordial 24 u. p., which is as weak as 'aniseed' should ever be made. It may be reduced by sweetened water.

II. Instead of distilling off the spirit, merely pass it through a wine-bag, to take off the seed, lower it with clear soft water, and sweeten as before.

III. Instead of 1 lb. of aniseed, add enough of the essential oil, dissolved in spirit of wine, to produce the desired flavor; 2 drachms of the oil is fully equal to 1 lb. of the seeds.

CORDIAL, CINNAMON. This is seldom made with cinnamon, but with either the essential oil, or bark of cassia. It is preferred colored, and therefore may be prepared by simple digestion. If the oil be used, 1 dr. will be found to be enough for 2 or 3 gallons of spirit. The addition of 2 or 3 drops each of essence of lemon and orange peel, with about a spoonful of essence of cardamoms to each gallon, will improve it. Some persons add to the above quantity 1 drachm of cardamom seeds and 1 oz. each of dried orange and lemon peel. 1 oz. of oil of cassia is considered to be equal to 8 lbs. of the buds, or bark. If wanted dark it may be colored with burnt sugar. The quantity of sugar is 1½ lb. to the gallon.

CORDIAL, PEPPERMINT. Add English oil of peppermint 2 oz. to rectified spirit of wine 1 quart, agitate well in a corked bottle, capable of holding pints or more, then pour it into a cask having a capacity of upwards of 100 galls.; add 36 galls. of perfectly white and flavorless proof spirit, agitate well for 10 minutes, then add 2 cwt. of the best refined lump sugar, previously dissolved in twice its weight of pure filtered rain water; rummage well, and further add sufficient clear rain water to make up the whole quantity to exactly 100 gallons; again rummage well; add 2 oz. alum, dissolved in 1 quart of rain water, and a third time agitate for 15 minutes, after which put in the bung and let it stand for a fortnight, when it will be fit for sale.

To Clean Marble Chimney-pieces.—Time, ten minutes. Equal quantities of soft soap and pearl-ash. Put the soap and pearl-ash on the chimney-piece with a soft flannel; let it lay on the marble for a few minutes. Wash it off with warm water not too hot; wash it over a second time with cold spring water.

For Bright Polished Grates.—Oil the bright part of the grate with good salad oil, dust over it some unslacked lime from a muslin bag. Let it remain one month, then rub it off with a fine rag. Polish it with a leather and a very little putty powder. If the grate is not in use put on the oil again.

To Take Stains Out of Marble.—Mix unslacked lime in finest powder with the stronger soap-lye pretty thick, and instantly with a painter's brush lay it on the whole of the marble. In two months' time wash it off perfectly clean. Then have ready a fine thick lather of soft soap, boiled in soft water, dip a brush in it, and scour the marble with powder not as common cleaning. This will, by very good rubbing, give a beautiful polish. Clear off the soap, and finish with a smooth hard brush till the end be effected.

To Take Rust Out of Steel.—Cover the steel with sweet oil well rubbed in, and in forty-eight hours use unslacked lime finely powdered, and rub until all the rust disappears.

Wash for the Hair.—Half an ounce of glycerine; half an ounce of spirit of rosemary; five ounces of water. To be well mixed together and shaken, and used night and morning.

To Cement Broken China.—Beat lime to a very fine, almost invisible dust; sift it through book muslin. Then tie it up in a piece of thin muslin, as powdered starch is sometimes used. Brush some white of egg over the edges of the china, dust the lime rapidly over them, put the edges together, and tie a string round the cup, etc., till it is firm.

Isinglass dissolved in spirits of wine, in the proportion of one ounce to two wineglassfuls of the spirits, is also a good cement.

For Removing Paint from Wood.—One pound of washing soda; two pounds of unslacked lime. Mix one pound of washing soda with two pounds of unslacked lime, and, if the paint is very strong on the wood, add half a pound of potash. Mix these ingredients together, and dilute with water until the mixture becomes rather thicker than whitewash, and then rub it on the paint with a piece of wood folded up in rag. The person who uses this preparation must be careful not to touch it with the hands.

To Clean Paper-hangings.—First blow the dust off with the bellows. Divide a white loaf of eight days old into eight parts. Take the crust into your hand and, beginning at the top of the paper, wipe it downward in the lightest manner with the crumbs. Do not cross or go upward. The dirt of the paper and the crumbs will fall together. Observe—you must not wipe above half a yard at a stroke, and, after doing all the upper part, go round again, beginning a little above where you left off. If you do not clean it very lightly, you will make the dirt adhere to the paper.

TO REMOVE PAINT STAINS FROM GLASS WINDOWS.—It frequently happens that painters splash the plate or other glass windows when they are painting the sills. When this is the case, melt some soda in very hot water and wash them with it, using a soft flannel. It will entirely remove the paint.

TOOTH POWDER.—A quarter of an ounce of bole armenian; a quarter of an ounce of bark; a quarter of an ounce of powdered camphor; a quarter of an ounce of powdered myrrh. Mix the ingredients very thoroughly together. Tooth powders should be kept closely covered in wooden boxes. The prescription is for equal quantities of the above ingredients, but one ounce of the whole mixed is enough at a time, unless a chemist is not of easy access.

TO WASH COLORED PRINTS AND WASHING SILKS.—Put a little bran into lukewarm water, wash quickly through; rinse in cold water also, quickly. Hang to dry in a room without fire or sunshine. Iron on wrong side with a coolish iron. No soap to be used.

TO CLEAN AN OLD SILK DRESS.—Unpick the dress, and brush it with a velvet brush. Then grate two large potatoes into a quart of water; let it stand to settle; strain it off quite clear, and sponge the dress with it. Iron it on the wrong side, as the ironed side will be shiny.

CASTOR OIL POMADE FOR THE HAIR.—Four ounces of castor oil; two ounces of prepared lard; two drachms of white wax; essence of jessamine, or otto of rose. Melt the fat together, and, when well mixed, and becoming cool, add whatever scent you prefer, and stir it constantly until cold; then pour it into pots or bottles for use.

COLD CREAM.—Half a pint of rosewater; four ounces of oil of almonds; three drachms of white wax; three drachms of spermaceti. Melt the white wax and spermaceti together with the oil of almonds. Then beat them all up, adding the rosewater slowly until it is cold. Put it in a pot, and pour some rosewater on the top.

A WINTER SOAP FOR CHAPPED OR ROUGH HANDS.—Three pounds of common yellow soap; one ounce of camphor dissolved in one ounce of rose and one ounce of lavender water. Beat three pounds of common yellow soap, and one ounce of camphor dissolved in one ounce of rose and one ounce of lavender water in a mortar until it becomes a paste. Make it into balls to dry, and set it in a cool place for the winter. The best time to make it is in the spring.

TABLE POLISH.—Half a pint of spirits of wine; an ounce and a half of gum shellac; half an ounce of gum benzoin; half an ounce of gum sandrac. Put the whole in a bottle for a day or two, and shake it a few times. When the gums are dissolved it is fit for use. When the polish is laid on thick enough, take a clean wad and cloth; put a little clean spirits of wine on the wad, the same as you did with the polish, rub it the same way, but very lightly, and until quite dry. You must then put a little oil on the cloth, and rub as in laying on the polish.

NATURE makes us poor only when we want necessaries; but custom gives the name of poverty to the want of superfluities.

Cure for Drunkenness.

1. Dr. Kain, an American physician, recommends tartar emetic for the cure of habitual drunkenness. "Possessing," he observes, "no positive taste itself, it communicates a disgusting quality to those fluids in which it is dissolved. I have often seen persons who, from taking a medicine in the form of antimonial wine, could never afterwards drink wine. Nothing, therefore, seems better calculated to form our indication of breaking up the association in the patients feelings, between his disease and the relief to be obtained from stimulating liquors. These liquors, with the addition of a very small quantity of emetic tartar, instead of relieving, increase the sensation of loathing of food, and quickly produce in the patient an indomitable repugnance to the vehicle of its administration. My method of prescribing it has varied according to the habits, age, and constitution of the patient. I give it only in alterative and slightly nauseating doses. A convenient preparation of the medicine is 8 grains dissolved in 4 oz. of boiling water, ½ an oz. of the solution to be put in a ½ pint, or quart of the patient's favorite liquor, and to be taken daily in divided portions. If severe vomiting and purging ensue, I should direct laudanum to allay the irritation, and diminish the dose. In every patient it should be varied according to its effects. In some cases, the change suddenly produced in the patient's habits has brought on considerable lassitude and debility, which were of but short duration. In a majority of cases, no other effect has been perceptible than slight nausea, some diarrhœa, and a gradal but very uniform distaste to the menstruum." A similar plan has been proposed by Mr. Chambers.

2. Infuse a little of the star-shoot plant in the liquor, at drinking which disgust will be gradually excited.

DENTRIFICE—The juice of the common strawberry has been recommended as an elegant natural dentifrice, as it readily dissolves the tartareous incrustations on the teeth, and imparts an agreeable odor to the breath.

TO DYE GLOVES.—Leather gloves, if not greasy may be dyed with any of the ordinary dyes by brushing the latter over the gloves stretched out smooth. The surface alone should be wetted, and a second or third coat may be given after the former one has become dry. When the last coat has become thoroughly dry, the superfluous color should be rubbed out, a smooth surface given them by rubbing with a polished stick or piece of ivory, and the whole gone over with a sponge dipped in white of egg.

TO CLEAN GLOVES.—I. (Dry cleaning.) Lay them out flat; then rub into them a mixture of finely powdered fuller's earth and alum; swep it off with a brush, sprinkle them with dry bran and whiting; lastly dust them well. This will not do if they are very dirty.

II. Wash them with soap and water; then stretch them on wooden hands, or pull them into shape 'without wringing them;' next rub them with pipe-clay, or yellow ochre, or a mixture of the two in any required shade, made into a paste with beer: let them dry 'gradually,' and when about 'half' dry, rub them well so as to smooth them and put them into shape; then dry them, brush out the superfluous color, cover them with paper, and smooth them with a warm iron. Other color may be employed to mix with the pipe-clay beside yellow ochre.

DRYING OIL.—Linseed Oil boiled along with oxide of lead, (litharge,) by which it acquires the property of drying quickly when exposed in a thin stratum to the air. It is much used in the preparation of paints and varnishes.

DRAWINGS, Chalk and Pencil—These may be fixed so as not to suffer from abrasion, by washing them with skimmed milk, or with water holding in solution a little isinglass. When the former is used, great care must be taken to deprive it of the whole of the cream, as, if the latter substance be present it will grease the drawing. An easy way of applying these fluids, is to pour them into a shallow vessel, and to lay the drawing flat upon the surface, then to place it on blotting paper in an inclined position to drain and dry.

GILDING OF PORCELAIN, GLASS, &c.—This is performed by blending powdered gold with gum water and a little borax, and applying it by means of a camel-hair pencil; the article is then heated sufficiently hot in an oven or furnace, by which means the gum is burnt, and the borax vitrifying cements the gold to the surface. When cold it is polished off with a burnisher. Names, dates, or any fancy device may thus be permanently and easily fixed on glass, china, earthenware, &c.

GILDING OF SILK, &c.—Silks, satins, woollens, ivory, bones, &c., may be readily gilded by immersing them in a solution of nitro-muriate (terchloride) of gold, (1 of the salt to 3 or 4 water), and then exposing them to the action of hydrogen gas. The latter part of the process may readily be performed by pouring some diluted sulphuric acid, or zinc or iron filings, in a bottle, and placing it under a jar or similar vessel, inverted, at the top of which the articles to be gilded are to be suspended.

The foregoing experiment may be very prettily and advantageously varied as follows;—paint flowers or other ornaments with a very fine camel-hair pencil, dipped in the above-mentioned solution of gold, on pieces of silk, satin, &c., and hold them over a Florence flask, from which hydrogen gas is evolved, during the decomposition of the water by sulphuric acid and iron filings. The painted flowers, &c., in a few minutes will shine with all the splendor of the purest gold. A coating of this kind will not tarnish on exposure to the air, or in washing.

GILDING VARNISH.—This is oil gilding applied to equipages, picture-frames, furniture, &c., the surface being highly varnished and polished before it receives the size or gold color; and after the gilding has become quite dry, a coat of spirit varnish, fumed with the chafing dish as above, is applied, followed by two or three coats of the best copal varnish, after which, the work is carefully polished with tripoli and water.

Gilders' Varnish—Prep.—Beeswax 4 oz., verdigris and sulphate of copper, of each 1 oz; mix.

FIRE EATING.—The power of resisting the action f fire is given to the skin by frequently washing it ith diluted sulphuric acid, until the part becomes sufficiently callous. It is said that the following mixture is very efficacious:—dilute sulphuric acid 3 parts; sal ammoniac 1 part; juice of onions 2 parts; mix. It is the acid however, that produces the effect.

IMPRESSIONS FROM COINS—A very easy and elegant way of taking the impressions of medals and coins, not generally known, is as follows —Melt a little isinglass glue with brandy, and pour it thinly over the medal, so as to cover its whole surface; let it remain on for a day or two, till it has thoroughly dried and hardened, and then take it off, when it will be fine, clear, and as hard as a piece of Muscovy glass, and will have a very elegant impression of the coin. It will also resist the effects of damp air, which occasions all other kinds of glue to soften and bend if not prepared in this way. (Shaw.) If the wrong side of the isinglass be breathed on, and gold-leaf applied, it will adhere, and be seen on the other side, producing a very pleasing effect. Isinglass glue, made with water alone, will do 'nearly' as well as if brandy be used.

LEAF GILDING—This term is applied to the gilding of paper, vellum, &c., by applying leaf gold to the surface, previously prepared with a coating of gum-water, size or white of an egg. It is usually finished with an agate burnisher.

LETTER GILDING—The letters of sign-boards and similar ornamental gilding for outdoor work, is done by first covering the design with yellow or gold-color paint, then with oil gold size, and when this is nearly dry, applying the leaf-gold, observing to shield it properly from the wind, lest it be blown way or become crumpled before being properly attached. This gilding is usually varnished.

MAHOGANY STAINS—Pure Socotrine aloes 1 ounce dragon's blood ½ oz., rectified spirit 1 pint: dissolve and apply 2 or 3 coats to the surface of the wood finish off with wax or oil, tinged with alkanet

COSMETIC SIMPLE. Soft soap ½ lb.; melt over a slow fire with a gill of sweet oil, add half a teacupful of fine sand, and stir the mixture together until cold. The shelly sea-sand, sifted from the shells, has been found better than that which has no shells.

Remarks. This simple cosmetic, has for several years past been used by many ladies who are remarkable for the delicate softness and whiteness of their hands, which they, in a great measure, attribute to the use of it. Its cheapness is a strong recommendation.

ESSENCE OF PATCHOULI. Indian patchouli leaves 2 lbs.: rectified spirit of wine 9 pints; water 1 gallon. Macerate for 1 week, frequently shaking the vessel, then distil over exactly 1 gallon. A very fashionable perfume.

ESSENCE OF ROSES (ODOROUS)—Very fine article.—Attar of roses 1 ounce; spirit of wine 1 gallon. Mix in a close vessel and assist the solution by placing it in a bath of hot water. As soon as the spirit gets warm, take it from the water and shake till quite cold. The next day filter. Unless the spirit of wine be of more than the common strength, it will not retain the whole of the otto in solution in very cold weather.

FURS may be preserved from moths and insects by placing a little colocynth pulp, (bitter apples,) or spices, as cloves, pimento, &c., wrapped in muslin among them; or they may be washed in a very weak solution of corrosive sublimate in warm water, (10 or 15 grains to the pint), and afterwards carefully dried. Furs, as well as every other species of clothing should be kept in a clean, dry place.

COFFEE MILK.—Boil a dessert-spoonful of ground coffee in about a pint of milk, a quarter of an hour: then put into it a shaving or two of isinglass and clear it; let it boil a few minutes, and set it on the side of the fire to fine. This is a very fine breakfast, and should be sweetened with real Lisbon sugar

BAKERS' ITCH OINTMENT.—Mix well together one quarter ounce of ointment of nitrate of mercury, and one ounce of palm oil.

SOAP A LA ROSE.——New Olive Oil Soap 30 lbs., new tallow soap, 20 lbs., reduce them to shavings by sliding the bars along the face of an inverted plane, melt in an untinned copper pan by the heat of steam or a water bath, add 1½ oz. of finely ground vermilion, mix well, remove the heat, and when the mass has cooled a little, add essence of roses [otto?] 3 oz.; do. of cloves and cinnamon, of each, 1 ounce; bergamot, 2½ ounces; mix well, run the liquid mass through a tammy cloth, and put it into the frames. If the soaps employed are not new, 1 or 2 quarts of water must be added to make them melt easily. A very fine article.

SOAP AU BOUQUET.——Best tallow soap 30 lbs., essence of bergamot, 4 oz.; oils of cloves, sassafras, and thyme, of each, 1 oz., pure neroli, ½ oz.; finely powdered brown ochre, 7 oz. Mix as last. Very fine

SOAP, BITTER ALMOND.—Best white tallow soap ½ cwt., essence of bitter almonds 10 oz., mix as soap a la rose. Very fine.

SOAP, CINNAMON.—Best tallow soap 30 lbs., best palm oil soap 20 lbs., essence of cinnamon 7 ounces, do. of sassafras and bergamot, of each, 1½ oz., finely powdered yellow ochre 1 lb. Mix as soap a la rose. Very fine.

SOAP, MUSK.—Best tallow soap 30 lbs., palm oil soap 20 lbs., powdered cloves, pale roses, and gilliflowers, of each, 4½ oz.; essences of bergamot and musk, of each, 3½ oz.; Spanish brown 4 oz. Mix as a la rose. Very fine.

SOAP, ORANGE FLOWER.—Best tallow soap, 30 lbs palm oil soap, 20 lbs., essences of Portugal and ambergris, of each 7½ oz., yellowish green color [ochre and indigo] 8½ oz., vermilion 1½ oz. Mix as soap a la rose. Very fine.

SOAP, PALM OIL.—Made of palm oil and caustic soda lye. Has a pleasant odor of violets and a lively color

ALMOND SOAP is made from almond oil and caustic soda, and is chiefly used for the toilet.—Curd Soap is made with tallow and soda. Mottled Soap, with refuse kitchen stuff, &c.

Printing Ink.

PRINTING INK. 10 or 12 gallons of linseed oil are set over the fire in an iron pot capable of containing at least as much more, to allow of its swelling without running over. When it boils it is kept stirred with an iron ladle, and if it does not take fire of itself soon after the smoke begins to rise, it is kindled by means of a piece of burning paper, stuck in the cleft end of a long stick. The pot is then shortly afterwards removed from the fire, and the oil is suffered to burn for about half an hour, or till a sample of the varnish cooled upon a pallet knife, may be drawn into strings of about half an inch long, between the fingers. The flame is now extinguished by the application of a closely-fitting tin cover, and as soon as the froth of the ebullition has subsided, black rosin is added, in the proportion of 6 lbs. to every 6 quarts of oil thus treated; the mixture is next stirred until the rosin is dissolved, when 1¾ lbs. of brown soap, cut into slices is further added, (cautiously), and the ingredients are again stirred with the spatula until united, the pot being once more placed over the fire to promote the combination. When this is effected, the varnish is removed from the heat, and after thorough stirring, covered over and set aside. It is necessary to prepare two kinds of this varnish, varying in consistence, from more or less boiling, to be occasionally mixed together as circumstances may require; that which answers well in hot weather being too thick in cold, and vice versa. Large characters also require a thinner ink than small ones. A good varnish may be drawn into threads like glue, and is very thick and tenacious.

2.—Making the ink. (Black.) Finely powdered indigo and Prussian blue, of each, 2½ ounces; best mineral lampblack, 4 lbs; best vegetable lampblack, 3½ lbs.; put them into a suitable vessel and mix in gradually the warm varnish. The mixture must now be submitted to careful grinding, either in a mill or with a slab and muller. On the large scale steam power is employed for this purpose,

Printing Ink Continued.

(An extemporaneous superfine ink). Balsam of copaiba (pure) 9 oz.; lampblack 3 oz.; indigo and Prussian blue, of each 5 dr.; Indian red ¾ oz.; yellow soap (dry) 3 oz.; grind to an impalpable smoothness. Canada balsam may be substitued for balsam of copaiba where the smell of the latter is objectionable, but it dries quicker.

Remarks. Old linseed oil is preferable to new. Yellow rosin soap is preferred for black and dark colored inks, and white curd soap for light ones. Vegetable lampblack takes the most varnish. The addition of indigo and Prussian blue is to correct the brown color of the black. The Indian red is added to increase the body and richness of the color. Some persons find much trouble in grinding up the indigo, from its running into a mass and clogging the mill; but this may be avoided by mixing it as above, or by first grinding it with a sufficient quantity of Canada balsam or copaiba, and using a proportionate quantity of varnish and that of a little thicker consistence The French employ nut oil instead of linseed. Mr Savage obtained the large medal of the Society of Arts for his black ink made as above. It is unrivalled. Colored inks are made in a similar way. The pigments used are. Carmine, lakes, vermilion, chrome red, red lead, orange red, Indian red, Venetian red, orange chrome, chrome yellow, burnt terra di Siena, gall stone, Roman ocnre, yellow do., verdigris, Scheele's green, Schweinfurth's do., blues and yellows mixed for greens, indigo, Prussian blue, Antwerp do., cobalt do., charcoal do., lustre, umber, sepia, &c. &c.

PAPER, COPYING. Make a stiff ointment with butter or lard and lampblack, and smear it thinly and evenly over soft writing paper, by means of a piece of flannel, then wipe off the redundant portion with a piece of soft rag. Placed on paper and written on with a style of solid pen. By repeating the arrangement, two or three copies of a letter may be obtained at once. This paper, set up in a case, forms the ordinary 'manifold writer.'

THE ART OF INLAYING AND ORNAMENTING PAPIER MACHE'.—The articles required are a small pair of cutting nippers, a half-round file, some gold size, Vegetable Black, Black Japan, two large camel's hair brushes, in quills, various powder colors, such as Lakes. Vermillion, Italian Pink, Prussian Blue, French Ultramarine, Emerald Green, &c. Copal Varnish, Spirit of Turpentine, Gold Leaf, Pumice Stone. Pumice Powder, Putty Powder, Palette Knife and Slab, Papier Mache and Pearl. Having roughly sketched your design upon the Papier Mache, and decided upon the part to be inlaid with Pearl, take your nippers and cut or nip the Pearl to your shape. which is afterwards to be finished with the file, to the exact form required. You will now mix in a gallipot, a small quantity of Gold Size and Vegetable Black, to the consistency of Treacle, and taking a large brush, lay a rather thick coating upon the whole of the Papier Mache. You will then stick on the pieces of Pearl before cut out, according to your design, and let it remain until dry, which will be 24 hours. The surface of your Papier Mache being perfectly dry, take Black Japan and give it a thick and even coating over the whole surface, not excepting the Pearl. It will require to be placed in an oven of more sort, quite free from dust, and heated about 145 degrees; but this is not particular, so long as it does not get hotter. It will be dry in 24 hours, when to test its dryness, dip a rag in Spirit of Turpentine, and brush the edge of the Papier Mache; if it soils the rag, it is not dry, and requires to be again stoved. The articles require four coats of Japan, and the above process to be repeated on each coat, the beauty of the articles entirely depending on the Japan being perfectly dry and hard. A piece of Pumice Stone rubbed flat on a flag, must now be dipped in water, and rubbed on the Papier Mache until it brings the whole to a level surface, and shows the Pearl. Fine Pumice Powder and water upon a bit of list is now applied to remove the scratches made by the Pumice Stone, polish with Putty Powder upon a piece of wash-leather.

If your design consist of flowers, &c. color the parts as required with Powder colors, mixed up with Copal Varnish, and diluted with Turpentine, using nature as a guide. The ornamental parts not consisting of flowers, are to be painted and gilded according to your fancy. For Gilding, take Gold Size and mix a little Chrome Yellow, with which draw your design, and when partially dry in 5 or 10 minutes cut Gold Leaf in small pieces, apply it, and dab it on with cotton wool. In 5 or 10 minutes after rub the cotton lightly over the surface, to remove the superfluous pieces of gold. When the coloring is dry, varnish over those parts which have been painted or gilded, with Copal Varnish, and let it dry 24 hours, and the article is complete.

BALLS, LAXATIVE, (for horses). Aloes, ginger and soft soap, of each 3 drachms; mix with treacle for 1 ball. Cordial and laxative.

BALLS, FEVER, (for horses). Tartar emetic 2 oz.; nitre 8 oz.; liquorice 6 oz.; all in fine powder; mix with treacle for 12 balls.

BALLS, GARLIC (for horses). Garlic 1 oz.; liquorice powder enough to make a ball. Use, for cronic coughs.

BALLS, MANGE (for horses). Crude antimony 2 oz., calomel 1 oz.; opium ½ oz.; flowers of sulphur 1 lb.; mix with treacle and divide into 12 balls. A piece the size of a horse bean to that of a small nut, is a capital medicine for dogs.

BALLS, STOMACHIC (for horses). Powdered Gentian 4 oz.; powdered ginger and carbonate of soda, of each 2 oz.; soft soap 8 oz.; mix and divide into 8 balls.

BALLS, TONIC (for horses). Gentian ½ oz.; opium ½ drachm; cascarilla, myrrh, and carbonate of soda, of each 1 drachm; soft soap ½ oz. Form into one ball.

BALLS, SULPHUR (for horses). Flowers of sulphur 1 lb.; powdered antimony 3 oz.; red sulphuret of mercury (pure) 2 oz.; powdered gum 1 oz.; treacle to mix. For 12 balls. Said to make the coat slick; also for mange, &c.

BALLS, STRENGTHENING (for horses). Powdered calomba and cascarilla, of each ¼ oz.; soft soap ¾ oz.; chalk ⅛ oz; make into a ball. For looseness.

BALLS, WORM (for horses). Aloes 5 drachms; Castile soap ½ oz.; calomel and ginger, of each 1½ drachms; oil of cloves and cassia, of each 6 drops; treacle to make a ball.

BALLS, GRIPE (for horses). Liquorice, black pepper, ginger, and prepared chalk, all in powder, of each 4 oz.; oils of caraway, cloves, and cassia, each 1 drachm; treacle to mix. For 12 balls.

BALLS, INFLUENZA (for horses). Barbadoes aloes, nitre, and Venice turpentine, of each 1 lb.; gentian 2 lbs.; ginger ½ lb.; treacle to mix. Divide into 1½ oz. balls.

BALLS, COLIC (for horses). Powdered opium ¼ oz.; Castile soap and camphor, each 1 oz.; powdered ginger and cassia, each ½ oz.; liquorice powder 2 oz; treacle to make 4 balls.

BALLS, CORDIAL (for horses). Aniseed, caraway seed, and cumin seed, of each 4 lbs.; ginger 2 lbs.; all in powder; treacle q. s. to mix. Product 21 lbs. To be made up in balls weighing 1¾ oz. each.

BALLS, COUGH (for horses). Cordial ball mass 4 lbs.; gum amoniacum 4 oz.; powdered squills 1 oz.; treacle to mix. Divide into 4 dozen balls.

BALLS, FARCY (for horses). Corrosive sublimate 10 grains; liquorice powder 1 oz.; oil of aniseed ½ drachm; mix with treacle for 1 ball.

BALLS, MERCURIAL (for horses). Calomel 1 oz.; aloes 2 oz.; rhubarb ¾ oz.; liquorice powder 14 oz.; treacle to mix. Divide into 12 balls. Laxative and alterative.

BALLS, ALTERATIVE (for horses). Calomel, sulphuret of antimony, and powdered opium, of each ½ oz.; powdered gum guaiacam 2½ oz.; Castile soap 12 oz.; treacle to mix. Divide into 12 balls. Use, for weak horses with a bad constitution.

II. Calomel ½ oz.; powdered aloes 1½ oz.; starch 6 oz.; soft soap 8 oz. Make them into a mass, and divide into 12 balls. Use—to improve the constitution.

Arabian Charm for Taming Horses.

The horse castor is a wart or excrescence which grows on every horse's fore-legs, and generally on the hind-legs. It has a peculiar rank, musty smell, and is easily pulled off. For the Oil of Cumin the horse is said to have an instinctive passion, and the Oil of Rhodium possesses some very peculiar properties for animals.

Procure some horse castor and grate it fine--also get some Oil of Rhodium and Oil of Cumin, and keep the three separate in air-tight bottles. Rub a little Oil of Cumin upon your hand, and approach the horse in the field on the windward side, so that he can smell the Cumin—when he approaches, immediately rub your hand gently upon the horse's nose, getting a little Oil on it. Then give him a little of the castor on a piece of loaf sugar, apple or potato. Then put eight drops of the Oil of Rhodium into a lady's silver thimble.—Take the thimble between the thumb and middle finger of your right hand, with the forefinger stopping the mouth of the thimble, to prevent the Oil from running out whilst you are opening the mouth of the horse. As soon as you have opened the horse's mouth, empty the the thimble upon his tongue and he is your servant.

ARTIFICIAL YEAST.—Honey 5 oz., cream of tartar 1 oz., malt 16 oz., water at 122 deg. F. 3 pints; stir together, and when the temperature falls to 65 deg., cover it up and keep it at that temperature till yeast is formed.

TO ATTRACT RATS.—Two dr. of oil of aniseed, 2 drops of nitrous acid, and 2 gr. of musk. Oil of rhodium is also supposed to be very attractive to these vermin Assafœtida with these oils is also used.

RHEUMATISM.—Take two eggs, one gill of vinegar, one gill of New England Rum, one tea-spoonful of spirits of turpentine, one tea-spoonful of sun-fish oil. Beat the eggs up well first, then add a small quantity of each article at a time. until all are mixed, stirring the mixture all the time. Bathe the affected parts with it two or three times a day.

BRITISH HERB TOBACCO.—The principal ingredient in this compound is dried coltsfoot leaves, to which a smaller portion of thyme, wood-betony, eye-bright, and rosemary are added.

HAIR DEPILATORY.—Quick lime 16 oz., pearlash 2 oz., liver of sulpher 2 oz. Reduce to a fine powder, and keep it in a close bottle. To be mixed with water, and applied to the skin, and scraped off in 2 or 3 minutes with a wooden knife. [Use caution, to prevent injury.]

DUPUYTREN'S POMADE.—Beef marrow 6 oz., nervine balsam 2 oz., (This is made by melting together 4 oz. each of beef marrow and oil of mace, and adding 2 dr. of balsam of tolu, and 1 dr. each of oil of cloves and camphor, dissolved in ½ oz. of rectified spirit.) Peruvian balsam 2 oz., oil of almonds 1½ oz., extract of cantharides 16 gr.; melt the marrow and nervine balsam with the oil, strain, add the balsam of Peru, and lastly the extract, dissolved in a drachm of rectified spirit.

ROUGE.—Rouge is prepared from carmine, and the colouring matter of safflower, by mixing them with finely levigated French chalk or talc, generally with the addition of a few drops of olive or almond oil. Sometimes fine white starch is used as the reducing ingredient.

HAIR DYE.—Nitrate of silver 11 dr., nitric acid 1 dr., distilled water 1 pint, sap green 3 dr., gum arabic 1 dr.; mix.

HAIR DYE.—Litharge 2 parts, slaked lime 1 part, chalk 2 parts, all finely powdered, and accurately mixed. When required for use, mix the powder with warm water, and dip a brush in the mixture, and rub the hair well with it. After two hours, let the hair be washed.

TOOTHACHE.--Opium 5 gr., oil of cloves 3 drops, extract of henbane 5 gr., extract of belladonna, 10 gr., powdered pellitory sufficient to form a paste.

ROSE TOOTH PASTE.—Cuttle-fish bone 3 oz. prepared or precipitated chalk 2 oz., orris 1 oz., lake or rose pink to give it a pale rose colour, otto of rose 16 drops, honey of roses q. s.

FILLING FOR TEETH.--Gutta percha, softened by heat is recommended. Dr. Rollfs advises melting a piece of caoutchouc at the end of a wire, and introducing it while warm.

GOLD FACTITIOUS.—Platina 7, copper 16, zinc 1: fuse together.

COMMON GOLD.—Copper 16, silver 1, Gold 2.

Bailey's Itch Ointment.—Olive oil 1 lb, suet 1 lb, alkanet root 2 oz. Melt, and macerate until coloured; then strain, and add 3 oz. each of alum, nitre and sulphate of zinc, in very fine powder; adding vermillion to colour it, and oil of aniseed, lavender, and thyme to perfume.

Caustic for Corns.—Tincture of iodine 4 dr., iodide of iron 12 gr., chloride of antimony 4 dr.; mix, and apply with a camel-hair brush, after paring the corn. It is said to cure in three times.

Consumption.—Rum ½ pint, linseed oil, honey, garlic (beaten to a pulp,) and loaf sugar, of each 4 oz., yolks of 5 eggs; mix: a teaspoonful night and morning.

Sweet's Salve.—Melt together 8 ounces of rosin and two ounces of beeswax; then add the following mixture in powder, bole armenia, nitre, camphor, of each one ounce: stir them well together, then pour the whole in to cold water, and work it in the water, until it can be taken out and formed into rolls or cakes.

Opodeldoc.—White soap, 2 ounces, camphor 1 ounce oil of rosemary 2 drachms, oil of origanum 2 drachms strong aqua ammonia one ounce, proof alcohol 1½ pints Dissolve together.

Infants' Cordial.—Pleurisy Root, scull-cap, skunk-cabbage, hops, cramp bark, prickly-ash berries, calamus angelica seed, sassafras, of each, in powder, one ounce ginger, capsicum, of each, two drachms. Pour on six pints of boiling water, when cold, add three pints of good Holland Gin, and two pounds of loaf sugar. Let it stand two weeks, frequently shaking. [We have substituted this for Godfrey's, as it is far superior.]

Milk of Roses.—Mix one oz. of fine olive oil with 10 drops of oil of tartar, and a pint of rose-water

Macassar Oil.—The oil made by the natives in the island is obtained by boiling the kernel of the fruit of a tree resembling the walnut, called in Malay, badeau. The oil is mixed with other ingredients, and has a smell approaching to that of creosote. But the Macassar oil sold in this country has probably no relation to the above, except in name. The following is given by Gray;—Olive oil 1 lb., oil of origanum 1 dr.; others add 1¼ dr. of oil of rosemary.

Eau de Cologne.—English oil of lavender, oil of bergamot, oil of lemon, oil of neroli, of each 1 oz.; oil of cinnamon ½ oz.; spirit of rosemary and spirit of balm, (eau des Carmes,) of each 15 oz., highly rectified spirit 7½ pints. Let them stand together for 14 days, then distil in a water-bath.

Eau d'Ange.—Flowering tops of myrtle 16 oz., rectified spirit a gallon; digest, and distil to dryness in a water-bath; or dissolve ¼ oz. essential oil of myrtle in 3 pints of rectified spirit. Mr. Gray gives under this name a water without spirit—water 2 pints, benzoin 2 oz., storax 1 oz., cinnamon 1 dr., cloves 2 dr., calamus a stick, coriander seeds a pinch; distil.

Russian Tooth Powder.—Peruvian bark 2 oz., orris root 1 oz., sal ammoniac ½ oz., catechu 6 dr., myrrh 6 dr., oil of cloves 6 or 8 drops.

Artificial Bears' Grease.—Prepared suet 3 oz., lard 1 oz. olive oil 1 oz. oil of cloves 10 drops, compound tincture of benzoin 1 dr.; mix.

Beetle Poison.—Put a drachm of phosphorus in a flask with 2 oz. of water: plunge the flask into hot water, and when the phosphorus is melted pour the contents into a mortar with 2 or 3 oz. of lard. Triturate briskly, adding water, and ½ lb of flour with 1 or 2 oz. of brown sugar.

Cockroach Poison.—Equal parts of Plaster of Paris, with oatmeal.

Arsenical Paste.—Melt 2 lb of suet in an earthen vessel over a slow fire, and add 2 lb of wheat flour, 3 oz. of levigated white arsenic, 2½ dr. of lamp-black, 15 drops of oil of aniseed. It may be used alone, or mixed with bread, crumbs, &c. [For destroying rats and mice

Washes for Vermin in Plants.—Infuse one lb of tobacco in a gallon of boiling water, in a covered vessel, till cold.

For Lice in Vines.—Boil ½ lb of tobacco in 2 quarts of water; strain, and add ½ lb of soft soap, and ¼ lb of sulphur. Mix.

For Aphides.—Boil 2 oz. of lime and 1 oz. of sulphur in water, and strain.

For Red Spiders.—A teaspoonful of salt in a gallon of water. In a few days wash the plant with pure water.

TO MARK ON GASS.—Glass may be written on, for tem porary purposes, by French chalk; pencils of this substance will be found convenient. Glass may be written on with ink, if the surface be clean and dry, and the pen held nearly perpendicular. The shell-lac ink is the best for labels, as it resists damp, &c. "To scratch glass," a scratching diamond is used; or a piece of flint, or crystal of quartz, or the point of a small 3-square file. "To engrave on glass," fluoric acid is used, either in the liquid state or in vapor. The glass must be warmed, and coated with wax or engravers' cement, and the writing or design traced through the wax with a brad awl or other pointed instrument. The liquid fluoric acid is poured on it, and left to act on the uncovered portions of the glass; or the fluor spar may be powder ed and made into a paste with oil of vitriol, and laid over the prepared surface, and covered with lead foil or tea lead: or bruised fluor spar is put on a Wedgewood evaporating basin, with sufficient oil of vitriol to form a thin paste, and the prepared glass laid over the basin, so that the vapors may act on the portions from which the wax has been removed. "To cut glass," (besides the usual method of dividing cut glass by a glazier's diamond,) the following means may be used:—To divide glass tubes or rods, form a deep mark around them with the edge of a sharp three-square file, then with a hand placed on either side of the mark, break the rod with a slightly stretching as well as bending motion. A diamond or sharp flint may be substituted for a file. Flasks, globes and retorts, may be divided by means of iron rings, having a stem fixed in a wooden handle. Make the ring red-hot, and apply it to the flask, &c. If the vessel does not break where it came in contact with the ring, wet the part, and it will generally separate. Another method is to twist together 2 or 3 threads of cotton, such as is used for wicks, moisten them with spirit of wine, and encircle the flask with them; then holding the flask horizontally, set fire to the wick, and turn the flask with the fingers, so as to keep the flame in the direction of the thread. If the separation does not take place the first time, the process may be repeated after the glass has cooled. By these means a com mon oil flask may be divided into an evaporating dish and a funnel. By means of a stout iron rod, fixed in a wooden handle, and terminating in a blunt point and heated to redness, broken retorts, globes and flasks, may be converted into useful evaporating dishes, &c. If any crack exists, it may easily be led in any direction, as it will follow the motion of the heated iron. If no crack exists, one must be produced by applying the point of the heated rod to any convenient spot on the edge of the broken glass, touching it afterwards with a moistened finger, if necessary. The edges of glass thus divided are rendered less apt to break by heating them in the flame of a blow-pipe, or grinding them smooth with emery on a flat stone. See Faraday's Manipulations.

To Silver Glass.—The term "silvering" is applied to the process of coating the surface of glass with amalgamated tinfoil, in forming mirrors. The tinfoil is rubbed over with quicksilver, and more of the latter poured over it: the plate of glass, perfectly clean and dry, is then applied to it in such a way as to exclude all air bubbles, and to bring the glass and foil into perfect contact. The plate, after being inclined so as to allow the superfluous quicksilver to drain off, is loaded with weights, under which it remains till the adhesion is complete. To convex and concave mirrors, the amalgamated foil is applied by accurately fitting plaster moulds. The interior of globes is silvered by introducing a liquid amalgam, and turning about the globe till every part is covered with it. But a method of literally silvering glass has lately been patented by Mr. Drayton. He mixes 1 oz. of nitrate of silver, 3 oz. of water, 1 oz. of liquid ammonia, and 3 oz. of spirit of wine, and filters the solution after it has stood 3 or 4 hours. To every ounce of solution he adds ¼ oz. of sugar (grape sugar, if possible,) dissolved in equal quantities of water and alcohol. The surface to be silvered is covered with this liquid, and a temperature of 160 degrees F. maintained, till the deposition of the silver is complete. When quite dry, the coated surface is covered with mastic varnish.

Cement for Steam Pipes.—Good linseed oil varnish, ground with equal weights of white lead, oxide of manganese and pipe-clay.

INKS.—The following are specimens of the most useful kinds of Ink:—

Black Writing Ink.—Bruised Aleppo galls 6 oz., soft water 6 pints; boil together, add 4 oz. of sulphate of iron and 4 oz. of gum Arabic. Put the whole in a bottle, and keep it in a warm place, shaking it occasionally. In 2 months pour it off into glass bottles, and add to each pint a grain of corrosive sublimate, or 3 or 4 drops of creosote. Add 1 oz. of brown sugar to the above, and it will make good Copying Ink.

Red Writing Ink.—Best ground Brazil wood 4 oz., diluted acetic acid ½ pint, alum ½ oz.; boil them slowly in a covered tinned copper, or enamelled saucepan, for an hour, strain, and add ½ oz. gum. Some direct the Brazil wood to infuse for 2 or 3 days before boiling.

Blue Ink.—Prepare a solution of iodide of iron from iodine, iron and water; add to the solution half as much iodine as first used. Pour this solution into semi-saturated solution of ferro-prussiate of potash, containing nearly as much of the salt as the whole weight of iodine. Collect the precipitate, wash it, and finally dissolve it in water, to form the blue ink. The solution from which the precipitate is separated, evaporated to dryness, and the residue fused, re-dissolved and crystallized, yields pure iodide of potassium. This process is patented.

Gold and Silver Ink.—Fine bronze powder, or gold or silver leaf, ground with a little sulphate of potash, and washed from the salt, is mixed with water and a sufficient quantity of gum.

Ink for Marking Linen.—Nitrate of silver 100 gr., distilled water 1 oz., gum Arabic 2 dr., sap green a scruple; dissolve. The linen is first to be wetted with the following "pounce," dried and rubbed smooth, then written on by a clean quill or bone pen dipped in the ink. Pounce: Subcarbonate of soda 1 oz., water 8 oz.

Indelible Ink.—Take 20 parts of Dantzig potash, 10 of tanned leather parings, and 5 of sulphur; boil them in an iron pot with sufficient water to dryness; then raise the heat, stirring the matter constantly, till the whole becomes soft, taking care that it does not ignite. Add sufficient water, and filter through cloth. It must be kept from the air. It resists many chemical agents.

CEMENT FOR GLASS, CHINA, &c.—Isinglass 1 oz., distilled water 6 oz., boil to 3 oz., and add 1½ oz. of rectified spirit. Boil for a minute or two, strain, and add, while hot, first ½ oz. of a milky emulsion of ammoniac, and then 5 dr. of tincture of mastic. [There are various kinds of this cement sold, and some of the improvements introduced have not been made public.]

COPPERSMITHS' CEMENT.—Powdered quicklime, mixed with bullock's blood, and applied immediately.

GILDING.—Leaf gold is affixed to various surfaces, properly prepared by gold size, or other adhesive medium. Metallic surfaces are coated with gold by means of amalgam of gold and mercury, applied with a wire brush, wet with an acid solution of mercury, made by dissolving 10 parts of mercury in 11 of nitric acid, by a gentle heat, and adding 2½ parts of water. The article thus coated is heated over charcoal till the mercury is dissipated, and afterwards burnished. To give it a redder color, it is covered with gilder's wax, (a compound of verdigris, ochre, alum and yellow wax,) again exposed to heat, and afterwards washed and cleaned by a scratch brush and vinegar. An inferior kind of gilding is effected by dissolving gold, with a fifth of its weight of copper, in nitro-muriatic acid, dipping rags in the solution, drying and burning them, and rubbing the ashes on the metallic surface with a cork dipped in salt and water.

ELECTRO-GILDING, by Elkington's patent process, is thus performed :—A solution of 5 oz. of gold is prepared and boiled till it ceases to give out yellow vapors : the clear solution is mixed with 4 gallons of water, 20 lb. of bicarbonate of potash added, and the whole boiled for 2 hours. The articles, properly cleaned, are suspended on wires, and moved about in the liquid from a few seconds to a minute, then washed, dried, and colored in the usual way. The solution used in gilding with the voltaic apparatus is made by dissolving ¼ oz. of oxide of gold, with 2 oz. of cyanide of potassium, in a pint of distilled water.

BALLS FOR CLEANING CLOTHES—Bath-brick 4 parts, pipe-clay 8 parts, pumice 1, soft-soap 1 ; ochre, umber, or other color, to bring it to the desired shade, q. s. ; ox-gall to form a paste. Make into balls, and dry them.

To Stain Wood a Mahogany Colour (dark.)—Boil ½ lb of madder, and 2 oz. of logwood, in a gallon of water, and brush the wood well over with the hot liquid When dry, go over the whole with a solution of 2 drachms of pearlash in a quart of water.

To Stain Maple a Mahogany Colour.—Dragon's blood ½ oz., alkanet ¼ oz., aloes 1 dr., spirit of wine 16 ounces. Apply it with a sponge or brush.

Rosewood.—Boil 8 oz. of logwood in 3 pints of water until reduced to half: apply it boiling hot two or three times, letting it dry between each. Afterwards put on the streaks with a camel-hair pencil dipped in a solution of copperas and verdigris in decoction of logwood

Ebony.—Wash the wood repeatedly with a solution of sulphate of iron; let it dry, then apply a hot decoction of logwood and nutgalls for two or three times. When dry, wipe it with a wet sponge, and when dry, polish with linseed oil.

French Polish.—Orange shell-lac 22 oz., rectified spirit 4 pints: dissolve.

Etching Fluids. For Steel.—Mix 10 parts of pure hydrochloric acid, 70 of distilled water, and a solution of 2 parts of chlorate of potash in 20 of water. Dilute before using with from 100 to 200 parts of water. For Copper.—Iodine 2 parts, iodide of potassium 5 parts, water 5 to 8 parts.

Silvering Compound.—Nitrate of silver 1 part, cyanide of potassium (Liebig's) 3 parts, water sufficient to form a thick paste. Apply it with a rag. A bath for the same purpose is made by dissolving 100 parts of sulphite of soda, and 15 of nitrate of silver, in water and dipping the article to be silvered into it.

Tracing Paper.—Paper well wetted with Canada balsam and camphine, and dried.

Shampoo Liquor.—Rum 3 quarts, spirit of wine 1 pint, water 1 pint, tincture of cantharides ½ oz., carbonate of ammonia ½ oz., salt of tartar one oz. Rub it on, and afterwards wash with water. By omitting the salt of tartar it nearly resembles the balm of Columbia.

Waterproof Compound.—Suet 8 oz. linseed oil 8 oz., yellow bees'-wax 6 oz., neatsfoot oil 1½ oz., lamp-black 1 oz., litharge ½ oz Melt together, and stir till cold.

COURT PLASTER is made by repeatedly brushing over stretched sarcenet with a solution of 1 part of isinglass in 8 of water, mixed with 8 parts of proof spirit, and finishing with a coat of tincture of Benzoin, or of balsam of Peru.

KITTOE'S LOTION FOR SUNBURNS, FRECKLES, &c.—Muriate of ammonia 1 dr., spring water a pint, lavender water 2 dr. Apply with a sponge 2 or 3 times a day.

VIRGIN'S MILK.—Simple tincture of benzoin 2 dr orange-flower water 8 oz. It may be varied by using rose or elder-flower water.

COLORING FOR BRANDY, &c.—Sugar melted in a ladle till it is brown, and then dissolved in water or lime water.

COLORS FOR LIQUERS.—Pink is given by cochineal, yellow by saffron or safflower, violet by litmus, blue by sulphate of indigo, saturated with chalk; green by the last, with tincture of saffron, or by sap green.

TO PRESERVE BUTTER.—Powder finely, and mix together, 2 parts of the best salt, 1 of loaf sugar, and 1 of nitre. To each pound of butter, well cleansed from the milk, add 1 oz. of this compound. It should not be used under a month. [Butter that has an unpleasant flavor is said to be improved by the addition of 2½ dr. of bicarbonate of soda to 3 lbs. of butter. A turnipy flavor may be prevented by only feeding the cows with turnips immediately after milking them.]

TO PRESERVE EGGS.—Jayne's liquid (expired patent) is thus made:—Take a bushel of lime, 2 lb. of salt, ½ lb. of cream of tartar, and water sufficient to form a solution strong enough to float an egg. In this liquid it is stated, eggs may be preserved for two years.

HOW TO MAKE FLY POISON—A common poison for flies consists of white arsenic or king's yellow, with sugar, &c., but the use of such compounds may lead to fatal accidents. A sweetened infusion of quassia answers the same purpose, and is free from danger. Pepper, with milk, is also used; and also some adhesive compounds, by which they are fatally entangled.

Indian Ink.—Real lamp-black, produced by combustion of linseed oil, ground with gum, and infusion of galls. It is prepared both in a liquid and solid form, the latter being dried in the sun.

BED-BUG POISON.—Scotch snuff mixed with soft soap

Sympathetic or Secret Inks.

[The solutions used should be so nearly colourless that the writing is not seen till the agent is applied to render it visible.]

1. Digest 1 oz. of taffre, or oxide of cobalt, at a gentle heat, with 4 oz. of nitro-muriatic acid till no more is dissolved, then add 1 oz. of common salt, and 16 oz. of water. If this be written with and the paper held to the fire, the writing becomes green, unless the cobalt should be quite pure, in which case it will be blue. The addition of a little nitrate of iron will impart the property of becoming green. It is used in chemical landscapes for the foliage.

3. Boil oxide of cobalt in acetic acid. If a little common salt be added, the writing becomes green when heated; but with nitre it becomes a pale rose-colour.

6. A solution of sulphate—or preferably, persulphate—of iron. It becomes black when washed with infusion of galls; BLUE, by prusiate of potash. [This constitutes colourless ink, which becomes visible when written with on paper containing galls, or tannin, or prusiate of potash.]

FATTENING CALVES.—Aniseed ¼ lb, fenugree ¼ lb, linseed meal 1 lb; make it into a paste with milk, and cram them with it.

BLAKE'S TOOTHACHE.—Finely powdered alum 1 dr., spirit nitric ether 7 dr.

BRITISH OIL.—Oil of turpentine, and linseed oil, of each 8 oz.; oil of amber, and oil of juniper, of each 4 oz.; true Barbadoes tar 3 oz.; American Petroleum (seneca oil) 1 oz.; mix.

To PRESERVE MILK.—Milk the cow into glass bottles, and seal them to keek out the air.

THE

SECRET OF BEAUTY.

Personal Beauty.

There are many things, both in nature and science, that are adapted to the personal improvement of all, which may be resorted to with commendable pride. It is our duty to make the best use of all our faculties tending to the improvement of both mind and body. Filthiness in every shape is always disgusting; and those regardless of their personal appearance are a species of leprous sores on the body of society. Neatness and cleanliness of person and dress, with a clear, beautiful skin, white teeth, and soft curling hair, attract the admiration of all; while the opposite, even when bedecked in the most gorgeous and expensive habiliments, are disliked and contemned.

The means here set forth, to enable all to enhance their charms, are within the reach of those even in the most humble circumstances, and at a very trifling cost. They are the result of much laborious research and years of extensive experience. Many of the following recipes are richly worth ten times the cost of the whole.

IMPROVING THE COMPLEXION AND CLEARNESS OF THE SKIN.

Cleanliness is always of essential importance, not only as regards the looks or appearance, but as concerns our health and longevity. Free and frequent ablutions in cold water, especially of the hands, face and neck, cannot be too highly recommended, using very little soap, and that of the finest and best quality. Friction with a brush or coarse towel is likewise serviceable. Persons accustoming themselves to daily ablutions in cold water are not liable to take cold, or suffer from the most inclement weather and exposure, as those who neglect it, or use warm instead of cold water. They seldom have cold feet, coughs, or sore throat. Too much cannot be said in favor of cold water; it makes the skin clear, ruddy and beautiful, as nature intended it should be, while those using warm water in its stead are generally suffering from cold; they are more liable to contract disease; their skin becomes wrinkled, losing its beauty and clearness.

It is best to change your under garments on going to bed, never sleeping in clothes you have worn through the day, but use clothing of the *same kind.* After your meals, remain quiet for an hour or so, if your business or duties will allow, as exercise is injurious at such times. Sleep, good and sound, is essential to health and personal appearance, while a restless night leaves its traces on the countenance. Many persons, especially those called nervous, hardly ever know what a good night's rest is. The following, when observed, will usually enable them to enjoy that luxury: Use friction with a flesh brush, or coarse towel, freely over the body on going to bed; take from two to five drops of spirits of hartshorn in a little water, or as much super-carbonate of soda as will lie on a ten-cent piece. If not then inclined to sleep, commence counting while in bed, moderately, one, two, three, and so on till you reach five hundred, if drowsiness is not sooner induced; most persons will find themselves overtaken with sleep before they reach that number. Sometimes a tepid bath before using the friction will facilitate the disposition to rest. From one to three grains of lactucarium, (a preparation made from lettuce,) may occasionally be resorted to; it has less injurious effects than opium, which is not unfrequently resorted to.

Those afflicted with headache during the night, should bathe the head with cold water, leave off the night-cap, use friction to the feet, and wear woollen or worsted stockings in bed.

REMEDY FOR COLD FEET.

Cold feet may be prevented by rubbing them and the ankles briskly with the hand, or a towel, until a glow of heat is experienced. Daily washing the feet in cold water and rubbing till dry, promotes that action that nature requires, and will do much towards promoting health, prevent taking cold, or suffering from cold feet.

To Remove Freckles,

TAN AND BLOTCHES, IMPROVE THE COMPLEXION, AND BEUTIFY THE SKIN, FACE, NECK AND HANDS.

Take half a pound of good white soap cut it into small thin pieces, and put it into one gallon of boiling soft water, stirring it until it is all dissolved. When it is cold, add one quart of alcohol, and half an ounce of the oil of rosemary. Mix the whole well together, and it is fit for use, and may be used as freely as desired.

Or you may take horse-radish, which grows abundantly throughout the country, grate or scrape it, and put it into cold sweet-milk; let it stand an hour or two, and it is fit for use. It is an excellent article, costs comparatively nothing, and is easily prepared, and may be used in place of the above, and as long as required to remove the imperfections.

Or this: Take the water of a blacksmith's forge, where he has often quenched his red-hot iron, and wash the parts with that. You can make the same article by repeatedly immersing a red-hot iron in a basin of water.

WHITE, SOFT, DELICATE HANDS.

Use none but good soap, and while the hands are wet, before wiping them, rub in some cold cream.

(as hereafter directed to make,) and sleep in kid or leather gloves. Too frequent wetting the skin makes it rough.

To Beautify and Preserve the Teeth.

The Teeth were intended to be ornaments, as well as instruments to masticate our food and with proper care would answer the purpose of their formation as long as we require them. But we too often neglect and suffer them to become receptacles of filth, and consequently to decay. Children should be early taught to keep their teeth clean, and impressed with the importance of their preservation. They should be washed twice a day, and especially at night, taking care to remove every particle of food or other extraneous substances that may have collected around them. Whoever will follow this course will have no occasion for the following preparations. But to those who have neglected so important a duty, we give the following recipes:—

DISINFECTING AND DECOLORIZING TOOTH-POWDER.

Take one part of chloride of lime and twenty-four parts of prepared chalk; mix them together and add otto of roses or any perfume you like, and use twice a day with a stiff brush. This will destroy the bad breath arising from the teeth, and remove all stains from them, arising from tobacco or other causes. *A mouth wash*, for the same purposes, may be made by dissolving three drachms of chloride of lime in two ounces (about half a gill) of soft water. Pour off the clear liquor, and add two ounces of spirits to it, and scent with such perfumes as you like.

ORRIS TOOTH-POWDER FOR ORDINARY USE.

Take four ounces of prepared chalk, rubbed down to a fine powder, and one ounce of finely powdered orris root, mix them well together, add three drops of otto of roses, and three drops of oil of cloves, or any other perfume you like, or you may use it without any scent.

ORRIS TOOTH PASTE.

May be made by adding honey or molasses (sugar-house molasses is the best) enough to the orris tooth-powder to make it into a paste, to be perfumed or not as you desire. A stiff brush is best in using either.

CHARCOAL TOOTH PASTE.

Take powdered charcoal, and mix it with honey or molasses and a little water, to the consistence you want, and flavor it to suit your taste.

Persons accustomed from childhood to keeping their teeth and gums clean, will seldom require much of anything more than water and a tooth-brush. It is mostly where the teeth have been neglected, as is too commonly the case, that artificial means are required, and for all such the above are particularly recommended.

CURE FOR SPONGY GUMS.

Use equal parts of common table-salt, white sugar, and flowers of sulphur, powdered fine, and mixed together.

A NATURAL DENTIFRICE.

May be found in the common strawberry; its juice dissolves the tartar, cleanses the teeth and gums, makes the breath sweet, and leaves a pleasant taste in the mouth.

CAMPHOR CREAM FOR CHAPPED HANDS OR FACE.

Take oil of almonds, or sweet oil, two ounces, spermaceti and good sweet lard, of each one ounce, melt them together, and set it aside to cool; when nearly cold, stir in one ounce of finely powdered white sugar and a quarter of an ounce of finely powdered gum camphor. and keep stirring till it is well mixed; rub it well on the parts affected three times a day, or oftener if necessary. Always rub a little well in immediately after washing your hands.

COLD CREAM FOR SOFTENING THE SKIN.

Take good sweet lard two ounces, oil of almonds or sweet oil one ounce. melt together over a slow fire, set aside, and while cooling add half an ounce to one ounce of rose-water, and keep stirring and beating it up till it is cold and becomes light and creamy. A little of it rubbed into the skin after washing and before wiping, will keep the skin smooth and soft, and prevent its becoming rough. It is excellent to use on the face after shaving.

LIP SALVE.

Take equal parts of mutton suet, spermaceti, white or yellow wax. oil of almonds or sweet oil, and finely powdered white sugar. If you want it colored, add a little alkanet root, while it is melted, and boil a few minutes, and then strain it off and it will be a beautiful red. If you want it scented, add a few drops of otto of roses, or any scent you may desire.

MOSQUITOE BITES, AND STINGS OF WASPS AND OTHER INSECTS.

Pennyroyal, the herb or essence, or spirits of camphor, will usually keep away mosquitoes, by keeping it about you, and wetting your skin and clothes with it. Where they have bitten you, apply a little of very strong spirits of hartshorn. and it will stop the itching and prevent any swelling or soreness. It is well to keep a little of it always about you, for it will save you from much annoyance.

RINGWORM.

Throw into water as much blue vitriol as it will dissolve. making it as strong as possible, and touch the affected part with the solution several times a day. Where this fails, apply some strong old citrine ointment two or three times a day. An occasional small dose of salts or a seidlitz powder will be beneficial. What is called barber's itch may be treated in the same way.

BLOTCHED FACE.

Take four grains of zinc and two ounces of water; dissolve it, and touch the blotches frequently with the lotion; live on plain, simple food; keep the bowels open with seidlitz powders or epsom salts; and if not sufficient, take one grain of hydriodate of potass twice a day, every other week for two or three months, if necessary. You may dissolve one drachm of the hydriodate of potass in half a pint of water, and sweeten to your taste, and take a teaspoonful twice a day, which will be the same as the grain dose above. In obstinate cases of ringworm, or barber's itch, this medicine, taken as above, will be highly beneficial.

POMATUM.

Melt together four ounces of mutton tallow, (or beef tallow will do,) one ounce of yellow or white bees-wax, and while it is cooling, stir in a few drops of oil of bergamot, or any other perfume you like, and before it gets cold and stiff pour it into a paper or tin mould, the size and shape you wish.

ROSE HAIR, OR FLESH POWDER.

Take one pound of finely powdered starch, two to five drops of otto of roses dropped on a piece of white loaf sugar, and rubbed down very fine together, mix all well together, and keep it in a bottle or dry, close vessel; use as desired for the skin where it is chafed or fretted, especially for children or infants. This powder is equal to the best hair or flesh powder of the shops, and only costs half the money.

CHILBLAINS.

Where ulceration attends chilblains, poultice the part a short time with bread and milk, and then dress with basilicon ointment, to which add some spirits of turpentine. Where there is no ulceration, and the skin is not broken, apply a mixture of one part of spirits of salt, and seven parts of soft water, rubbing it well in with the hand, on going to bed, repeating it two or three nights. The feet may feel a little tender, but the tenderness will soon pass away.

COLOGNE WATER.

Take oil bergamot, oil rosemary, oil lemon, and oil lavender, each one drachm; oil cloves, ten drops; oil cinnamon, six drops; otto roses, four drops; musk, two grains; alcohol, three pints; mix all together, and it will soon be fit for use. By omitting the musk and roses, it lessens the cost and is still very good. By adding from fifteen to twenty drops of the oil of neroli, you will greatly improve the perfume, but the pure oil of neroli is very costly, and the common and inferior is of but little use. It is very important that you procure good alcohol, that which is entirely free from all unpleasant odor. Lavender water is made by adding the oil of lavender to alcohol, in such proportions as you desire. say about half an ounce to the pint. It makes a very cheap and pleasant perfume.

ROSY CHEEKS AND LIPS.

Take a very small quantity of Carmine, or Rose Pink, and rub on the cheeks and lips, and you have a beautiful color. For white tints, use common starch, powdered very fine; never use chalk or any mineral substance, as it is injurious to the skin, and after a while makes it look wrinkled and old.

A Rouge may be made by taking a little sweet lard about the size of a pea, and as much "Bloom of Beauty" as will equal the size of a pea ; rub them well together on a piece of white paper with the finger, until it is thoroughly mixed ; then take a piece of raw cotton, compress it, and dip it in the "Bloom of Beauty," so that a little will adhere and rub it on the face till you get the desired tint. By this means you can imitate the natural color exactly. Free exercise in the open air and a free use of cold water, are nature's means of imparting a healthy and ruddy hue to all her children.

Bright Eyes.

To Preserve the Eyesight for Life, to Relieve the Far-Sighted, and to Restore Impaired Vision.

Where the eyesight has failed from age, or too constant and long-continued use, the following directions will secure you from dependence upon spectacles. The eyes were intended by our Creator, like the other parts of our bodies, to last us through life ; but man's abuse of them has doomed him to resort to glasses to make up for what his imprudence has deprived him of.

Commence in early life to wash the face and eyes in cold water, dipping the face into it so far as to cover the eyes ; then open and shut them a few times, so as to wash the lids and balls, taking care to wipe them inwards, towards the nose, and never outwards, taking care not to press upon the balls so as to flatten them. The late lamented and venerated John Quincy Adams, and several others we could mention, preserved their eyesight unimpaired through life by this simple process.

This care and attention to the eyes will not only ensure their preservation, but will also keep them bright and sparkling through life, and avoid that dead and flattened appearance so common in the aged and often the middle aged.

Near-sighted people should, by gentle pressure

upon the eye-balls, depress or flatten them—using cold water freely, as before directed.

TO PRESERVE THE EYESIGHT.

Whenever the sight is impaired from age or too much use, or any imprudence or neglect, you must wash the parts two or three times a day with cold water, as before directed, taking the same precaution, in wiping them inwards, towards the nose, without pressing directly on the balls, so as to flatten them. Press gently your thumb and second finger on the outer corner of each eye, and hold them in that position for a few seconds at a time, then draw them slowly and gently out, as though you wished to make them protrude. Occasionally press your thumb and finger on the top of the eye-balls, and also on the bottom of them, using all these means to make the eye more prominent, and, as we commonly say, to stick out. Never press upon the front of the eye, so as to depress or flatten it, except where you are troubled with short or near-sightedness. These manipulations must be followed up repeatedly through the day, but never so hard as to produce pain or inflammation. The free use of cold water must not be dispensed with, but followed up with the manipulations till the vision is restored. A little practice will enable any one to apply the pressure as directed ; and a few weeks, if not a few days, will prove the utility of the practice. Those just beginning to experience the failing of their sight, will find a few seconds' pressure as above directed, to give immediate and sensible relief.

I have known what is commonly called squint-eyes entirely cured by these manipulations. In such cases you must press your thumb or finger so as to press, or tend to press, the eye into its proper position. Follow up this course for some time, with a free use of the cold water, as before directed, and by perseverance you will remove all the obliquity of vision, and make your eyes to see perfectly straight

Those who do not wish to dip their faces into a basin of cold water, and open and shut their eyes in it, so as to bring them in full and free contact with the water, can use eye-glasses made for that purpose; in which case they should renew the water three or four times during each operation.

The above instructions on the preservation of the eyes cannot be too highly appreciated, nor too generally adopted, and are worth ten times the cost of this whole work, and if universally practiced, there would be no further use for spectacles, and but little demand for occulists. Cold water to the eyes as well as to the whole body, is nature's panacea, but being so simple, is too little heeded.

Where the eyes are weak or inflamed, the following eye-water will prove very efficacious: Take of sulphate of zinc, commonly called white vitriol, one drachm; sugar of lead, four scruples; dissolve each separately in twelve ounces (which is three gills), of soft water, then add both together, and shake well and set aside to settle, after which pour off the liquor and throw away the settling; apply it to the eyes with the finger three to six times a day. If it makes them smart too much, reduce it by adding more water.

STYES.

Styes are often very troublesome. They are caused by the obstruction of some of the small glands in the edge of the eyelids. When they first appear, apply a leech to the inflamed part, and if somewhat advanced, apply a warm bread and milk poultice, and as soon as matter is formed, open it with a lancet or needle and let it out; then apply a little weak citrine ointment.

Beauty of Form.

Cure for Corpulency or Fatness.

Corpulence is a disease that sometimes proves fatal. The difficulty of breathing with which very corpulent people are oppressed, is caused by an accumulation of fat on the kidneys, which obstructs the motion of the diaphragm; whilst the heart and large blood vessels being equally encumbered, a slowness of pulse is produced, and possibly apoplexy and death. Corpulence generally arises from indulgence of the appetite, or in taking too much sleep. In ordinary cases, a system of training will remove it. But, in robust habits, we must alter the diet, or increase the exercise; we prefer the latter; and, in addition, let the person lie on a horse-hair mattress, and not sleep more than six hours—say from 10 p. m. to 4 a. m. Strong exercise, succeeded by change of clothes when perspiration has been produced, with considerable friction of the skin at each change of apparel, morning and evening, as before directed, will usually prevent excessive corpulence. If, however, it fail, a vegetable diet must be adopted. All butter, cream, beer, wine and spirits, must be abandoned, except that quantity of brandy allowed for meals as before directed; this system, with exercise, [if possible in the open air.] and in the intervals of exercise, having the mind properly applied, will, we engage, reduce any ordinary case of obesity, and make the individual active both in mind and body. When this is effected, the return to animal food must be gradual, and the state of the stomach and bowels must be attended to.

Many ladies who are not troubled with general obesity of the system, have a superabundant development of the breast; the modern mode of reducing this is by a preparation of iodine; but as this is a dangerous internal medicine in unprofessional hands, we shall recommend its external use, thus: Take

Iodine of zinc,—1 drachm,
Hog's lard.—1 ounce;

mix well, and rub daily into each breast a piece about the size of a nutmeg, a linen bandage so placed as gently to compress the breast, without pressing upon the nipple, will assist its operation. We need scarcely say, this must not be done during lactation or pregnancy.

Some of the old practitioners recommend pounded mint applied to the breasts, to check their exuberant growth, accompanied with bandages; but to bandages as a general rule, we decidedly object;—when necessary, they must be used with care as just stated.

LEANNESS, when accompanied with decrease of strength, must also arise from disease, and we recommend attention to the general health, as it may be the herald of consumption; but if no decrease of strength accompanies it, though not a disease, it is still an enemy to beauty, as all angular development is in opposition to gracefulness of figure. We must therefore adopt a system, if we wish to produce that approach to *embonpoint* which is necessary to the beautiful. A diet at once nourishing and strengthening little exercise, from ten to twelve hours sleep, [say from 10 P. M. till 9 A. M.]—a soft bed, complete tranquillity of mind, little excitement even of a pleasurable character, good mild ale at dinner and supper, [but abstinence from spirits of all sorts.] cream at breakfast and tea, with plenty of sugar, is necessary to the accomplishment of our object. If the bosom participates in the general leanness, its growth may be encouraged by having it loosely clothed, avoiding all pressure; and friction by the hand for an hour or two every day will assist much in its development; but *nothing* will more effectually *prevent it*, than the artificial padding usually worn to supply the natural deficiency, except it be the artificial bosom, said to be made of Indian rubber, but which we only speak of from report; this would most effectually stop their growth, destroy its complexion, and probably produce disease, by a complete exclusion of the air, and repression of the natural exhalations.

THE CARE OF THE SKIN.

Being assured that the preservation of health in this important membrane is one of the most effective means of prolonging life, we shall be most explicit on the subject. From what has been already said, it must be manifest, that if the pores of the skin be stopped up, the operations of digestion must be impaired, acridity and corruption of the juices must ensue, ruining the surface of the skin, and laying the foundation for acute disease. Our great object, then, is to keep the pores open by cleanliness, and give it tone by bathing and gentle friction; and here, at the risk of being thought tautological, we shall enforce the necessity of all persons (ladies especially) passing a wet sponge over the WHOLE SURFACE of the body every morning and evening, or at any rate every morning, commencing with tepid water, and adopting cold water as soon as they can bear it;—then let the body be thoroughly dried with a soft towel, and rubbed with a soft flesh-brush. This habit will not only beautify the skin, and give it that transparency of complexion for which the Roman ladies were so eminent; but it will be the most effectual means of guarding against colds, and all the interruptions of the system of which they are the fruitful source; it has a double effect, it beautifies, and it fortifies the skin. The late Sir Astley Cooper has recorded, that to this habit he owed his robust health, and said that though he was in the practice of going out of hot crowded rooms at all times, night and day, without making any addition to his dress, yet he never caught a cold. It will, in fact, make woman look lovely, by removing from her everything that reminds us of mortality, leaving only that image of himself with which God has endowed her.

It is scarcely necessary to inform my fair readers that the skin will be dried and hardened by exposure to the burning heat of the sun, or to a high wind; when such exposure is unavoidable, the face should be slighty washed by the following preparation: Take one Teaspoonful of Soda, one pint of Water, one Teaspoonful of Cologne Water, mix and apply two or three times a day. On returning home, wash the face again with tepid water, and thoroughly dry it with a soft napkin. If exposed to dust or smoke, the face or neck should be wiped with a handkerchief as soon as convenient, if there be no opportunity of laving them. If sitting near the fire, persons who value their complexions must protect the face, &c., with a screen. If, from walking, or other exercise, or indeed from any cause whatever, there be moisture on the skin, a handkerchief should be applied by slight pressure, so as to absorb, not wipe it away: these are the minor cares, which, though apparently unimportant, are necessary, as their omission would destroy the appearance of the complexion.

PRECAUTIONS.—A few may still be necessary. Friction to the neck and arms should be performed by means of a flesh-brush, which, though soft, is sufficiently elastic to remove the scaly particles which sometimes appear after the application of water. When there is insufficient action in the skin the hair glove may be applied with advantage to the other parts of the body, care being taken to produce no abrasion of the skin.

All external applications are but temporary expedients, unless the stomach and intestines have their proper action.

NEVI MATERNI, or birth-marks, may be upon any part of the body, but usually appear upon the neck, face, or head; at an adult age these cannot be eradicated, but when they are observed upon an infant, the advice of a skilful surgeon should be taken. These marks are usually masses of blood-vessels, being veins when the blue color prevails, and arteries when the bright red predominates. We particularly caution mothers against external applications to such marks, without the advice of a physician.

MOLES.—The common mole is situated in the middle layer of the skin; the coloring matter is probably some chemical combination of iron; they are often elevated above the surface, and then the natural down of the skin over them is changed into a tuft of hair. Although they usually have their origin before birth, they sometimes appear at puberty or after life; some also that have been observed at birth, disappear at puberty. We must inform our fair readers, that the less moles are trifled with, the better, and admonish them particularly against the use of depilatorics to remove the hair from them, a fœtid suppurating wound is frequently the consequence of such attempts. A surgeon is the best adviser in this case.

FRECKLES.—These we can generally remove, by external applications, but if the liver or stomach is out of order. it must have the first attention, or no external application can thoroughly succeed. CAUSE OF FRECKLES.—The skin, we must inform our readers, has charcoal, or *carbon* (as the chemists term it) for its base, and in proportion as the other elements of which it is composed are driven off by heat, so will the spots upon the skin be more or less dark.

Oxygen is another element of which the skin is composed, and is disengaged from carbon by heat; if, however, iron is present, the oxygen, upon being released from the carbon, would immediately unite therewith. Now, as it is well known that there is a considerable quantity of iron in the blood, especially so in the blood of persons with red hair, the union of the oxygen with the iron will produce various shades of a rusty appearance, according to its purity and its mixture with the charcoal or carbon; the reader will therefore at once perceive the cause of freckles, which are the rusty appearances thus produced.

CURE OF FRECKLES.—For this purpose anoint the skin every night, for from three to seven days, with Almond Paste made as follows:—Take one ounce of Bitter Almonds, one ounce of Barley flour, and enough Honey to make all into a thin paste: if you think proper to attack the oxygen, apply this mixture to the freckles by means of camel-hair pencil:—Take one Teaspoonful of Soda, one gill of cold water, ten drops of Cologne water, mix; persevere for a week or ten days; if not successful, you may be more so by attacking the iron ; then use this mixture for two or three days :—Take one Teacupful of cold sour milk, a Tablespoonfull of grated Horse-Radish, let stand 12 hours, strain off and apply three times a day If none of these succeed, use the Lemon Cream.

Lemon Cream is made as follows :—Put two spoonsful of sweet cream into half pint of new milk ; squeeze into it the juice of one Lemon, add half teacupful of Spirits, and half Teaspoonful of Alum, and one Tablespoonful of Loaf Sugar ; boil for ten minutes, skim it, and when cold, apply three times a day.

Remember, however, that the stomach and the biliary system must at the same time be attended to, if they are out of order ; for, as before said, no external applications can eradicate those appearances effectually and permanently, while the cause of the evil lies deeper than the skin.

Yellow Appearances sometimes present themselves under the skin, frequently upon the neck—sometimes upon the face : sometimes they are smaller than a dime, sometimes larger than a dollar. A very effectual way to remove them is, by rubbing into them the flour of sulphur every night until they disappear ; this, however, sometimes creates a disagreeable odor, hence the very frequent rubbing of the part with roll brimstone has been adopted, and will commonly remove them without the same disagreeable results.

Sunburn is nearly related to freckles, and arises from much the same cause—use the same remedies.

Wrinkles.—These are still greater enemies to beauty than the preceding, but, fortunately, are usually not seen until the approach of old age, unless brought on by dissipation, or disease ; the latter are much the most rapid manufacturers of wrinkles.—By attention, a person with a good constitution may prevent the exhibition of these heralds of decay for years after the time of their common appearance—for wrinkles are not so certain an indication of old age, as they are of the wear and tear of the constitution ; we, in fact, do wrong in applying the term [as generally understood] "old age," to a certain number of years; the approach of this period should be calculated, not by time, but by the ravages of decay. Many persons, from disease, or more often, from profligacy, are old at thirty, while we see others of sixty with the animal spirits and activity of matured strength. Wrinkles are occasioned by the obstruction or obliteration of the finer blood vessels; when this occurs, the larger veins are loaded, and protrude, as may be seen in the veins on the back of the hands of very aged persons; while wrinkles are in other parts produced by the absence of the blood, caused by the obstruction and obliteration above alluded to; or, by the same process acting on the small pipes which convey that moisture to the skin which keeps it smooth, soft, and flexible. Our object then is, first, to prevent wrinkles, by preserving undiminished the action of the skin, and thus securing the assistance of the minor blood-vessels; and, secondly, to direct how wrinkles may be removed, if acquired. To effect the first object, cold water bathing is the best; observing, however, that as age advances, tepid water, instead of cold, must be used for the morning and evening ablutions. A warm bath, with friction for a quarter of an hour with a soft flesh brush [after being thoroughly dried], will be a great regenerator of the appearance. A nutritive, but not over phlogistic diet, is also necessary to ward off these unpleasant visitors; and we need hardly say, that temperance is indispensable, and early hours equally so; for late hours will, in some degree, retard our operations, or, at any rate, will prevent their proper and natural effect. The system recommended must be scrupulously followed, if wrinkles have appeared and are wished to be got rid of. We need here hardly repeat, that air and exercise are also indispensable; without these, health cannot be preserved; in the absence of health, little can be done by cosmetics, except in temporary appearance.

The philosophy of the operation of destroying

wrinkles is founded upon the opening, by stimulating the small thread-like blood vessels, and moisture pipes, which have been closed; if the stimulating process be pursued previous to the closing of these vessels, they will not be obliterated. Our readers will therefore perceive our directions are founded upon common sense, and that very little thought would have rendered our advice unnecessary.

THE WORM-PIMPLE, WITH BLACK POINTS, is one of the most common appearances, and not less unsightly than annoying. The cause of it is, obstruction of the pores of the skin, generally from want of attention; perspiration is allowed to accumulate and become hard in the mouths of these small pipes, irritation ensues, the pimple rises, and the black point becomes prominent. This point is, however, nothing more nor less than perspiration allowed to accumulate until it actually has the consistence of a paste, and is loaded with impurities. The only way to eradicate this appearance, when formed, is to press out the extraneous matter very carefully. To prevent its return, cleanliness and friction of the skin only are required, with ordinary attention to the digestive organs.

BEAUTY DERIVED FROM DRESS.

A few hints upon this subject may not be amiss. Ladies of fair complexion may even wear the purest white; they should, in the choice of colors, select such as are light and brilliant—rose, blue, or, if there be a slight tinge of brown in the carnation, light yellow; be it, however, observed, that a perfectly light complexion would become almost livid by being opposed to yellow. Bright colors brighten a light complexion, dark ones would give it the appearance of alabaster, destroy its life, and leave it without expression; on the contrary, if light colors were opposed to a dark complexion, it would appear dull, lifeless, and inanimate; the most suitable color for this is some of the varieties of yellow. Amber, for instance, is peculiarly suitable; violet, puce, dark blue, purple, dark green, or even black, make it appear more fair, become animated, and enable it frequently to bear away the palm from its blonde competitors.

The fashion of the form of a dress is frequently followed without any regard to the propriety of its adoption; but this is quite contrary to good taste. Nothing can look much more absurd than a short, stout figure adorned with a superfluity of flounces and trimmings, yet the power of fashion forces such exhibitions into continual notice; even when fashion has decreed the flounces and trimmings shall be worn, such a figure need not be made ridiculous, and be made to bear as near as possible a resemblance to the prince of a Christmas dinner-table; in such a case let the trimmings be placed as low as possible, and the dress be made very long; the body also should be as long as convenient, and be made to fit tight. If the dress then hangs in graceful folds, it will add much to the appearance of length.

The arrangements of the upper part of the person can also be made to add to, or to diminish the height. Much trimming about the neck of a short stout person must make her look shorter; her object should be to elongate the appearance of the neck, and thus further destroy the appearance of a superfluity of substance. Nature is especially kind to the ladies in giving them so many personal advantages. Their hair offers them another means of apparently increasing their stature; in so doing care must be taken not to raise the head-dress disproportionately, as, to the above figure, it would give the appearance of a mountain stuck upon a pigmy; it should, however, be elevated in some measure, and at the same time diminished as much in breadth as will be consistent with the features, for we must not destroy a charm while we are attempting to remedy an evil.

All parts, indeed, of a lady's dress may be made to improve her figure or her face; nor is the bonnet the least important--how many pretty faces have been spoiled by an ugly bonnet! fashion being the only thing attended to; a good taste will enable a person to avoid this. The trimmings may be generally so arranged as to suit a face by making the fashion meet them half-way; if fashion dictate an absurdly large or small bonnet, which is inappropriate to a certain physiognomy, let such a person adopt that degree of addition or diminution which will be sufficient to be within the bounds of fashion without spoiling her appearance, and she may depend that the "graceful" will always ensure more admirers than the fashionable.

Everything that we have said upon a short figure must of course be reversed with a tall one. Trimmings and flounces may be adopted *ad libitum*; the dress should be made full, and the lines being broken by the flounces, the height of the figure will be diminished; if this is required to be done still more, the dress should not reach the ground; thus the eye stops as it were in its survey, and the artifice is not perceived.

PERFUMES AND ARTICLES FOR THE TOILETTE, THE COMPLEXION, &c.

Cologne Water.—Take 38 drops of essence of cedrat, 38 do. of bergamotte, 60 do. of oranges, 38 do. of citronella, 32 do. of neroli, 26 do. of melisse, 1 pint of alcohol. Mix, and let stand two weeks; then strain through filtering paper, or fine muslin.

Honey Water.—Take 1 ounce essence bergamotte, 3 drachms of oil of lavender, half a drachm of oil of cloves, half a drachm of aromatic vinegar, 6 grains of musk, a pint and a half of alcohol. Mix, and let stand two weeks, then strain.

The Delectible Odor.—Take four ounces of rose-water, 4 do. of orange-flower water, 1 drachm of oil of cloves, 1 drachm of oil of lavender, 2 drachms of oil of bergamotte, 2 grains of musk, and 1 pint of alcohol. Dissolve the musk and ambergris in the spirit of wine, then mix the whole well.

Lavender Water.—Take a pint of alcohol, essential oil of lavender, one ounce; put all into a quart bottle and shake well.

Aromatic Vinegar.—Take 1 ounce of dried tops of rosemary, 1 ounce of dried leaves of sage, 1 ounce of dried flowers of lavender, I drachm of cloves, 1 drachm of camphor, one pint and a half of distilled vinegar. Macerate for fourteen days, with heat, and then filter. Used to produce a fine soft feeling of the hands and face.

Macassar Oil.—Take 1 quart of olive oil, 2½ ounces of alcohol, 1 ounce of cinnamon powder, 5 drachms of bergamotte. Heat them together in a large pipkin, then remove it from the fire, and add 4 small pieces of alkanet root; keep it closely covered for six hours, let it then be filtered through a funnel lined with fine flannel.

Cold Cream.—Take 2 drachms of white wax, 2 drachms of spermaceti, 2 ounces of hog's-lard; put altogether into a jar, which place into boiling water and stir till all is melted; take it out of the water, and stir till nearly cold, then pour the mixture into rose-water, and with the hand work it thoroughly, changing the water until the cream is very white. Return it to the jar, and as soon as it is melted, add 1 drachm of oil of almonds, and any perfume you approve. Let these be thoroughly incorporated, then remove it. When cold, put it up in rose-water; if you wish to keep it in the greatest perfection, change the rose-water every day.

Lip Honey.—Take 2 ounces of fine honey, 1 ounce of purified wax, and half an ounce of myrrh. Mix over a slow fire, and add milk of roses, Eau-de-Cologne, or any perfume you may prefer.

Preventive Wash for Sunburn.—Take 2 drachms of borax, 1 drachm of Roman alum, 1 drachm of camphor, half an ounce of sugar-candy, 1 pound of ox-gall. Mix and stir well together, and repeat the stirring three or four times a day, until it becomes transparent. Then strain it through filtering or blotting-paper, and it will be fit for use. Wash the face with the mixture before you go into the sun.

How to Cure Sunburn, Tan, Freckles, &c.—Dip a bunch of green grapes in a basin of water; sprinkle it with powdered alum and salt mixed; wrap the grapes in paper, and bake them under hot ashes; then express the juice, and wash the face with the liquid, which will usually remove either freckles, tan or sunburn.

How to Cure Pimples.—Put into a pint bottle half a pint of spirits and as many strawberries as the spirits will cover, close the mouth of the bottle with a piece of bladder. and let it remain exposed to the sun for a week; then strain it through a linen cloth, add as many more strawberries as the liquid will cover, and add half an ounce of camphor; soak a pledget of lint in the mixture, and apply it to the parts.

To Cure Wrinkles.—Take of barley-water 1 pint, and strain through a piece of fine linen, add a dozen drops of the balm of Mecca, shake it well together until the balm is thoroughly incorporated with the water, which will be effected when the water assumes a whitish or turgid appearance. Before applying, wash the face with soft water; we have heard that if used once a day it will beautify the face, preserve the freshness of youth, and give a surprising brilliancy to the skin.

How to Have a Sweet Breath.—When the breath is affected by constipation of the bowels, which is very often the case, the following mixture will be useful:—Take 4 drachms of Epsom-salts, 8 drachms of tincture of Columba, 6 ounces of infusion of roses. Well shake the phial each time you take the draught, which should be every other morning, for a month or six weeks, a wine-glass full at each time.

How to Remove Warts.—Take nitrate of silver, 1 drachm, pure water, 1 ounce. Apply to the warts very often with a camel's-hair brush. This is poisonous if it gets into the stomach; be careful to label it such.

How to Cure Frostbite, or Chilblains.—Take liquor of subacetate of lead, 1 ounce, camphorated spirits of wine, 2 ounces; mix, and rub into the hands or feet two or three times a day; oftener if convenient.

N.B.—This is an excellent application, and well worthy of attention. Occasionally soak the feet in warm water going to bed, and then apply the liniment.

Balm of Mecca.—Take of Balsam of Tolu 1 ounce, alcohol, 1 pint, oil of lemon, 1 tea-spoonful. Mix all in a bottle, and shake occasionally for two weeks. This is used as a cosmetic for beautifying the complexion, curing pimples, blotches, &c.

How to Cure Corns.—Take 2 ounces of gum ammoniac, 2 ounces of yellow wax, 6 drachms of verdigris; mix them together, and spread the composition on a piece of linen or soft leather, first rubbing down the corn with an instrument like a file; it is to be purchased at most chemists. A file not too coarse will, however, answer the same purpose. Let the plaster be renewed in a fortnight, if necessary.

The Celebrated "Bath of Modesty" for Beautifying the Skin.—Take 4 ounces of sweet almonds, peeled, 1 pound of pine-apple kernels, 1 pound of elecampane, 10 handsful of linseed, 1 ounce of marsh mallow roots, 1 ounce of white lily roots. Pound all these till reduced to a paste, and tie it up in several small bags, which are to be thrown into a tepid bath, andjoressed till the water becomes milky.

The Wonderful Virgin Milk, for the Complexion, &c.—Take equal parts of gum benzoin and styrax, dissolve in a sufficient quantity of alcohol; the spirits will then become a reddish tincture, and exhale a very fragrant smell. Some people add a little Balm of Gilead. Drop a few drops into a glass of clear water, and by stirring the water, it instantly changes milky. Ladies use it successfully to clear the complexion.

HOW TO DRESS.

The Dress of Ladies.

Of the Color of Dress.—This, which we have placed first, is one of the most important considerations, and one upon which the greatest amount of ignorance has been shown. Not only at present, but formerly as we can see by paintings and by still older illuminations, various colors have been in vogue without the slightest regard to the complexions of those who wore them; nay, sometimes people have been dressed according to the picture of their armorial bearings, in *two* colors, exactly divided down the middle, red and blue; or like John of Gaunt, *temp.* Richard II., blue and white.

Out of three primitive colors, red. blue and yellow, there are endless mixtures and variations, and some of these can skillfully be adapted to any complexion; but to do so, these two rules must be observed: the rule of Harmony and of judicious Contrast.

Red, and its dark variations, may be worn by dark persons, and will harmonise with their complexion. Crimson and brilliant red are vulgar and unsuitable, but purple and dark maroon, worn by brunettes, and persons of a dark complexion, are both becoming and genteel, either in evening or winter dresses.

Light Red and Pink, approaching flesh tints, are becoming, both to dark and to fair, to the former especially, because they, by contrast, set off the complexion. Fair persons venturing upon such dresses or trimmings by daylight, should have clear and excellent complexions, or the brightness of the color, from a similarity of tint, will make their faces appear dirty and clouded.

CHOCOLATE colors, and warm browns partaking of red, may be worn by either fair or dark persons, provided they be not too pale, in which case the contrast will render the face chalky or death-like. The great art, as regards color of dress, is to enhance the tints of the complexion, care being taken to let the flesh appear of a healthy natural hue, and to avoid wearing those colors which heighten or destroy either the red, yellow, or white, in the natural flesh tints.

YELLOW in dress, as well as ORANGE, is also more becoming to dark than to fair persons. Primrose is to be expected as becoming to fair persons. The trimmings of this color, the flowers and ribbons, should be violet, such contrast being agreeable to art and nature.

MAIZE color is becoming to all complexions, especially to those which are brilliant.

GRAIN is more becoming to fair than to dark persons, because in the fair complexion, brilliancy and depth of color are more frequently found. Pale green should never be worn by the dark, it rendering them sickly and cadaverous in look. To those of a fair and brilliant complexion it is most becoming. For trimmings and flowers ladies cannot do better than to study nature, there being in the leaves of flowers every imaginable tint of green, whilst the flowers themselves are various in their hue. Thus ribbons of every kind both harmonise and contrast with green; green and white; green and rose color; green and purp'e; green and yellow; green and blue; but generally speaking these two colors are the most difficult to harmonise.—Yellow-greens, blue-greens, gray-greens, are all found in the leaves of flowers; the yellow and scarlet tulip has a gray-green leaf; the crimson geranium a yellow green; these must be studied, blue not harmonizing with the light greens, and *vice versa*.

The FORM of the dress, in which *Fashion* is to be included, next demands our attention.

The gown seems to promise in the future, as in the past, to be the destined covering for the female, but this is capable of much variation. The position of the band or waist will materially alter the look of the robe. The compression of the waist, entirely a modern invention—for the ancients, as we can see by the nude statues and draped figures of their sculptors, never dreamt of so ignorant a mode—is one of the most injurious which could possibly have obtained. By the use of stays, the space occupied by the stomach, the heart, and the lungs, the most essential organs of life, is diminished to such an extent as to render them diseased, and their action is, of course, impeded. The result of this externally, is a clouded, unhealthy appearance of the skin, a redness in the face and nose, and an enlargement of the feet, the hands, and the abdomen. A small waist is only beautiful so far as it is natural, and diagrams of the skeleton in the natural form, and in the artificial state, will, at first sight, bear out what we say. When ladies are about to become mothers the effects are still more disastrous; curvature of the spine, club-foot, other deformities, and even death of the infant itself, may be set down to it.

Smallness of waist may also be obtained naturally; by proper exercise in walking, the hips become enlarged, and by attention to the exercise of the arms, the carriage become more upright, and the chest is expanded, the contrast of these gives smallness to the waist.

"We are inclined to think," says a writer in the Quarterly Review, "that the female dress of the present day is in as favorable a state as the most vehement advocates for what is called nature and simplicity could desire. It is a costume in which they can dress quickly, walk nimbly, eat plentifully, stoop easily, loll gracefully; and, in short, performs all the duties of life without let or hindrance. The head is left to its natural size, the skin to its native purity, the waist at its proper region, the heels at their level. The dress is one calculated to bring out the natural beauties of the person, and each of them has, as far as we can see, fair play." To this opinion we subscribe to a certain extent, and an education in taste should prevent our readers from running into the extravagances of the past; from wearing hoops, which make the head look like the apex, and the bottom of the figure like the base of a pyramid; from wearing, as in George the Fourth's day, the waist immediately under the arm-pits; or from wearing high-heeled shoes, which cramp and deform the feet. Present fashion, however, has a tendency to run towards both the first and last items, the hoop and high heels,—let our readers avoid them.

The gown should fall gracefully from the hips, as free as possible from the odious "bustle," which Sam Slick ridicules in American ladies as an hideous deformity, looking like an unnatural hump.—It should fall in long full folds, and expand gradually to the feet, which it should touch, but not entirely cover.

Flounces should only be worn by those of a tall graceful figure, and then they should be made of a light material, gauze, muslin, or of stuff akin to it, so that they fall in gracefully with the outline of the dress. When made of any rich stuff, which stands out stiffly, they break the graceful flow of the dress.

Flounces, by marking the height, at regular intervals, take away from it, and make a short figure look shorter. For this reason, short persons should not wear stripes running in parallel rings round the dress. Perpendicular stripes upon a dress make the wearer look taller, like the flutes in a composite.

The out-door costume of ladies is not complete without a shawl or a mantle. Shaws are difficult to wear gracefully. Women should not drag it tight to their shoulders and stick out their elbows, but fold it loosely and gracefully, so that it fully envelopes the figure.

Black silk scarfs and mantles are particularly graceful, but they should be full, and not, as is the prevailing fashion, "scant." If a lady has a very fine figure, she may look well in an article which will expose that figure fully; but unless she be so, she should always wear a *full* mantle. Those of transparent gauze, or rich lace, which show the figure through the material, are, under the most advantageous circumstances, vulgar and ugly.—The reason is that they answer no purpose, either for warmth or covering, and seem to confess that they are worn for show and to exhibit the vanity of the wearer.

The *Bonnet*, which common consent has for so many years made the sole covering of the female head, is a very artificial and exceedingly useless article. It is dear without being ornamental; it does not cover the head, and, to quote a very good authority, "it is, at best, an unmeaning thing, without any character of its own, and never becoming to a face that has much." The present fashion of bonnets worn off the head so as to show the bare prominent face and dressed hair of the wearer, is odious, and at the same time immodest.

If our readers object to the foregoing, that some ladies look very pretty in bonnets, we can only say that they would look just as pretty without them, or that they owe their prettiness to a frame-work filled with pretty-colored flowers, ribbons, or lace, and not to the bonnet.

The rules which we have given for the color of the dress must, of course, apply to the covering for the head; the colors must, to look well, contrast or harmonise with the complexion.

Texture, material, and pattern, should suit not only the taste, but also the purse. There are few greater evils in this country than an inordinate passion for dress. Nothing is so silly nor so contemptible as to see a young person dressed beyond her station and her means. It is a lie, a deception which discovers itself. That fabric which looks joyous, proper, and at home upon the person of a lady who has a carriage to ride in and exhibit her dress, looks not only absurd, but worse, upon the body of one who is obliged to go constantly on foot through dirty streets or dusty lanes. No one looks so well dressed as those who are dressed properly, neatly, and whose attire sets them at their ease. A lady who is so over-dressed as to be constantly afraid of spoiling her gown, can never be graceful, since she cannot be at her ease.

With regard to the hair, little can here be said. In this respect the nature and the color of the face must be studied. Ringlets make round faces look longer, and more oval; plain bands make the face which is too long, lose part of that length. This should be studied. It is manifestly absurd to render oneself hideous merely to follow the fashion, as the courtiers of the French king did, who, when they found his majesty obliged to wear a wig, immediately shaved their heads and did so too.

The proper dress of the foot is certainly to be studied. In this, as in all things else, fitness for the occasion will constitute taste. Thus, a thin shoe in winter would be vulgar, because useless and dangerous to the wearer's health, and a thick boot in summer would be out of place.

Heeled boots are not entirely to be objected to; but care should be taken that the heel be not high, for if so, it entirely destroys the grace of the body, by throwing it out of its perpendicular; and a lady, instead of becoming like a graceful pillar, resembles rather a leaning tower, and that most awkwardly so.

Boots and Shoes should be well, nay, scientifically made. Few persons show such entire ignorance as those immersed in trade, who produce merely such articles, as by pandering to the perverted ideas of the untaught and vulgar (rich and poor), will sell. This is especially true of the dress-maker and boot-maker; the latter understands very little of the form of the foot, nor of its anatomical necessities. Modern boots and shoes are therefore often made narrow, just where they should be wide; and the foot, instead of being beautiful in shape, and graceful in its action, becomes long, narrow, distorted, and ungraceful when used.

If the preceding rules be adhered to, the dress of a lady, chosen with regard to propriety, station, and her acquirements, cannot fail to be useful, graceful, and in good taste. Let her never, on account of economy, wear either what she deems an ugly or an ungraceful garment; such garments never put her at her ease, and are neglected and cast aside long before they have done her their true service. We are careful only of those things which suit us and which we believe adorn us, and the mere fact of believing that we look well, goes a great way towards making us do so. Fashion should be sacrificed to taste, or, at best, followed at a distance; it does not do to be *entirely out*, nor *completely in*, what is called "fashion," many things being embraced under that term which are frivolous, unmeaning, and sometimes meretricious.

Lastly, a becoming modesty is always to be retained, and this may be ever done compatibly with extreme taste and ornament. If this is not done, it will have the worst effects, and not alone in the dress will it be found, but in the look and bearing which accompanies the costume. If a swimming, careless walk be indulged in, a lady, like Delilah, in Samson Agonistes, will be judged of at a distance

THE DRESS OF GENTLEMEN.

A very graceful Latin author, who was a dandy in his time, declares that it is difficult to say anything smart upon a common subject. And if so, what more common and ugly than the present dress of the male sex? Woman, happy creature, may adorn herself and make herself look charming—but man, poor man, with his stiff coat and stiffer collar, with his straight boot and straighter hat, what can he do? He indeed has been subjected to various rough hints and severe rebukes upon this subject, but it has apparently had no effect upon him, or rather upon his tailor. Caricaturists without number have assailed him; critics have pointed out the senselessness and uselessness of various parts of his costume; but still the coat remains the same; the tails of which are of no use, and collars rolled back so as to encumber the neck and spoil the appearance of the shoulders. So much do they contribute to this effect, that it is apparent to all, and we have but to point out an illustration, and the truth of our statement will be at once seen and acknowledged.

We had better, to begin with an unpleasant subject, first commence upon a man's coat. And here, indeed, we have some slight glimpses of hope and partial reform. "Men," it has been written, "are restricted to a costume which expresses nothing beyond a general sense of their own unfitness to be seen," and a little while ago it was true; but lately the overcoat has become, from the introduction of the short cloak or *poncho*, more flowing and artistic, and, were it not that the stupidly straight and scanty Noah's-Ark coat has been with senseless young men somewhat in vogue, we might indulge in a pleasing hope that something more useful, more elegant, and more comfortable, would ere long be adopted.

But to the coat, that contrivance which "covers only one-half of a man's person, and does not fit that." The coat in morning costume, and gentlemen should bear in mind that in the early part of the day they only can appear in colored and light garments, according to the strict rules of etiquette. The coat of a morning may be of various colors. These should be adapted to the complexion and figure of the wearer; and when so, do certainly set a [illegible] off to more advantage than in the evening-dress. The latter should always be black, varied with a white waiscoat, and a white cravat, which are both very difficult "to look well in," as the phrase goes; that is, they suit very few people—

Beau Brummel had a natural antipathy to a white waistcoat with black coat and trowsers, and very naturally compared a man dressed thus to a jackdaw. Bulwer, the most supercilious and insufferable of coxcombs, that is to say, in print, will allow a man to have only a thin gold chain appended to his watch upon such occasions; but recently etiquette has banished watches, probably because only men of business and not men of fashion need them, and allows only the eye-glass.

The shirt-front, says my Lady Etiquette, should be plain, in small folds, and without studs or buttons, upon which we may reasonably conclude that it should fasten behind.

Of shirt-collars, what shall we say? In the good old days, before the Croats of the Emperor Alexander taught us to wear dreadfully stiff-neck coverings, called after them *cravats*, the collars to the shirt were very small indeed, and before then we had fine lace affairs which were graceful and elegant. But now the collars are senseless, uncomfortable, and useless. Detached from the shirt, they are only put on for certain dandified purposes, and they are altogether so ridiculous, that is, when in the extreme of fashion, that we prefer to say nothing more about them.

The cravat, or necktie, is an improvement on the old stiff stock, and perhaps our variable climate will not allow us to banish it altogether. Science tells us, however, that the freer the neck the better the health, and consequently small neckties are not only more graceful, but also more healthful.

Of the trowsers little need be said. When full at the bottom they serve to hide a large foot. If colored trowsers are worn, those patterns should be chosen which conform to the rules of taste. Bars running across the legs should be avoided, and also all large staring patterns. Stripes down the side, or stripes of any sort, should be worn only by those who are tall, and whose legs are straight, or else the eye running along the stripe will quickly discover any deviation from the perpendicular.

The colors of the nether integuments may be various, but light colors do not suit town, and they are only worn to advantage in the country.

We may add a few general maxims, applied to both sexes, and our task will be done.

"All affectation in dress," says Chesterfield, "implies a flaw in the understanding." One should, therefore, avoid being singular, or attracting the notice, and the tongues of the sarcastic, by being eccentric.

Never dress against any one. Choose those garments which suit you, and look well upon you, perfectly irrespective of the fact that a lady or gentleman in the same village or street may excel you.

When dressed for company, strive to appear as easy and natural as if you were in undress. Nothing is more distressing to a sensitive person, or more ridiculous than to see a lady laboring under the consciousness of a fine gown; or a gentleman who is stiff, awkward, and ungainly in a bran-new coat.

Dress according to your age It is both painful and ridiculous to see an old lady dressed as a belle of four-and-twenty, or an old fellow, old enough for a grandfather, affecting the costume and the manners of a *beau*.

Young men should be *well* dressed, not foppishly, but neatly and well. An untidy person at five-and-twenty, degenerates, very frequently, into a sloven and a boor at fifty.

Be not too negligent, nor too studied in your attire; and lastly, let your behavior and conversation suit the clothes you wear, so that those who know you may feel that, after all, dress and external appearance is the least portion of a LADY OR GENTLEMAN.

THE

GUIDE TO HEALTH;

OR HOW

To Live a Hundred Years.

Origin of Life.

ORIGIN OF LIFE.—Life originates in a cell or vesicle. This cell is a growth, a formation, a vegetation. Whether the living being is to be minute or monstrous, simple or compound, a creature of a day, or a being of immortality, a cell or microscopic point is the origin of its existence. It is from this cell or vesicle, the vital force, as it is termed, evolves the range of diversified results we see in all animated nature. Of the particular nature of this vital force, how it is produced, how applied or how it excites to form and motion, there is much mystery. We can watch the workings of life; we can learn some of its laws, but of life itself, or of vital force, there is much guess-work. The vital force has been classed with heat, light, electricity, and nerve force; but whether it is a different or a combination of these separate forces, it is certain that this vital force or principle alone produces, sustains, and controls the action of animated beings. Where this is present there is life; where it is exhausted there is death.

The first visible state of a human being is a small pulpy or jelly-like substance, approaching the nature of albumen or white of egg. In this pulpy cell or globule, various particles of more solid matter begin to appear. These particles of matter, acting by force of vitality, gradually increase in bulk and density, until they come in contact with each other. These different points of contact are slowly modified into joints or hinges; and thus by degrees, a distinct framework or skeleton is formed. During the formation of this bony fabric, the surrounding pulpy matter also accumulate, and changes in form until at length that degree of organization is produced which constitutes a fœtus, or child in the womb. This process must prove the position, that a child can only possess a full and sound constitution provided the mother during the process of gestation observes all the conditions essential to her own life and health. These conditions are, plenty of pure air; a sufficiency of nourishing food, rightly taken; cleanliness; sufficient exercise to the various organs of the body: a moderate temprature; cheerful enjoyments; and a mind free from care.

Among the many astonishing discoveries of modern science, the most interesting is that of the various changes of the rudimentary organization. The organs of the different beings, before they can attain to the rank assigned them in the animal scale, must first pass through many of the phases which the same organs assume in the classes beneath them. Thus, while the future man is a simple pulpy structure of the lowest zoophite, the brain at first is wanting, and is subsequently like a fish's, a reptile's, a bird's. About twenty-one weeks after its development, the brain resembles that of the squirrel, or marmot.

The human heart also, as in certain animals low in the scale, is at first wanting; then it is like a fish's; at another period the human embryo is furnished with gills like a fish. These transformations explain the mystery of monstrous births. A person born with a hare lip, weasel-features, hawk-features, or the like, represents the condition or state of development, during which the mother may have been most affected. The transformations of insects afford beautiful illustrations of the same law; every one has observed that the frog, before it becomes a reptile, remains some time as a tadpole, among the lowest class of fishes. It has the gills, and is essentially a fish. How important, therefore, for a mother to know the laws of her being, so as to avoid the many accidents and evils attending the state of pregnancy!

Peculiarities of Organization.

Peculiarities of Organization.—Our bodies are subject to organic laws, as much as inanimate bodies are to the mechanical and chemical laws which surround them: and we can as little escape the consequences of neglect or violation of these natural laws, as we can place ourselves beyond the laws of gravitation. The first thing, therefore, is to acquire a knowledge of these laws, so far as they relate to health, and it is for this purpose this book is written.

By a knowledge of the organization of man and the external means at his disposal, we more easily ascertain the mode of sustaining our health and prolonging our life. An engineer first ascertains the knowledge of the structure, uses and power of his machine, adapts the materials and the surrounding circumstances to its wants, and then applies its powers to its specific purposes. So must we first learn the structure of our vital machine, its wants and powers, and then supply the one and direct the other.

Physiologists have divided mankind into several classes, as to temperaments, according to the predominating traits in their constitution. These temperaments are usually distributed into four classes, but they are seldom found pure in mixed society; however, a knowledge of the distinguishing characteristics in each will afford the best means of perceiving which predominates in any individual.—The *phlegmatic* or *lymphatic* temperament is the least intellectual. Its external indications are a pale, soft skin—fair and thin hair—placid or flabby features—flesh inclined to corpulency—muscles weak, vital action languid, and mental and physical functions feeble. People of this temperament, not being easily excited, require a stimulating diet, as beef, mutton, coffee; their regimen should embrace gymnastics, cheerful society, and active employment. Their diseases are likely to be those of a torpid character, as costiveness, jaundice, atrophy.

Sanguine temperaments are known by the animated, often florid countenance,—plump muscle, light hair, frequent pulse, and greater energy than the previous class. The sanguine are more people of action than of thought, and sooner affected with the trying or pleasing scenes of life. Stimulating food, drink, or an excited situation, creates an unnatural activity of heart and muscles, and therefore is dangerous to the persons of this temperament. The diseases peculiar to the sanguine are those of excitement, acute inflammation, fevers, hæmorrhages, which require anti-phlogistic remedies. The diet should be spare and unstimulating.

The Bilious temperament consists in dark hair and eyes, yellow or brown skin, not large but firm muscles, no corpulency, countenance exhibiting firmness, decision, and harshness, and a general manifestation of energy and activity. This class of persons neither need the stimulating diet of the lymphatic, nor the spare diet of the sanguine. The persons of this temperament require a full and generous diet suited to support their energy and activity. The diseases to which they are most liable are bilious affections, colic, stomach complaints, rheumatism, and the like.

THE NERVOUS TEMPERAMENT shows delicacy of form and constitutional sensibility—the nervous system greatly preponderates, and the mind of the nervous person passes from one subject to another with the utmost facility. They are very sensitive to external influence, both upon their body and mind. Their diseases are those of the nerves inflammation of brain, fever, debility, &c. Their diet should be mild, cooling, and nutritious. Their training should be judicious, out-doors, much walking, wood-sawing, and cricket-playing.

These different temperaments are variously affected by diet and outward circumstances. The sanguine and the ardent need a cooling diet; the phlegmatic require exciting food; the irritable should live on bread, fish, vegetables, milk, and the like. The dyspeptic should be careful of a slowly digesting diet; so also, when the habits change, should the food be altered to suit the new circumstances.

A Practical Lesson on the Seasons.

A Practical Lesson on the Seasons.—The temperature of a country influences not only the organization of the inhabitants, but also the diseases to which they are liable; hence we observe in the northern countries different constitutions and states of disease from those in more southerly regions. Without entering into a minute description of the diseases common to particular districts of our country, we content ourselves with such general observations on the subject as may be absolutely useful and necessary.

The influence of heat on animal life is as remarkable as it is on vegetation. When heat is abstracted to a great degree animals become torpid, and death speedily ensues; on the other hand, high degrees of heat produce stimulating effects, which are followed by depression and exhaustion. Animals generate heat, and maintain nearly the same degree of warmth in all climates. The effects of heat on the surface of the body are a derivation of the fluids from the internal organs, and, whilst the functions of the skin are carried on with considerable vigor, the healthy action of the inner organs are greatly diminished; in fact, the natural healthy balance of the body is destroyed. This readily accounts for the frequency of cholera, fever, and diseases of the liver in warm climates. The internal organs are enfeebled by excessive heat. Cold acts differently; by cold, the fluids are driven from the surface, and propelled upon the internal organs. Depending on the degree of coldness, and the predisposition to disease in any particular organ, disease to a greater or lesser extent may be produced in any part of the body. If that condition of the brain exist which would tend to apoplexy, should an exciting cause present itself, the warm surface of the body, chilled by cold, may prove to be such exciting cause and the disease will be produced. The same may be said of congestion of the lungs, liver, stomach, bowels, &c., &c. The greater and more sudden the change, generally the more serious and fatal the disease.

The practical lessons to be learned from these observations are, the importance of maintaining a uniform temperature, through the clothing, according to the season of the year, and climate. In cold seasons active exercise and partaking of an animal or stimulating diet may be necessary. On removal from a temperate to a cold climate, we should have recourse to furs, animal food, stimulating drinks, exercise and sports, to counteract the effects of cold. In warm seasons exercise should be less active, the diet less stimulating, less in quantity, and frequent ablutions should be had recourse to. On changing a temperate for a tropical climate, the woolen should be laid aside for cotton clothing, the stimulating animal diet and vinous drinks for those much simpler and milder; and calm repose, to a considerable extent, from active exercise.

EFFECTS OF LIGHT ON HEALTH.—Light is also a stimulant, the utility of which may be inferred from the ill effects produced by its absence—called

Etiolation, or blanching, which may frequently be observed among miners, sailors much confined to the holds of ships, and those residents of large towns who suffer from dark basements or other defective isolation. Light is equally necessary to the elaboration of the most important vegetable products. It is a most important curative agent, or condition of health, to both animal and vegetable life. The sick are often kept in dark rooms, but they ought rather to have an extra share of the sun and light. Light is the source of life. The remedy is obvious; but in diseases of an acute character, particularly of the eye, light must be partially or entirely excluded. Direct exposure to the rays of the vertical sun may induce acute disease, particularly of the brain as "sun-stroke," and should be avoided.

On Natural Stimulants.

On Natural Stimulants.—Electricity is a powerful stimulant. Of the usual electric states of the earth and atmosphere, our senses take little cognizance, but before or after a thunderstorm, when the electric equilibrium between the earth and clouds is being restored; then the electrical effects on nervous, susceptible persons, particularly females, show themselves by producing restlessness, anxiety, languor, oppression of the breathing, headache, sickness, fainting &c., and the fatal consequences of a stroke by lightning, sufficiently demonstrate the terrific power of the Electric fluid in excess.

The nerves are hollow tubes and contain a subtle transparent fluid, which is generally supposed to be the medium of sensation. The nerve therefore is something like the connecting wire of an electric telegraph, carrying, when required to do so, instant intelligence, by a motive sense, to the point where it is wanted for use; while the arteries may be compared to a railway, by which bodily substances are really carried from place to place, in regular order and time.

The practical lesson taught by these cursory observations is that in order to resist the effects of this powerful agent, the tone of the system should be improved as much as possible, and confidence excited by certain precautions which should be taken against serious electrical effects. Houses should be protected by lightning rods, and during a thunderstorm it is advisable to assume the horizontal rather than the upright form: to keep in the middle of an apartment rather than near the doors or windows; resting on a mattress, and carefully avoiding the wearing or contact with metallic substances, and the sheltering under trees.

The Causes of Fevers and Agues.

The Causes of Fevers and Agues.—Exhalations from the surface of the earth are fruitful sources of disease, and proceed principally from the decay of vegetable or animal matters. In hot and moist seasons, the putrefactive process goes on much more rapidly than in the opposite states of the atmosphere, and the air becomes more particularly charged with the noxious exhalations proceeding from particular localities.

The particular sources of miasms are swamps, lands subject to inundations, jungles, stagnant waters, marshes, mud, ill drained and ill-cultivated land, the densely populated and filthy parts of large towns, and the over-crowded state of the public burial grounds. The diseases produced by these causes are principally agues, remittant and continued fevers, the yellow fever, the plague and the cholera.

If we look at the mortality of some of these diseases, self-preservation, as well as enlightened benevolence, should prompt us to correct the sources of them, as well as to adopt all the sanitary means necessary for promoting the public health. In every situation visited by ENDEMIC diseases, the land should be well drained and cultivated; water should not be allowed to remain stagnant, embankments should be raised, and every possible attention paid to the cleanliness of the more filthy districts of towns. Dwelling-houses should be built on elevated situations, and windward of any particular pestilential source during the prevailing winds of that part of the country. The moist night-air should be carefully excluded, and moisture, which is the usual vehicle of the noxious exhalation, should in every instance be particularly counteracted.

Too great stress cannot be laid on the necessity of inculcating habits of universal obedience to the physical laws of our nature. The inhabitants of miasmatic districts should have recourse to a regular and generous diet; if no other than the marsh water can be procured, it should be purified by boiling and filtration.

Advice to Females.

ADVICE TO FEMALES.—In relation to health and disease, the physical and mental distinctions of sex occupy as important a position as do their appearance. The general distinction between the male and female may be summed up in the peculiar delicacy of organization of the latter. In woman we observe a more exalted sensibility, and stronger feelings and passions than in man. This fact naturally infers the propriety of that education of the female which should particularly invigorate the system. Her education has been too exclusively mental and sedentary; while not the least important improvement of society may be anticipated from the attention now being devoted to physical education and improvement. It does not require much physiological knowledge to know that the more delicate conformation of the female demands greater attention to her physical education. Active amusements in the pure open air are not less required by the female than by the male.

The increased sensibility of the surface in the female requires an adequate extent of clothing. A smaller quantity of a more digestible, and less excitant diet is generally required by the female.

Trades and Professions.

Trades and Professions.—It is deeply to be lamented that, notwithstanding the improvements that have been made in this respect, so many of the occupations of life are still destructive of health and happiness. Although many of these evils are irremovable, there can be no doubt that occupations are injurious, more by reason of the excessive length of time of labor, than of any inherent unhealthy tendency. If men generally were less ignorant of the laws of the animal economy, and applied their knowledge to the counteraction of the morbific influences to which they are daily exposed, they would escape many of the miseries which they now endure.

The Farmer, of all the individuals employed in the open air, probably enjoys the best health and longest life. The digestive organs, however, of many of the farmers are frequently deranged in consequence of too much salt meat and too much cider; and from their residence in some districts they are particularly the subjects of endemic diseases.

Commercial or other travellers, coachmen, conductors, boatmen, sailors, masons, builders, butchers, porters, and other out-door occupations, although exposed to great vicissitudes of weather, are very healthy. Their complaints generally take the form of pulmonary and rheumatic. Attention to food and raiment would obviate them. Butchers, from their abundant supply of animal food, become subject to plethoric complaints. Remedy: the food should be a due admixture of vegetable with the animal.

Tailors, dressmakers,' shoemakers, saddlers, engravers, painters, clerks, printers, and professional men, suffer more or less from the sedentary nature of their employments, from long-continued confinement, and from the impurity of the air they breathe. The contamination of the air, of course, depends on the size of the room they work in; the number of persons in a room, and the means of ventilation.

An eminent writer depicts forcibly the fruitful source of disease in some occupations through the position of the body. The eyes of the tailor must necessarily be near his cloth, which, being a heavy material, cannot be kept elevated by the hands. Hence the stooping and constrained posture, which induces curvatures of the spine, deformity, an awkward gait, and, very frequently, fistulo in ano. The remedy suggested is, that the table to support the cloth should have semi-circular holes cut in it to fit the body of the workman, with a seat placed at a sufficient distance below, that the body may be prevented stooping. The usual posture of the shoemaker, from the pressure in the region of the stomach, induces frequent derangement of the stomach and bowels, which might be partly obviated by more firmly grasping the shoe between the knees, thus removing the pressure from the epigastrium.

Compositors, tenders of machinery, drivers of cars, &c., where a constant standing posture is maintained, are liable to an inward inclination of the knees, and a varicose or dilated state of the veins of the lower extremities. The remedy lies in varying the employment, or in repeated intervals of relaxation.

SEDENTARY occupations are productive of indigestion and its train of ills, and should be counteracted by regular and systematic exercise in the open air. Dress-making, lace-running, machine-sewing, embroidering, engraving, which, from the minuteness of the work, are injurious to the vision can only be prevented inflicting serious evils to the eyes by seasonable and judicious intermission of these employments.

WORKERS IN WOOL, leather, provision dealers, cooks, rectifiers of spirits, brewers, bricklayers, plasterers, tobacconists, rape and mustard crushers, grooms, glue and size boilers, tallow-chandlers, tanners, millers, bakers, dyers, founders, cutlers, and the like, carried on in an atmosphere containing steam, dust, vapors, gaseous exhalations, strong odors and excess of heat, are more or less unhealthy, according to the noxious qualities of the artificial admixture. Dust, from whatever material evolved, is injurious to the respiratory organs, in proportion to the mechanical irritation it produces in the membrane lining the bronchial tubes. The gases evolved in some employments affect the digestive more than the respiratory organs. The volatilization of lead, mercury, and some other minerals used in manufactories, have a most deleterious effect on the human being. Daily bathing, open air exercise, and variation of employment are the only remedies. The apartments for such labors should be spacious and lofty, properly ventilated, and few workers in them.

PAINTERS and PLUMBERS, from the particles of lead exerting an injurious effect on the mucus membrane of the digestive organs, are advised to wash thoroughly before meals, and change the dress as frequently as possible. Employments in which injurious substances are applied to the skin, as painters, bricklayers, dyers, drug-mixers, &c., may always prevent ill-effects by a rigorous habit of cleanliness.

Digestion.

DIGESTION.—To every individual a good digestion is the key of life. Unpossessed of this, wealth, honor, success, virtue, or happiness, are either beyond man's reach, or cannot be enjoyed, if reached. It is hardly necessary to observe that the object of digestion is to supply the blood with those nutritious particles of food which will repair the waste and provide for the growth of the body; hence its due performance is essentially necessary to health, and its impairment is productive of innumerable diseases. Dr. Johnson said, "The study of the stomach was the study of morality," and he was right, for the stomach is the real gateway to virtue or to vigor. The philosophy of digestion consists in using but two or three kinds of food at one meal —in cutting meat as finely as possible before putting into the mouth, in chewing it thoroughly, eating slowly, and taking but little liquid either before, at, or after a meal. The following sections will be found to embrace the most important suggestions and facts connected with this subject, either for the healthy, invalid, or dyspeptic.

Diet.

DIET.—The principles of diet require to be understood by those who respect their digestive powers. The sweet and salt food should not be mixed; nor should fish and fruit. Every meal should consist of food of one general character. Breakfast, for instance, of bread, butter, meat, eggs, rice, potatoes. Dinner of fish or meat, with appropriate vegetables. Supper of light farinaceous food or fruits.

The food also should accord in its elements with the elements of which the body is composed. The specific effects of diet should be noticed upon par ticular temperaments, in particular seasons, and for particular occupations. For instance, brandy and fat meats produce heat, and if excessively indulged in during the hot season or in a hot climate, MUST produce eruptions, fevers, and liver complaints. On the contrary, moderately used during cold weather, or in a damp, non-electric state of atmosphere, both fat meats and brandy may be beneficial. (Brandy is used here as an illustration, not recommended as a beverage. It, of course, is often necessary as a medicine.) Again, every one is acquainted with the singular effects of alcoholic drinks upon different persons. Some they stupify, some they gladden and enlighten, and some they convert into pugnacious animals. Precisely in the same manner, though in a less startling degree, does certain foods operate upon different constitutions. The very temper, virtue, or vice of an individual depends much upon the physiological adaptation of his meals to his constitution, temperament, peculiar wear and tear of system and the seasons. The body and the soul, the brain and the stomach, depend for their harmonious action upon the food embracing those elements only which have been wasted in the human frame. We cannot here discuss the details; enough for the reflecting is all for which we have space.

Digestibility of Food.

DIGESTIBILITY OF FOOD.—The natural diet of man in temperate regions consists of a mixture of animal and vegetable, which is best suited to his wants. The relative proportion of each must be regulated by the circumstances, temperament, occupation, and climate of every individual. A larger quantity of animal food being required by those whose avocations require them to fast long, to labor hard, who live in cold or moist climes, and during the winter season; and of vegetable food by those whose mode of life is of an opposite kind.

Of course there are many constitutions and temperaments, for which vegetable food is best adapted; the author is also well aware that much more animal food is eaten by the majority than ought to be.

The various kinds of food enumerated here are arranged according to their digestibility. Thus, MEATS are facile of digestion so;—1, Mutton,—2, Beef,—3, Lamb,—4, Veal—5, Pork.

GAME.—1, Hare,—2, Partridge,—3, Pheasant,—4, Venison,—5, Canvass-Back,—6, Snipe,—7, Woodcock.

FISH.—1, Whiting,—2, Haddock,—3, Cod,—4, Soles and Flounders,—5, Crabs,—6, Raw Oysters, —7, Lobsters,—8, Fresh-water fish,—9, Turbot—10, Salmon,—11, Cooked Oysters,—12, Herrings, Sprats, &c. The theory recently adopted is, that sea fish, besides being nearly as nutritive as butcher's meat, contains more or less iodine, and therefore prevents the production of scrofulous or tubercular disease, such as pulmonary consumption—The beneficial effects of cod-liver oil on this class of diseases is attributed to the iodine it contains. It should be recollected that fat is much more indigestible than lean. Good meat means that the animal should have been in GOOD CONDITION, and have attained its full growth when slaughtered. Lamb and Veal have been very ERRONEOUSLY considered by some as a proper article of diet for the invalid and convalescent. Mutton, beef, or chicken, is superior. Pork is difficult of digestion, though nutritive.

The digestibility of the various meats depends much on the cooking. BROILED meats are the most digestible, then ROASTED, BAKED and FRIED. UNDERDONE meat is more digestible than OVERDONE.—Hashes and stews are not very digestible. Salted meats, cured hams, tongues, &c., are not the best articles for persons of impaired digestive powers. The glandular parts of animals, as kidney, liver, tripe, heart, tongue, &c., are less easy of digestion than the muscular parts of animals. Fish should always be eaten with a considerable quantity of salt, and, if a greasy fish, with vinegar.

Milk agrees with most stomachs, and is nutritious. To prevent constipation of the bowels, milk should be thickened, for those who use it much, with flour, oatmeal, or arrow-root. Cream is less digestible than milk. Butter less digestible than cream. Dyspeptics should beware of it.—Cheese is less digestible than butter.

Eggs are both nutritious and easily digested, if SPARINGLY cooked. The white of the egg is not good for the dyspeptic, if cooked. The preferable way of preparing the egg for food is by beating it with tea, coffee, or other drink. The egg, when raw, is a mild laxative; when cooked, astringent.

Vegetable Food.

The individual articles are arranged, as before, in the order of their digestibility.

1, Wheat flour,—2, Rice,—3, Rye,—4, Oatmeal, —5, Indian and Barley meal,—6, Bean and Peas meal.

HERBS, ROOTS.—1, Asparagus,—2, Cauliflower,—3. French beans,—4, Potatoes,—5. Spinach,—6, Turnips,—7, Kidney Beans,—8, Cabbage, greens, &c.,—9, Carrots, 10, Tomatoes,—11, Parsnips,—12, Peas.

SALADS—1, Water-cress,—2, Lettuce,—3, Celery, —4. Radish,—5, Onion,—6, Cucumber.

FRUITS.—1. Orange,—2, Strawberry, Raspberry, Huckleberry,—3, Pine apple,—4, Grape,—5, Currant, Gooseberry,—6, Peach, Apricot, Nectarine,—7 Apple, Pear,—8, Cherry,—9, Plum,—10, Walnut, Chestnut, Filbert,—11, Melon.

Bread from wheat flour is more nutritious and digestible than that from any other grain. The better baked it is, without being burned, it is the more digestible. For the same reason the bread of small loaves is better than that of larger ones. Toasted is more digestible than untoasted bread. Stale is better than new bread. Bread made from flour mixed with bran is more digestible than without it. Pastry, when plainly made, is not unsuitable for healthy stomachs; but let dyspeptics discard all kinds of pastry. Rice is easily digested, as also oats and corn. Gruel, made from these grains, is very nutritious and digestible. Barley-water is an excellent drink. In summer the proportion of herbs and roots to animal food should be very large. The lettuce, in consequence of its narcotic principle, should not be eaten in the evening. Radishes should be carefully scraped. Onions are not good for an impaired digestion. The best time for eating fruit is the forenoon.

TAPIOCA, ARROW-ROOT, SAGO, belong to the starch principle, amd are nutritious and easily digested substances. Honey is easily digested. Sugar, very nutritious, but not so digestible as honey. Molasses digestible and slightly laxative.

Vegetable diet, such as bread, potatoes, milk, and fruit, is the best adapted for infancy and childhood; and it should be the business of parents to watch the effects of the various food children eat, and take a note of them for future guidance. By this means, indigestion, costiveness or diarrhœa may be avoided.

Salt taken in proper quantity is conducive to health. Vinegar, in health, facilitates the digestion of food. Mustard and pepper are stimulants, and should be used moderately. Pickles should not be eaten by the dyspeptic or the sedentarily employed citizen.

According to the strength of the infusion, tea is a stimulant or sedative. Coffee is more nutritious but less digestible than tea. Cocoa less digestible than either. It must be remembered that although tea and coffee aid digestion and conserve the tissues of the system, yet, like all stimulants, if too freely indulged in, they weaken the sensibility of the stomach and derange its functions. In fact, dilutents of any kind, in large quantities, relax the coats of that organ and impair its efficiency.

Water is best fitted for man to drink; it is suitable for every constitution, and is more effectual than almost any other liquid in allaying thirst, thereby showing that it is the beverage designed to supply the loss of fluid to which we are perpetually subject.

How to Eat, and When to Eat.

The quality of the food is of much consequence. Bread that is sound in the grain, and well leavened and nicely baked, gives more strength to the body, than if of either indifferent grain, or badly managed in the making. One pound of flesh from a well-fed three-year old ox, will give as much strength as two pounds from an old or lean animal. Low-priced food is always the least profitable for use; and unwholesome food is a great cause of sickness.

The true method of taking food is to furnish nature with the means of getting all she needs, and no more—the wise study is to ascertain just what elements the body requires, and to find them in the food. People should not eat and drink themselves into a fever or a nausea, simply because there is a drug store at the corner of the street.

The time of eating, as well as the quantity of food, must be regulated by the appetite indicating the wants of the system. Many of the arrangements in regard to meals are sanctioned by habit and custom, and are perhaps as good as can be adopted. The times of eating, however, should be regular Breakfast and dinner should be the principal meals, and the time of the latter should be soon after the middle of the day. The principal meal should not be eaten, even in health, much less by a dyspeptic, in a state of fatigue; neither should laborious exertion be had recourse to immediately after. Food seldom leaves the stomach in less than three, and often not before four or five hours, consequently the interval between the meals should not be less than five hours. LIGHT FEEDING IS THE SECRET OF LIFE.

How to Clothe the Body.

The first use of clothing is to keep the body at a healthy temperature. The standard temperature of the human body is 98 degrees, while the temperature of our capricious clime is everything by turns and nothing long; hence, for want of due attention to the regulation of the clothing, lung and bronchial complaints are universal. The average amount of secretion from the skin, during twenty-four hours, in this climate, is about thirty ounces. Disease is most certainly induced by tne sudden suppression of this secretion by exposure to cold, the surface of the body becoming chilled, and the blood, which should be circulating through it, being forced internally. The sympathy between the skin and all the internal organs, as the stomach, bowels and lungs, is very minute, and shows the importance of maintaining an equable uniform temperature of the body. The warmth of different kinds of clothing depends on the readiness with which they conduct heat; those which feel cold to the touch, are good conductors of heat, and those which feel warm, are bad conductors of heat; the former afford the least protection against cold, the latter the greatest. Tne following is the order in which the articles are best adapted for winter wear: 1, Furs; 2, Woolen cloths; 3, Cotton; 4, Silk. For summer wear, linen is a good conductor; but cotton, not so readily absorbing the transpired fluids of the system, or the moisture of the air, is generally preferred. Materials for clothing should be as destitute as possible of the property of absorbing and retaining moisture, because moisture renders apparel a good conductor of heat. Hence, damp clothing should never be worn, as it retains less heat than dry.

In this variable climate, a bad conductor of heat should be worn next the skin; the best for this purpose is flannel. If thin and very fine flannel cannot be borne, calico should be substituted in the summer, and the flannel lined with calico in the winter. The flannel clothing next to the skin should not be worn during the night, being then unnecessary and injurious. All parts of the dress should fit loosely. Close-fitting garments are always associated with *Apoplexy, Costiveness, Headaches, and bad Breath.*

How to Warm the Feet.

An important appendage to the clothing of the body is that of the feet. Their clothing should be strictly regulated by the temperature of the atmosphere, and according to the surface of the earth. There is scarcely a disease of the body of which coldness and dampness of the feet may not be the exciting cause. Besides, by the intimate sympathy subsisting between the surface of the body and the various internal organs, coldness of the feet acts prejudicially on these latter, by the suppression of much perspiration, and the determination of the blood to the inner parts of the body. Throat and chest affections, stomach and bowel disorders, and apoplexies, are induced by coldness and moistness of the feet. Where there is a difficulty in keeping the feet warm, lamb's wool or worsted stockings should be used. The shoes ought also to be made large, and as near to the shape of the foot as possible; and in damp weather a layer of cork should be included in the sole of the shoe, which, of course, should be thick.

What to Sleep on.

A mattress is preferable to a feather-bed. The latter is relaxing, weakening and, from the animal matters of the feathers decaying, not very sweet. A cotton mattress has none of these objections. It is even preferable to hair and wool, being free from the odors of grease and staleness to which they are subject. Few and light-bed clothes are preferable to many and heavy ones. Warm light-bed clothing is especially desirable for old persons; from neglect of this they are often in cold weather subject to a great mortality.

It has been found, by experience, that prepared corn husks make the best, sweetest, and healthiest of beds. Few persons who have thoroughly tried the corn husks, would be willing to exchange them for either feather, hair or wool.

Bathing.

The surface of the skin is daily covered with excretions, oil, scales, salts, perspiration, and the like, and, to maintain purity of blood and body, daily ablution is required. Water removes the salts, and soap the oily excretions. If the health is good, and the body full of animal life, the cold bath may be used in summer, and the tepid in winter. Besides answering the end of cleanliness. *cold bathing* exerts a tonic effect on the system, and diminishes the susceptibility of the surface of the body to the variations of temperature. But to those of feeble body, or cold flesh, and not easily warmed after the cold bath, we recommend the tepid or warm bath in its stead. Sponging the body daily with cold water is exceedingly conducive to health. If cold water alone produces too great a chilliness of the surface, vinegar or salt may be added to it, in the proportion of one part of vinegar to four parts of water.

The conditions of bathing are that the colder the water the shorter should be the immersion. Bathing should not be indulged in if fatigued, during the fulness of the stomach, nor after drinking stimulating liquors. Cold bathing is more beneficial when the mind is free and active—in a state of despondency the *warm* bath is preferable. All persons subject to pulmonary or rheumatic complaints should bathe once a day in either a cold, tepid, or warm bath, if they desire to lengthen their days.

Bodily Exercise.

The body possesses no fewer than four hundred muscles, and each muscle is designed to serve some particular end. A sound state of body requires that *every one* of these muscles be brought into daily action in proper circumstances. The laws of life declare that only by a certain amount of daily exercise will *each* muscle gain in strength and soundness; otherwise it must become feeble, delicate, and dead. Exercise, therefore, must not be confined to any particular set of muscles, but should be as general as possible. Horse exercise is better than riding in a carriage, but walking is better than either. Quick walking is better than slow, and running than either, but a judicious combination is preferable to either separately. Next to exercise of the legs is that of the arms. Dumb-bells, skipping-rope, rowing, gymnastic feats with poles, ropes, fencing, ten-pins, billiards, base-ball, cricket, sawing wood, planing boards, digging a garden, are all highly serviceable. Exercise should not only call into action, occasionally, the different parts of the body, but should, for the maintenance of health, be regularly and daily followed, if possible in an elevated, dry, and rather cold than warm situation. The degree of exercise must depend upon the age and strength of the individual, but should be short of absolute fatigue. Active exercise should not be taken immediately *before* nor *after* eating. Nor should persons rest suddenly from active, perspiring, exercise, and sit in a cold situation. Such sudden change is dangerous.

Development of the Voice and Lungs.

The laws of the lungs imply that a large chest is the result of expanding and distending the lungs as much as possible at every inspiration. The lungs being a kind of bellows, speaking, singing, and reading aloud is a beneficial means of working them, and extending their capacity. Besides, these operations strengthen the voice and the muscles of the throat, and perfect the pronunciation. Wind instruments, if commenced to be played upon in early youth, by those of good constitutions, are capital developers of the chest and lungs. But reciting, singing, and reading aloud, should be encouraged in every family.

Mental Exercise.

The training of the body to perfection is strictly harmonious with the highest mental cultivation. If exercise is beneficial for the body, so also is it beneficial to the mind. But in both cases the exercise must be conducted in subservience to the laws of nature—that is the corporeal and mental natures should be evenly balanced. The future prospects of the rising generation will be better promoted by attention to the physical education in just proportion to the mental than by an overstrained attention to the mental only. Thousands are annually sacrificed by this partial attention to the education of youth. If exclusive attention be paid by the horticulturist to the leaves and blossoms of a plant, to the neglect of the root and stem on which they are dependent, the plant will perish; so if the mental powers of youth be cultivated to the exclusion of a robust body disease and an early death is the certain penalty.

Recreation.

Amusements and recreation are subjects of rational study It is a law of our nature that we cannot secure a sound body and sane mind, without indulging in bodily sports and mental amusements. There are medical properties in laughing, romping, and joking. Stern etiquette and decorum originated in a diseased system—they are associated with feebleness, plots, and paltriness. Wisdom lies midway between the extremes of labor and relaxation. The longest livers have been they who indulged in moderate hilarity, and unbent the body and mind from the drudgery of the current labors of life. The penalty paid by the lazy and idle is debility, bodily and mental lassitude, indigestion, disturbed sleep, bad health, and early death. The penalty paid by "all work and no play," is a desire for stimulants, general insensibility, grossness of feeling, and avarice. It is better to companion

> "Sport that wrinkled Care derides,
> And Laughter holding both his sides."

How to Sleep.

Sleep is as necessary for the renovation and healthful repose of the nervous system, and the mind, as food and drink are for the muscles, bones, and other parts of the body. Rest alone, unaccompanied by the oblivial state of insensibility called sleep, will not restore the lost vigor occasioned by long-continued efforts. At the close of a laborious day the muscles relax, and become languid, the eyes grow dim and heavy, the blood flows lazily, the head nods, the mind becomes oblivious. Now it is that the nervous power, ceasing from labor, obtains refreshment and renewal for the coming day. How necessary therefore that the sleep should be sound!

Sleep, like the taking of food, should be regular. Too little causes languor and an early exhaustion; too much produces heavy, benumbing influences on body and mind. The quantity of sleep required is considerably influenced by the amount of labor during the day, by habit, also by the health and constitution of individuals. The feeble, nervous, irritable, scantily fed, and intemperate, will require more sleep than those who are muscular, temperate, good-natured, and fairly fed. In childhood more sleep is required than in manhood. Seven or eight hours may be said to be an average time for sleep, which should not be commenced immediately after taking food. The most certain promoters of a sound rest are, avoiding sleep during the day, taking fair exercise and labor, mental peace, temperate and wholesome supply of food, a properly ventilated and large bed-room, light bed-clothing, warm feet, and the head moderately elevated.

Ventilation.

The common air is a fluid composed mainly of two gases in certain proportions; namely, oxygen as 20, and nitrogen as 80 parts in a hundred, with a minute addition of carbonic acid gas. Such is air in the state we require it for respiration. If these proportions are in any way deranged by breathing, miasm from stagnant water, marshes, privies, or the like, it cannot be breathed without producing injurious results. Breathing air once destroys it for further respiration. One person consumes or breathes half a cubic foot of air every minute; and a room of sixteen feet square and nine feet high will give sufficient air for four persons for one hour, yet hundreds sit that length of time in a theatre sucking in each other's poisoned breath! It will be seen that a continued supply of fresh air for all apartments is as necessary as a supply of heat in cold weather. In public boarding-houses, hotels, taverns, cabins of steamboats, and the sleeping-places below deck, are to be found the daily nurseries of fatal diseases. Churches, lecture-rooms, theatres, and school-rooms, are generally imperfectly ventilated, and greatly assist in cutting short the thread of life.

What functions of the body is more important than respiration? Its oject is to change the impure venous blood which has been circulated through the system, into the purer arterial blood through contact with the minute air-cells in the lungs. This renovation of the blood must necessarily depend upon the power of the lungs and the purity of the atmosphere. But the atmosphere becomes abridged of its purity by densely crowded towns and rooms, drains, marshes, privies, &c.; hence the necessity of a free ventilation of cities, and the *continual* exchange, in apartments, of a contaminated air for one of a purer kind. The air of a room is rarified by heat, and rendered less efficient in æration of the blood, consequently rooms should not be over-heated. Generally speaking, fires should not be burned in bed-rooms, neither should gas-lights be used The curtains of beds should be kept drawn, and as little carpeting used as possible. Warming of beds not only renders the air deficient in quality for healthy respiration, but gives a morbid sensibility to the surface of the skin, and debilitates the body. Sitting-rooms should not be over-heated; yet fires, when judiciously managed, are important means to ventilation, the moderately heated air passing up the chimney and being constantly replaced by colder air entering by the doors or windows. In every apartment there should be two constant currents; one outward carrying off the foul air, and one inward, bringing in pure air.

Never rent a human habitation near air-infecting nuisances, such as a distillery, cow-stables, swill-milk factory, hog-pen, soap-factory, slaughter-house, bone-boiling establishment, tallow-melting places, grave-yards, or other pestilence producing influence

The purest air in cities is contaminated enough, without locating ourselves near these death-dealing nuisances, where it is still worse.

Influence of the Passions on the Body.

The reciprocal influence of the body and mind on each other, and in the production of disease, is well known to medical men. The imagination is a frequent and powerful agent in the production and eradication of diseases. The passions of excessive joy, fear, or anger, sometimes cause sudden death. Everything which tends to discompose or agitate the mind, whether it be excessive sorrow, rage or fear, envy or revenge, love or despair, tends to injure the health and abridge life. In individuals subject to anxiety and depression produced by adversity in love, business, or the other wear and tear of ordinary life, we find the indigestive are usually the first to suffer. Flatulence, spasmodic affections of the liver, sallow appearance of the features, sighings, palpitation, rupture of the heart, and apoplexy, follow the indigestive symptoms

The most important part of the REMEDIAL MEASURES, in these cases where the passions have been allowed to obtain an undue ascendancy, will be found in the cultivation of the powers of judgment. Care and anxiety should be discouraged, and application to studies should be interchanged with active exercise in the open air, and various kinds of amusement and recreation adopted.

How to Preserve the Teeth.

Much of the health depends on the state of the teeth. Teeth are lost from want of care, and some few from defects in families. But almost all teeth may be preserved by thorough cleanliness with a good brush and water after every meal. Small particles of food are liable to remain in the irregularities of the teeth, and the spittle and the warmth of the mouth soon hasten their decay, which if not removed, breed thousands of minute living animals to eat through the hard enamel. Dirty teeth are therefore not only emblematic of their early decay, but also of the general habits of the person.

How to Preserve the Eye-sight.

When the general health is robust it is astonishing what an amount of labor the organs will endure; but when the body is depressed, especially by mental disturbance, they are easily deranged by too close application to business. When they have become weak, much of their preservation depends on the proper management of light to which they are exposed. When the light is in excess it should be diminished, and when it is deficient labor should be discontinued. The light blue of the sky and the verdure of the fields are the natural colors to which the eye is naturally adapted, and which it will endure with most ease.

Long fasting and frequent heats and colds; keeping the head too long in a hanging posture; violent head-aches, excessive venery, and diseases as small-pox and measles, are hurtful to the eyes.—All kinds of excess, particularly the immoderate use of ardent spirits, is injurious to the eye-sight.

The following precautions will be useful. Never use glasses if *it is possible to do without them.*—When the sight is too short close the eyes, press the finger gently outward from the nose across the eyes. Short sight is caused by too great roundness of the eye, and rubbing them from their inner towards their outer angles flattens them, and thus lengthens or extends the angle of vision. But as long sight is caused by too great flatness of the eyes, passing the fingers from their outward angles inwardly, rounds them up, and thus preserves the sight. Never use a writing desk or table with your face towards a window. In such a case the rays of light come directly upon the pupil of the eye, causing a forced contraction thereof, and injury of the sight. Always sit so that your face turns *from*, not towards the window, while reading or writing. It is best to read *with the light coming over your left side;* then the light illumes the paper, and does not shine upon the eye-ball. Beware of reading or working by an oscillatory or flickering light, as it produces constant attraction and dilatation of the pupil. It is always hurtful and fatiguing to the eye to read in an omnibus, railroad car, or steamboat, as the constant vibration keeps the paper or book in continual motion. A shade of light-blue paper over a lamp ameliorates the light, and enables the eyes to endure application with less fatigue.

How to Preserve the Hearing.

The ear is one of the most necessary instruments of a pleasurable existence, and its health and preservation of the utmost importance. The external ear is both an ornament and an adaptation for catching sounds, which are conveyed along the small opening till they strike the *drum* of the ear, an elastic membrane of its inner extremity, attached to the bones forming the interior of the ear, in the way that parchment is attached to the end of a common drum. The hollow drum of the ear being full of air, sound is formed by the air striking against its outer side; a chain of small bones then conveys the sound to the auditory nerve, which communicates it to the brain.

The functions of the ear may be injured by ulcers, wounds, cold in the head, fevers, excessive noise, or general debility. The prevention is in keeping up the general health by diet, exercise, and air.—When deafness is the effect of dryness, a few drops of oil of almonds poured into them, and afterwards washed out with a syringe and soap and warm water is considered beneficial. If deafness arises from too much moisture, it may be drained off by an issue, and by cleanliness of the ears. But neither the ears nor eyes should be tampered with; they are delicate organs, and if their functions are failing, good medical advice should be resorted to.—Prevention is what this treatise aims at, and that will be best accomplished by keeping up a vigorous tone of body, keeping the head free from heats and colds, and the feet free from damp and wet.

Childhood.

When ushered into life, man enters on an independent existence in a far more helpless state than other animals; many of them being able to walk, and look for their food immediately on attaining life, while a child would die if left to itself. On first entering on the stage of life a child requires to be carefully preserved from all shocks, and gradually to be accustomed to the stimulus of the external agents by which it is surrounded. Its food should be simple and nourishing; it ought to sleep much, to be kept dry, to have its skin washed in tepid water with a piece of flannel or sponge, morning and evening. Weaning should not long be deferred after the teeth have appeared. Weaning should be gradual. A child's happiness here, and hereafter, greatly depends upon the right physiological training given to it from one to four years.

Spring and Winter of Life.

When childhood merges into adolescence—when the vigorous development of every organ of the body is progressing, it is necessary to note the yearly changes and condition of the frame, and accommodate the treatment to them. A generous diet is especially necessary, but stimulating food or drink must be avoided. Air, pure and plenty of it, night and day, is heaven's best gift to youth, as well as age. Plenty of out-door exercise, energetic amusements, mirth and jollity, will make youth grow, and send it to sleep as sound as the robin. Cold bathing should be pursued daily, with a due attention to the temperature of the surface of the body.—Bathing should be brief, if the youth feels chilled or fatigued.

Now-a days, old age comes on apace. Should the laws of physical health, as briefly laid down in this work, be observed during youth, man, and womanhood, few outward symptoms of old age would appear before one hundred years! But how is it to-day? The wild hog, the swan, the parrot, the eagle, the toad, the serpent, the elephant, and many other animals obeying the instincts of their being, live to periods varying from seventy to several hundreds of years; while man, who possesses *reason*, yet who neglects to employ that *reason to a knowledge of his own organization*, dies of old age at an average of some forty years! Every day of our lives we see hundreds carried off at all ages, from the suckling of four months, to the premature and toothless old man of forty. Time, or the number of years, has little to do with old age. And no wonder, for nearly all live in continual transgression of the laws of the vital economy. We eat unwholesome food, take improper quantities, at improper times; we drink improper liquids, breathe impure air, sleep in confined bed-rooms, sit in close parlors, clothe ourselves unsuitably to the temperature, or the ribs chest and lungs; we take too much or too little exercise, and we study *cure* rather than *prevention*, and yet wonder at premature old age! How few can truthfully repeat these words:

Though I look old, yet I am strong and lusty;
For, in my youth, I never did apply
Hot and rebellious liquors in my blood;
Nor did not, with unbashful forehead, woo
The means of weakness and debility;
Therefore, my age—is as a lusty winter,
Frosty, but kindly.

Old age is the one in which much care is demanded as regards clothing, which at this period requires to be warm and thick, principally of woollens.—Fatigue should be avoided. In the place of active exercise, friction of the extremities with the hand, flannel, or flesh-brush, will be agreeable and useful to the aged and infirm. The diet of aged persons should be of soft materials, digestible and nutritious; and mild stimulants are frequently useful and necessary.

The Reason Why People Die.

Not one in a hundred dies a natural death.—Nearly all are murdered by slow or swift violations of the physical and organic laws—of those laws which we might all so easily understand and so easily comply with. Yet people believe that early deaths are scourges from God which we cannot avoid! The truth is, disease and premature death is only a scourge from God because we transgress his physical laws. We may be healthy and long-lived if we will; health and long life are in our own hands, if we only try as hard to obtain them as we do to get and grab the dollar!

Most people die because some one organ fails to perform its part in the work of life. If that organ was equal in power to the others at the start, there must have been some variation *from*, or failure in the conditions of being. This failure of any one or all of the organs, may arise from one of these causes—from some deficiency of the building up the body, in the developing of its organs, or from some mistake in the expenditure of life. These include dietary, labor, education, habits, stimulants, clothing, and the intemperance of the passions.

The number of sudden deaths of late years have been frequent and alarming and will become more so as men continue to sin against the laws of health. These sudden deaths usually occur under the influences of diseases arising from a plethoric state of the blood-vessels, such as apoplexy, convulsions, and affections of the brain and heart. These diseases originate in the abuse of the laws of health and life, particularly in an undue indulgence of the delicacies of the table after the wants of nature have been satisfied. Also in the use of artificial stimuli after the stomach has been stretched beyond its capacity for action; and by frequent and unnecessary use of fermented and spirituous liquors.—Under these circumstances, the most minute vessels of the body become gorged by a superflux of corrupt humors, and in the endeavor to obtain an equilibrium in the circulation, some important vessel becomes ruptured, or those parts of the system which are weak by previous disease give way, and a rush of fluid takes place, and the fabric is ruined. Light meals, daily washing, and constant exercise, can alone avert such sudden deaths.

What is Health?

The previous contents of this small volume will have led the reader to infer that Disease is not a substance, nor an enemy, but a *condition* of things. Disease is *discord*, or a want of equilibrium in the organization, arising either from hereditary constitutional predisposition, atmospherical changes, occupation, habits, local situation, injuries, or mental disturbances. It is well known that parents daguerreotype their own peculiarities of body and mind on their offspring, and hence the abundance of scrofula, cancer, gout, rheumatism, and nervous diseases. The only possible way of avoiding this sin of transmission, is by parents studying the laws of life, and never transgressing them.

It has already been shown, in another part of this work, how atmospherical changes operate upon the human being. When there is abundance of electricity in the air, we become overcharged with it, unless we adapt our food and clothing to counteract its superfluity. When the electricity is deficient, as in raw, moist weather, our raiment and food should be of a character to generate and retain the electricity of our bodies.

Occupations have been shown as developing bronchitis and pulmonary diseases, dyspepsia, constipation, asthma, near-sightedness and ophthalmia, according as they are protracted or exercised in certain positions and from confinement and bad ventilation. Leaving or varying the occupations, and transferring them to a purer atmosphere, the only remedies.

Habits of life greatly affect health. Intemperance in food, in drink, in labor, in recreation, in acquiring knowledge, in sleeping, in smoking, in indulging the passions—continually impair health and produce disease.

Disease, then, being a state of body, and not a superfluous or poisonous material, which needs to be cleansed or purged out of the body, food, dress, air, water, and exercise are the *only means of cure.* We are endowed with life, and permitted its enjoyment for a long or a short period, according to the obedience we render to the laws written on the muscles, bones, nerves, and tissues of our bodies. Disease is the penalty of disobedience. The only redemption from disease consists in *each person knowing himself and herself, and educating their bodies up to a state of energy and health.*

When and How to Use Medicines.

Medicines are by many persons supposed as essential means of promoting health. Medicines and disease are equally unnatural to the human economy. When disease exists, medicines are used to relieve it, by substituting a disease of its own, which nature tries to cure for herself. When we have brought ailment upon us by our own imprudence, the ailment of medicine is induced as the least of two evils. But both disease and medicine are alike evils to the body. In jaundice which arises from the inactivity of the liver, medicines are used to stimulate the liver and bowels, and they are worn out by this process, just as a piece of machinery would be worn out by being driven beyond its usual velocity. Such is the manner of medicines benefitting us.

The true way of preserving health is to live so as to avoid disease; the true way of curing disease is by closing the flood-gates of individual imprudences. Let every man and woman *manufacture* their own health, by the enlightened use of God's agents—food, clothing, air, water, and exercise.

How to Manage the Sick.

If it were but the interest of physicians to *discover* and *arrest disease*—if their interests did not consist in sickness and the infractions of the physical laws—good nurses for the management of the sick would soon become more important than either medicines or medical advice. Medicines themselves are of little use, if all the other matters appertaining to the welfare of the patient is neglected. It is not doctors the people need so much as nurses, and these require both a practical and theoretical knowledge of the principles and practices upon which health and comfort depend. Woman is the natural nurse of the child, sister, father, mother, and husband, and therefore every girl should become familiar with the principles of practical physiology. *Then* nurses would be kind, attentive, and firm, to their patients. A good nurse would adopt the best means of elevating the mental condition of the patient;

for despair, fear, or other agitation, is fatal to recovery. Many sink under the progress of disease, through the desponding looks and words of relatives and friends. A patient, if possible, should be washed all over each day, and the clothing changed so as to clear away the exhalations and excretions from the person. The sick-room should be thoroughly ventilated, to remove the poison exhaled by the victim of disease. No fumigation can be a substitute for ventilation. The temperature of the room should be as uniform as possible, say about 60 degrees Fahrenheit. The light should never be excluded, unless there is a strong case of brain fever. The proper period for cleaning and arranging the sick-room is in the morning, after the patient has enjoyed a night's rest. Never keep the medicines and drinks of the patient in his view; it is enough to have to take them at certain times, instead of having them always before the eye. Never whisper, exchange looks, or appear to commiserate the condition of a patient, lest he suspect the worst, and go down to death, when otherwise he might have recovered.

How to Live Long and Die Happy.

Dr. Monroe, in his anatomical lectures, has said: "The human frame, as a machine, is perfect—it contains within itself no marks by which we can possibly predict its decay; it is apparently intended to go on forever!" And whether Dr. Monroe's statement was literally meant or not, there is no doubt it was uttered in the unfeigned belief that a long life was within the reach of all who had a good constitution at the start. The words of the Deity are, "I will show mercy unto thousands of them that keep my commandments;" and it is every one's duty to study and observe these commandments.— This little work gives a summary of them. They are few and easily regarded—to wit, the alimentary canal should be regularly cleansed by good habits and suitable regimen; food to be chosen in accordance with the temperament of the body and temperature of the weather, and the kind and amount of labor, and all food MUST BE EATEN SLOWLY AND MASTICATED THOROUGHLY. Rise early and walk; go to bed early; sleep in a large room with a good ventilation; breathe pure air; take exercise in open air between meals, without great fatigue; bathe or sponge the body daily; form regular habits, and cultivate a cheerful and active state of mind. Always live with a conscience void of offence towards GOD and man; never rest contented with what this vain world *alone* can give you, but lay up for yourself treasure in heaven, by loving and serving God on earth. Try to do all the good you can, and thus go on your way rejoicing.

If these rules are strictly adhered to, even by those of dilapidated constitutions, they will be raised from ill health to vigor and comparative robustness.

> So may'st thou live, till like ripe fruit thou drop
> Into thy mother's lap; or be with ease
> Gather'd, not harshly pluck'd for death.
> This is old age.

A wise observance of these simple laws of nature will redeem its observers from the hell of ailments to the paradise of a pleasurable existence, and conduct them through life silently, gently, and serenely, to its far-off termination, when they may be able to exclaim—

> "And is this Death? Dread thing!
> If such thy visiting,
> How beautiful thou art!"

To all those born of healthy parents and of good constitution, an obedience to the laws of God and nature, as laid down in this brief treatise, will not only enable them to evade all the contingencies of bad health, and teach them how to KEEP YOUNG AND GOOD LOOKING, but also how to attain the patriarchal age of, at least, a hundred years.

A TREATISE

ON THE

Management of Bees.

ESTABLISHMENT OF AN APIARY.—The proper time for this purpose is about the beginning of March, as the stocks have then passed through the winter in safety; the combs are then empty of broods, and light of honey, and may be removed with safety and ease. *Stocks* should be selected by a competent judge, as the weight alone cannot always be relied on; such as weigh 12 lbs., and upwards, the number of bees being also observed, and that they are well combed to near the bottom, may be safely chosen.

As soon as they are brought home, they should be set in the *bee-house*, care being taken to keep them dry and from the attacks of vermin. The next day plaster the hive to the bee-board, leaving an entrance the size of the little finger.

If the season has passed, the first and early swarm should be selected, as late ones or casts are not worth keeping, unless two or three of them have been united.

The time for removing stocks, is in the evening; the hives should be raised by wedges some hours previous, unless the floor be moveable with the hive, otherwise many bees will remain on the floor at the removal, and prove very troublesome. When the floor is moveable, plaster the hive with mortar to the board, and pin a card pierced with holes before the entrance; in this way it will travel any distance in safety.

Swarms should be brought home the same evening that they are purchased; if delayed a day or two, combs will be worked, and subject to be broken in removing.

Management of Bees.—The best situation for bees is to the north, with a range of hills wooded on the summit, and toward the base enriched with heather; and southward, gardens where hardy winter greens have been allowed to flower, as early food for the bees. White mustard should also be sown very early, in patches near the hives; but not nearer than one yard. A few dwarf flowers may come within two feet, but tall ones would assist the insects to get up. To the West it may be desirable to have a shrubbery, a wood, a broomy common or heather moor.

The stations for the hives must be six yards asunder, and never nearer than three yards. The board on which they are placed ought to be of one piece; or if joined, the under side of the joining should be lined with a thinner board, fixed closely with wooden pins. The edges of this rounded standard should project four inches all round from the hive. Place it on three wooden pillars sixteen inches long, ten inches above the ground, but six inches of its length should be firmly thrust into the earth; in all, its length should be sixteen inches. The pillar in front should be an inch shorter than the other two, and the three pillars should be within twelve or fourteen inches of the outer edge of the board, to exclude rats and mice. For the same reason no tall-growing plant, no wall, nor any means of ascent should be within three or four feet of the hive. In fine weather the entrance to the hive must be four inches long, and an inch and a half in depth.

In the beginning of the fine season, when the bees can get food, or have stores remaining, the bee-master has nothing to do but to keep the ground about the hives clear from weeds, and from whatever might enable vermin to climb there. Yet as a thriving stock inclines very soon to swarm, the hives must be frequently looked after from eight in the morning till five in the afternoon. The symptoms are generally thus:—The little city seems crowded with inhabitants. They are continually in motion during the day; and after working-time they make loud noises. The drones may be seen flying about in the heat of the day, and the working bees go with a reeling motion and busy hum. When the bees come regularly out of the hive, let no noise, no interruption incommode them; but if they fly long, as if they were unsettled, some tinkling noise, or the loud report of a gun, will make the fugitives repair to the nearest lodgings. If there is an empty hive with combs and some honey in it, they will readily go there. If a new hive is used, remember to smooth it well within, and singe off loose straws. Perpendicular sticks should never be employed. Four cross sticks at equal distances will support the combs. Old hives do very well for late swarms, that are not to be preserved through the winter;—but box-hives are best for them, as the bees work fastest there. They are not, however, fit for being kept through the cold seasons.

It is to be observed, that great haste in forcing a swarm into the hive may disperse them. Give them time to settle undisturbed, though keep a steady eye on their motions; but whenever they gather into a cluster, lose no time in placing the hive over them. If the swarm rest on any thing that can be brought to the ground, spread a clean linen cloth; lay two sticks on it, two feet asunder; lay the body on which the swarm have fixed, gently on the sticks, covering it with the hive by a motion the least perceptible, and taking care that the edges of the hive rest upon the sticks. Cover hive and all with a cloth, for the sun might allure the bees to rise again When they have gone into the hive, cover it with its own board, and carry it cautiously to its station. Bees are apt to leave their hive even after they begin to work, so they must be watched till evening, and throughout the ensuing day. Whenever they are sure to remain, fix the hive to its board with a little lime round the edges; and crown it with green sods to keep out too great heat or rain.

If a hive divides into two swarms, it is a sign that each swarm has a queen. Put each into old hives or boxes, but they must be kept separate. If a clus ter of bees about the size of a small plum are seen together, the queen will generally be found there. Separate them, and with a drinking glass turned down, you may seize the queen. Put her and a score or two of her subjects, into a box full of holes, large enough to admit air, and yet not to allow the bees to escape. Feed her with honey-combs, and keep her in reserve in case of the death of a queen in one of the hives. When a hive ceases to work, it is a sure sign the queen is no more. Then the bee-master may wait an hour if the spare queen be taken late in the evening, (wet her wings to prevent her escape), and introduced to the desponding society, they will receive her gladly, and begin to work.

If a hive fight among themselves, be assured there are two queens; and they will destroy each other, if one is not taken away.

When bees are to swarm a second or more times they do not come out in clusters: but they make a sound called *bellings*, which may be heard; ceasing for a little, and renewed again and again. If there are different tones, it is certain there are several young queens in the hive. It is only by putting the ear close to it that the sound can be heard distinctly.

To take the honey without destroying the bees.—In the dusk of the evening, when the bees are quietly lodged, approach the hive, and turn it gently over. Having steadily placed it in a small pit, previously dug to receive it, with its bottom upwards, cover it with a clean new hive, which has been properly prepared, with a few sticks across the inside of it, and rubbed with aromatic herbs. Having carefully adjusted the mouth of each hive to the other, so that no aperture remains between them, take a small stick, and beat gently round the sides of the lower hive for about ten minutes or a quarter of an hour, in which time the bees will leave their cells in the lower hive, ascend, and adhere to the upper one. Then gently lift the new hive, with all its little tenants, and place it on the stand from which the other hive was taken. This should be done some time in the week preceding Midsummer-day, that the bees may have time, before the summer flowers have faded, to lay in a new stock of honey, which they will not fail to do for their subsistence through the winter.

The color of the honey shows whether it is fine or inferior. If it be wanted to press some in the comb, choose the fairest and those that have not been broken: wrap each comb in white paper, such as lines the blue cover of loaf sugar. Set it edgewise as it stood in the hive, and it may be preserved many months. The combs meant to be drained must be cut in slices. Lay them on a hair-search, supported by a rack over the jar, in wich the honey is to remain, for the less it is stirred after draining, it keeps the better. Fill the jar to the brim, as a little scum must be taken off when it has settled. A bladder well washed in lukewarm water, ought to be laid over the double fold of white paper with which it is covered.

To keep hives for winter.—They must not be more than three years old, and well stocked with bees. A hive for preserving should weigh from thirty to forty pounds. Place them in October where they are to remain. Stocks of less weight than 21 lbs. in September should never be kept. In most cases light stocks will require feeding, which may be done by inserting little troughs containing a mixture of equal parts of sugar and mild beer, into the hive in the evening, and removing them the next morning.

Mr. Cobbett on the management of Bees.—The best hives are those made of clean unblighted rye-straw. A swarm should always be put into a new hive, and the sticks should be new that are put into the hive for the bees to work on; for, if the hive be old, it is not so wholesome; and a thousand to one but it contains the embryons of moths and others insects injurious to bees. Over the hive itself there should be a cap of thatch, made also of clean rye-straw; and it should not only be new when first put on the hive, but a new one should be made to supply the place of the former one every three or four months; for, when the straw begins to get rotten, as it soon does, insects breed in it, it smells bad, and its effect on the bees is dangerous.

The hives should be placed on a bench, the legs of which mice and rats cannot creep up. Tin round the legs is best. But even this will not keep down ants, which are mortal enemies of bees. To keep these away, if they infest the hive, take a green stick and twist it round in the shape of a ring, to lay on the ground, round the legs of the bench, and at a few inches from it; and cover this stick with tar. This will keep away the ants.

Besides the hives and its cap, there should be a sort of shed, with top, back and ends, to give additional protection in winter, though, in summer, hives may be kept too hot, and in that case, the bees become sickly, and the produce light. The situation of the hive is to face the south-east; or, at any rate, to be sheltered from the north and the west. From the north always, and from the west in winter. If it be a very dry season in summer, it will contribute greatly to the success of the bees, to place clear water near their home, in a thing that they can conveniently drink out of; for, if they have to go a great way for drink, they have not too much time for work.

It is supposed that bees live only a year; at any rate, it is best never to keep the same stall or family over two years, except it be wanted to increase the number of hives. The swarm of this summer should always be taken in the autumn of the next year. It is whimsical to save the bees when the honey is taken. They must be fed; and if saved, they will die of old age before the next fall; and though young ones will supply the place of the dead, this is nothing like a good swarm put up during the summer.

A good stall of bees, that is to say, the produce of one, is always worth about two bushels of good wheat. The cost is nothing to the laborer. The main things are to keep away insects, mice, and birds, and especially a little bird called the bee-bird; and to keep all clean and fresh as to the hives and coverings. Never put a swarm into an old hive. If wasps or hornets annoy you, watch them home in the day-time; and, in the night, kill them by fire or boiling water. Fowls should not go where bees are, for they eat them.

ON THE DIFFERENT KINDS OF HIVES.—1. *The common hive.*—This hive is too well known to require any description. It should be made of good clean dry straw, and sufficiently thick and firm to protect the bees. The size of the hive should be proportionate to the size of the swarm placed in it. Care should be taken to avoid covering this hive with a hackle or turf, as it induces mice to build in it, and ultimately destroy both combs and bees. 2. *Glass hives.* There are various modifications of this useful kind of hive. That of Mr. Moulton consists in placing glasses on a board furnished with holes at the upper part of a straw hive of peculiar construction; when filled with honey they may be removed without injuryto the bees or disturbing the economy of the hive. The first year the glasses are only filled once, and generally produce about 8 lbs. of honey of superior quality; but the second and subsequent years the glassses may be worked twice or oftener. 3. *The double cottage straw hive.* This hive is worked by first hiving the bees in the lower hive, and after 10 days clearing the opening at the top, and affixing thereon another small hive either of glass or straw. When full, the latter may be removed. 4. *The box, hive and hexagon box, and straw hives*, may be worked in the common way, or by placing a glass hive over it. The management is very similar to the preceding varieties.

Bee Flowers.—Bees seldom fly more than a mile for their food; it is therefore advisable to encourage the growth of such flower as they appear to be most attached to. The following are said to be the most favorable for pasturage, and those that blossom early should be preferred.

Shrubs, &c.—Rosemary. Broom, Heath, Furze, Fruit Blossoms. *Flowers.*—Mignonnette, Lemon Thyme, Borage, White Clover, Bean Flowers.

Swarming.—As soon as a stock has increased to a certain number, which can barely find accomodation in the hive, an inclination to swarm is evinced as soon as a queen bee is ready to lead them. When the bees begin to carry in farina, or pellets on their thighs, it denotes that they have commenced breeding, which frequently begins in February, and does not finish till October. The indication of swarming is the clustering of the bees in great numbers below the resting-board. They never rise but in fine weather, and most frequently about noon: it becomes therefore necessary to observe the hives well during the swarming season, or from April to July. A second cast may generally be expected within 3 or 4 days after the first, but the interval seldom exceeds 8 or 10 days. Should they alight on a tree, the branch may be shaken over the hive or if *small*, cut off and placed in it, and the hive left on the spot, when the remaining bees will go into it. The hive should then be left near to where they settle until the evening, when it may be gently removed to the bee-house. Ringing a bell, or beating an old kettle, is a common way of collecting the bees together and making them alight.

Reinforcement of Weak Stock.—Weak swarms of bees should be strengthened. This is done, by hiving the swarms as usual, and in the evening striking the bottom of the hive containing the new swarm smartly, or a cloth spread upon the ground. The bees then fall in a cluster on the cloth, when the hive containing the stock to be reinforced must be placed over them as quickly as possible; after the lapse of about a quarter of an hour, they will have become united as one family. Another method is to invert the one hive and to place it in a bucket or pail, then to set the other hive over it; by the next morning the bees in the lower one will have ascended into the upper. The operation of reinforcing stocks is very economical, as it is found that one strong stock will produce more honey than two weak ones.

Weak Stocks.—Stocks weighing less than 18 or 20 lbs., cannot be safely brought through the winter without feeding. The best food is a mixture of sugar and water, or equal parts of sugar and beer.

TWENTY WAYS TO MAKE MONEY,

A VALUABLE COLLECTION OF

RARE AND PRACTICAL MONEY MAKING RECIPES.

(Series No. 2)

1st. **To make Silver Plating Powder,** for silvering brass, copper, &c., and for repairing worn out parts of plated goods.—Nitrate of silver, 30 grains; common table salt, 30 grains; cream tartar 3½ drachms. Mix all thoroughly, and make into a fine powder in a mortar. Moisten a soft cloth, dip into the powder, and rub over the surface to be plated for a few moments; then wash off with a solution of common salt in water, and rub dry with a cloth, and chalk or whiting.

2d. **To increase the laying of Eggs in Hens.**—Pulverized Cayenne Pepper, half ounce is to be given to one dozen hens, mixed with food every second day.

3d. **To make Violet or Purple Ink.**—Boil 16 ounces of Logwood in three quarts of of rain water, to 3 pints; then add 3 ounces of clean gum arabic and 5 ounces of alum (powdered). Shake till well dissolved. It would be well to strain through a wire sieve.

4th. **To clean Kid Gloves.**—Add 15 drops of strongest solution of ammonia to spirits of turpentine ½ pint. Having fitted the gloves on wooden hands or pegs, apply this mixture with a brush. Follow up this application with some fine pumice powder. Rub with some flannel or sponge dipped in the mixture. Rub off the sand, and repeat the same process twice or thrice, Hang in the air to dry, and, when dry, place in a drawer with some scent.

5th. **To make Matches without Sulphur or Phosphorus.**—Chlorate of potash, separately powdered, 6 drachms, vermilion one drachm, lycopodium one drachm, fine flour two drachms. Mix carefully the chlorate with the flour and lycopodium, avoiding *much friction*, then add the vermilion, and mix the whole with a mucilage made with---1 drachm of powdered gum arabic, 10 grains of tragaanth, 2 drachms of flour, and 4 ounces of hot water; mix, add sufficient water to bring it into a proper consistence, and dip in the wood previously dipped in a solution of 1 ounce of gum camphor, in 6 ounces of oil of turpentine.

6th. **To make Black Ink Powder.**—Sulphate of copper [blue stone] one ounce, gum arabic 2 ounces, green vitriol [copperas] 8 ounces, nutgalls, powdered, 1 pound, extract of logwood 1 pound. All are to be finely pulverized. About 1 ounce of this mixture will be required to make one pint of ink, to be put into boiling water. It should stand about two weeks before using.

7th. **Baking Powder.**—Baking soda six ounces, cream tartar 8 ounces. Each should be thoroughly dry before mixing. About a teaspoonfull, dissolved in warm milk or water, is sufficient for a quart of flour.

8th. **To make Syrup of Sarsaparilla.**—Take of Sarsaparilla root 1 pound, boiling water 5 quarts, sugar 1 pound. Cut or chop up the sarsaparilla root into short pieces, the shorter the better, put it into the water, let stand for 24 hours, then boil down to 2½ quarts, and strain the liquid *while hot.* Then add the sugar and boil gradually for about an hour. When cool put up into bottles or a jug, and keep corked. DOSE, from one to two table spoonfulls before each meal. This is a valuable medicine to *purify the blood,* and is used with great advantage in all cases of general debility or weakness from any cause whatever: also, for disease of the liver, dispepsia, or indigestion, scrofula, female weakness, loss of appetite, effects of syphilis or venereal disease, and in every case where the wish is to *build up* and *strengthen* the system. It should be used about two months or more at a time.

9th. **To make medicated Root Beer.**—For each gallon of water to be used, take hops, burdock, yellow dock, sarsaparilla, dandelion and spikenard roots, bruised, of each ½ ounce,; boil about 20 minutes, and strain while hot; add 8 or 10 drops of oils of spruce and sassafras, mixed in equal proportion. When cool enough not to scald your hand, put in 2 or 3 table spoonfuls of yeast, molasses two-thirds of a pint, or white sugar ½ pound, gives it about the right sweetness. Keep these proportions for as many gallons as you wish to make. You can use more or less of the roots to suit your taste, after trying it. It is best to get the dry roots, or dig them and let them dry, and of course you can add any other root known to possess medicinal properties desired in the beer. After all is mixed let it stand in a jar with a cloth thrown over it, to work about two hours, then bottle and set in a cool place. This a nice way to take alternatives, without taking medicines to operate on the bowels.

10th. **To make Ice Cream.**—Fresh cream ½ gallon, rich milk ½ gallon; white sugar 1 pound. Dissolve the sugar in the mixture and flavor with extract to suit your taste, or take the peel from a fresh lemon and steep one half of it in as little water as you can, and add this. It makes the lemon flavor better than the extract, and no flavor will so universally please as the lemon. Keep the same proportion for any amount desired. The juice of strawberries or raspberries gives a beautiful color and flavor to ice creams; or about ½ ounce of essence or extracts to a gallon, or to suit the taste. Have your ice well broke; 1 quart salt to a bucket of ice. About half an hour's constant stirring, and an occasional scraping down and beating together, will freeze it.

ICE CREAM, A CHEAPER KIND.

Milk 6 quarts, Oswego corn-starch ½ pound. First dissolve the starch in one quart of the milk, and then mix all together and just simmer a little; (not to boil). Sweeten and flavor to suit your taste as above.

CHICAGO PLAN OF MAKING ICE CREAM.

Irish moss 1½ ounce, milk 1 gallon. First soak the moss in a little cold water for an hour, and rinse it well to clear it of sand and a certain peculiar taste; then steep it for an hour in the milk just at the boiling point, but not to boil. It imparts a rich color and flavor without eggs or cream. The moss may be steeped *twice*. A few minutes rubbing, at the end of freezing, with the spatula against the side of the freezer, gives ice cream a smoothness not otherwise obtained, and makes it look nice.

11th. **To make Fever and Ague Pills.** —Quinine 20 grains, Dovers powders 10 grains, sub-carbonate of iron 10 grains. Mix with mucilage of gum arabic, and make into 20 pills. DOSE: two every hour, beginning four or five hours before the chill is expected. When the chills have been broken, take one pill night and morning for a month to prevent a return.

12th. **To make Axle Grease.**—One pound of black lead, ground fine and smooth with four pounds of lard. A little powdered gum camphor is sometimes added.

13th. **To Tan Raw Hyde.**—When taken from the animal spread it flesh side up; then put 2 parts of salt, 2 parts of salt petre and alum combined, make it fine, sprinkle it evenly over the surface, roll it up, let it alone a few days until dissolved; then take off what flesh remains, and nail the skin to the side of a house in the sun; stretch it tight. To make it soft like harness leather, put neatsfoot oil on it. Fasten it up in sun again; then rub out all the oil you can with a wedge shaped stick, and it is tanned with the hair on.

14th. **To make Refined Oil for Watches, Sewing Machines, &c.**—Take sweet oil 1 pint, put into a bottle and then put into the oil 2 ounces of thin sheet lead, in coils. Set the bottle where it will be exposed to the sun for a month, (shaking it up once a week) then strain through a fine wire or cloth sieve, and keep tightly corked.

15th. **How to make Transparent Soap.**—Slice 6 pounds of nice bar soap into thin shavings; put into a brass, tin or copper kettle, with 2 quarts of alcohol, and heat it gradually over a slow fire, stirring till all the soap is dissolved; then add one ounce of sassafras, and stir till all is mixed. You will then pour into pans 1½ inches deep, and, when cold, cut into bars or cakes as many be desired.

16th. **To make Self-raising Flour.**—This is made by adding 4 pounds of the following mixture to every 100 pounds of flour, and then mixing all completely. It must be kept perfectly dry, and, in using, mix quickly and *put into the oven at once.* Here is the mixture referred to above: carbonate of soda 56 pounds, tartaric acid 28 pounds, potato flour 112 pounds. Having used bread made from self-raising flour, we can testify that it is good.

17th. **To make Solid Candles from common Lard.**—Dissolve ¼ pound of alum and ¼ pound saltpetre in ½ pint of water on a slow fire; then take 3 pounds of lard, cut into small pieces, and put into the pot with this solution, stirring it constantly over a very moderate fire until the lard is dissolved; then let it simmer until all steam ceases to rise, and remove it at once from the fire. If you leave it too long it will get discolored. These Candles are harder and better than those made from tallow.

18th. **How to make Oroide Gold**—Spanish copper, 16 parts; silver, 4 parts; gold, 1 part. Melt together.

19th. **To make Renovating Mixture** FOR REMOVING GREASE SPOTS, &c.—Aqua ammonia 2 ounces, soft water 1 quart, salt petre one teaspoonfull, variegated soap one ounce. Mix all, shake well, and it will be a little better to stand a few hours or days before using, which gives the soap a chance to dissolve.

DIRECTIONS---Pour upon the place a sufficient amount to well cover any grease or oil which may get spilled or daubed upon coats, pants, carpets, &c. sponging and rubbing well, and applying again if necessary to saponify the grease in the garment; then wash off with clear cold water

20th. To make Magic copying or Impression and Duplicating Paper.—To make black paper, lamp black mixed with cold lard. Red paper, venetian red mixed with lard. Blue paper, prussian blue mixed with lard. Green paper, chrome green mixed with lard. The above ingredients to be mixed to the consistency of thick paste, and to be applied to the paper with a rag or brush; then take a flannel rag and rub till the color ceases coming off. Cut your sheets 4 inches wide and 6 inches long; put 8 sheets together, 2 of each color, and sell for 25 cents per package.

Directions for writing with this paper.—Lay down your paper upon which you wish to write, then lay on the copying paper, and over this lay any scrap of paper you choose; then take any hard pointed substance, and write as you would with a pen. To take impressions of flowers, leaves, &c., press them between this paper and a sheet of clean white paper, and then lay the leaf on another clean sheet of paper, and press the paper gently over it.

THE MAGIC MIRROR,

OR,

THE ART OF

ORNAMENTING GLASS.

This easy and cheap process of ornamenting glass with Paper is a pleasing and profitable employment. A thin paper is best, although you can use Lithographs, Photographs, Steel Plates, Wood-cuts, Pen or Pencil Writing, or in fact almost anything on paper. By this process you do not transfer the copy from the paper, but let the paper remain on the glass, and it forms a beautiful frosting.

Prepare the glass by applying a thin coat of the preparation with a brush; let it stand a day, or until it is dry, keeping it from the dust, then apply the preparation to the glass the second time, spreading it on thick. Let it stand 15 or 20 minutes, then place the copy smoothly on the glass, pressing it down firmly so as to exclude the air. If the paper is very thick, thin it on the back after you fasten it to the glass with a tooth or nail-brush, dipping the brush in water enough to keep the paper moist while you are thinning it. If you make the paper rough in thinning it, use a fine sand-paper to smooth it; then let it dry and get firmly set to the glass; then apply the preparation on the back to make it transparent.

There is no occasion for rubbing or thinning, unless the paper is thick.

If you wish to change the shade, place colore papers at the back.

Recipe for Preparation.—One ounce Balsam of Fir to one-half ounce Spirits of Turpentine. Mix and shake well together.

THE
ARABIAN HORSE-TAMER.

That obedience to man is a ruling principle in the nature of the horse; and therefore, to make him obey is *not* necessary to do violence to him. This disobedience is in fact forced upon him by conduct towards him which does violence to his nature.

That to make him obey, it is only necessary to make him *fully comprehend* what is required of him.

That he has originally no conception of his own strength or powers; and,

That it is the part of wisdom to keep him in ignorance, which can only be done by mastering him without force; that is, by kindness.

That in the horse, as well as in man, fear is the result of ignorance; and

That, therefore, it is only necessary to *accustom* him to any object of which he may at first stand in dread, to make him lose the sense of fear. Further,

That the best means of accomplishing this end is to allow him to examine the dreadful object himself, and *in the manner most natural to him.*

All which amounts to just this: that the horse is an intelligent creature, and that the only way to develop fully all his powers of usefulness to man is to treat him as such, and to *convince* him that his master is also his superior and his best friend.

Characteristics of the Horse.

INDICATIONS OF A HORSE'S DISPOSITION.

A long, thin neck indicates a good disposition; contrarywise if it be short and thick. A broad forehead, high between the ears, indicates a very vicious disposition.

The horse is unlike the dog, the bull, and most other quadrupeds, in two respects, both of which peculiarities run into one tendency. The horse has no weapons of defence, and hence is more dependent than other animals on his sense of *smell* for protection.

It is remarkable that, unlike other animals, the horse breathes only through his nostrils, and not through his mouth, like the ox and the dog.

Mechanical, Medicinal, Psychological.

Each of these terms is necessary in describing all that is comprehended in the philosophy of taming and training horses. The horse, like other animals, is controlled by *memory* and the *laws of association*. Hence he must be reached through one or each of his external senses—*smell, sight, hearing, and feeling*, and when they are reached, he may be controlled by mechanical force, and especially by psychology and the laws of association.

"For the mechanical process you will need a strong leather strap, three or four feet in length, with a buckle; also a pole (a fishing-rod)—the longer the better. On the end of the pole you may wind and fasten a small slip of cloth.

"For the medicinal you will need the oil of rhodium, oil of cummin, or oil of anise-seed. These should be kept in air-tight phials ready for use.—Have also in readiness the horse-castor, grated fine.

"That which partakes of the psychological you will find in your own mind,—your own love, will, and wisdom. If you have little or no instinctive love for the horse, of course you are not the person to control him. Men and women are often found who are said to have the natural gift of controlling the horse; they love horses from instinct, as it were. The secret in these cases consists in their intense love for the horse. If you love the horse, you will, you can. but know how to make the horse love you. Love in all grades of animals has its appropriate language; and when this lan guage is addressed to the horse, it excites love, of course. A blow with a whip or club does not come from love, but from combativeness, and it excites combativeness or fear in the horse. If you want to make a horse love you (and you must cause him to love you if you control him), why, of course, you must love him and treat him accordingly.

"Study the character of your horse, not the nature of horses in general, but of the horse you wish to control. Horses differ in their dispositions as really as men do; and each one is to be approached, attracted, pleased, and controlled accordingly.—The organs in our way are Fear and Combativeness, and both these functions are excited through the sense of smell. Observe that these objects against which this sense of smell warns the horse differ very much. One object or person may be offensive to one horse, another object to another.

To Catch a Wild Horse.

"If your horse be in the field, he must be cornered;" drive him into a yard, into the corner where he cannot escape. Rub your hands with the oil of cummin, or rhodium; have your pole, with the small piece of cloth wound on the further end, which must smell also of the oil. Approach him from the windward, and you may thus attract him, even before he is in the reach of your pole. Proceed gently until you can reach his back with the end of your pole. It is precisely as if your arm were elongated to the length of your pole; and you pat him and work and move the pole over his back, gradually and gently approaching his head. And thus, by passing the pole up and down his back, and occasionally carrying the end near his nose, he is attracted by the sense of smell, so that you may slowly shorten the distance between you and the horse, until you can with your hand rub a little oil of cummin or rhodium on his nose; and this done, you can with suitable assistance put on the bridle or halter, and thus secure him. A failure for a few times should not discourage you; repeat the process until you succeed. And if you fail with one of the oils, try another. With some horses you may succeed best by mixing equal parts of the oil of rhodium and anise seed. A small quantity of the rhodium may be dropped upon the grated castor, after it has been sprinkled upon an apple or a lump of sugar, and given him to eat; and rubbing his nose with either of these oils, and, at the same time, breathing into his nostrils, will often work like a "charm." But then it should be borne in mind that there is a difference in horses as really as in human beings. Horses that have large caution or fear, it is, of course, much more difficult to control. But the agreeable excitement of the sense of smell overcomes the sense of fear; and fear once subdued, it enables you to render your sphere agreeable to the horse, so that you may compel him to do your bidding.

To Make a Horse lie down.

First catch your horse, then strap the near foreleg up round the arm of the animal; lead him about on three legs until he becomes tired or weary; he will then allow you to handle him anywhere; then attach a strap with a ring to the off fore-fetlock; to this ring fasten another strap, which being brought over the horse's back to the near side, is put through the ring on the off fore-fetlock; return the end of the strap to the near side, keeping fast hold, and move the animal on, and pull; he will then be thrown upon his knees, when, after struggling some time, by gentle usage he will lie down. After unloosing the straps, put him through the same process as before, when the horse will lie down whenever required.

¶ Uniformity is necessary in our method. It is by the repetition, by the constant recurrence of certain motions, words, or actions, that we succeed. Many fail for the want of uniformity in their method.— They are loving and kind by spells; then they are harsh and cruel. The horse is "impressed," as it is said, with his master's wishes, when those wishes are often and uniformly expressed in motions, words and deeds! If man needs "precept upon precept, line upon line," &c., in order to learn his lessons well, how much more true is this of the horse, which is below man in consciousness and the reflective faculties.

Plan of Driving the Wildest Horse.

This is easily effected, by fastening up one foot. Bend the leg inward, so as to bring the bottom of the hoof neatly up to his body, and slip a strap over the joint, and up, until it is as high as the pastern-joint, at which you must have another small strap, to which the larger one must be fastened, so as to prevent it from slipping down. Your horse now stands on three legs, and you can manage him as you please, for he can neither kick, rear, run, or do anything of a serious nature. This simple operation will conjur a vicious horse quicker than any other way.

Teaching a Horse to Pace.

Buckle four pound weight around the ankles of his hind-legs (lead is preferable), ride your horse briskly with those weights upon his ankles, at the same time twitching each rein of the bridle alternately, by this means you will immediately throw him into a pace. After you have trained him in this way to some extent, change your leaded weights for something lighter; leather padding, or something equal to it will answer the purpose; let him wear these light weights until he is perfectly trained.—This process will make a smooth and easy pacer of any horse.

Horsemanship.

The rider should, in the first place, let the horse know that he is not afraid of him. Before mounting a horse, take the rein into the left hand, draw it tightly, put the left foot in the stirrup, and raise quickly. When you are seated, press your knees to he saddle, let your leg, from the knee, stand out; turn your toe in and heel out; sit upright in your saddle, throw your weight forward, one-third of it in the stirrups, and hold your reins tight. Should your horse scare, you are braced in your saddle, and he cannot throw you.

To Make a Horse Stand.

This lesson is to be first in the stable. Having put your bridle on, drop the reins over his neck, and commence caressing his face, and gently work backward until you take hold of his tail. Hold on to it, and step back till you are to the length of your arm, then gently let his tail fall, and forming a half circle, walk back to the head, all the while repeating, "Ho, boy!" Pat his face, rub his eyes, and again pass backward, and this time form a complete circle round him, but so near as to keep your hands on him. Continue to enlarge your circle, until you get off as far as the stable will allow. When he will stand still in this way, you can take him out on a lot and go through the same manipulations.

To Make a Horse Set on his Haunches.

First learn the horse to obey you, so that when you say "Ho!" he will remain still. Then, having learned him to lie down, let him get up on his fore-legs, and then stop him. The horse gets up in this way, and you have only to teach him to hold his position for awhile. It does not strain the horse to set, and you must always use the word "set" in connection with the feat. Also the word "down" when you wish him to fall.

To Make a Horse come down for Mounting

Stand by his side, and stooping down, put up one of his feet, set it as far forward as you can, to make him keep it there; then take up the other and put it forward as far as you can, not to have him put it up again. Then with a small stick lightly tap him on the back of the leg, near the pastem-joint, first one leg, then the other. he will soon put them a little farther forward, and then you may in the same way spread out his hind-legs. Continue this, day after day, until he will come down enough at the word "Lower." This trick is easily taught a young horse; but remember, it injures him to often mount him thus spread out.

To Make a Horse follow you.

Take your horse to the stable, put on a circingle and a bridle with short reins, which may be checked up a little and fastened to the circingle. Then lead him about a few times, and letting go the bridle, continue to caress him, as you constantly say "come along." If he lag, give him a light cut behind with a long whip. Continue this until you succeed. Do not forget the element of "LOVE" in this as well as other feats.

How to Handle Horse's Feet.

Should the colt refuse to have his feet handled he may be made to submit by reproving with the bridle and putting a small strap on the hind hoof; then pull on this strap and bring the foot up; then at the moment he kicks bring down on the mouth sharply with the bridle. In a short time he will submit to your control unconditionally. The same principle applies to the use of this under all circumstances. It is a means of reproof, and certainly has a powerful effect upon a horse.

Armenian Cement.—Soak Isinglass in water till soft then dissolve it in Proof Spirit, add a little Galbanum or Gum Ammoniac, and mix it with Tincture of Mastick.

It must be kept well stopped, and when wanted, liquefied by the phial being immersed in hot water. Used to cement jewels upon watch-cases; to mend china, or to replace leaves torn out of books.

To prevent Flies from Settling on Pictures, Picture Frames, or other Furniture.—Soak a large bundle of Leeks for five or six days in a pail of water, and then wash or sponge the pictures, &c. over with it.

A wash to be used to the Arm-pits when the perspiration is unpleasant.—Take pure spring water as cold as can be got, 2 pints; Tincture of Myrrh, 1 ounce; Sulphate of Zinc, ½ ounce; Rose Water, 2 ounces. Mix all together and sponge the arm-pits occasionally with it.

To cure Butter.—Take 2 parts of the best common Salt, one part of Sugar, and one part of Salt-petre. Beat them up and mix well together. Take one ounce of this to every pound of Butter, work it well into the mass and close it up for use.

Butter thus cured, appears of a rich marrowy consistence and fine color, and does not acquire a brittle hardness, nor taste salt. It will keep good for three years, if let stand three or four weeks before opening it.

To Moderate Perspiration.—Take Spring Water, 4 ounces; Diluted Sulphuric Acid, 40 drops; Compound Spirits of Lavender, 2 drachms. Mix. A table-spoonful twice a day; keeping the bowels regular by Rhubarb.

Wash to Whiten the Nails.—Take Diluted Sulphuric Acid, 2 drachms; Pump Water, 4 ounces; Tincture of Myrrh, 1 drachm. Mix. First cleanse with white Soap, and then dip the fingers into the wash.

Sore Throat.—Let the Throat be steamed with Hot Water, in which Hops are infused; apply the Hops, after having been scalded some time, externally to the diseased part of the throat.

To join Glass together.—Take a little Isinglass, and melt it in spirits of Wine; it will form a transparent glue, which will unite glass, so that the fracture will be almost imperceptible. The greatest care is necessary, that the spirits of wine shall not boil over into the fire.

To Renovate old Apple Trees.—Take fresh made Lime from the kiln, slake it well with water, and well dress the tree with a brush, and the insects and moss will be completely destroyed; the outer rind fall off, and a new, smooth, clean, healthy one formed, and the tree assume a most healthy appearance and produce the finest fruit.

To prevent the Smoking of a Lamp.—Soak the wick in strong vinegar, and dry it well before you use it; it will then burn both sweet and pleasant, and give much satisfaction for the trifling trouble in preparing it.

To make Silvering Powder.—Get from a Drug Store 1 oz. of what is called Hydrargirum, *Cum Creta*, and mix it with 4 oz. Prepared Chalk. Used to give a Silver Polish to Brass, Copper, Britannia Ware, &c. To be rubbed on with a dry cloth.

Nerve Ointment.—Take half a pint of Neatsfoot oil, one gill of Brandy, one gill of spirits of Turpentine and simmer them together fifteen minutes. Excellent for sprains, swellings, and Rheumatism.

To free plants from Leaf-Lice.—Mix 3 ounces of Flowers of Sulphur with a bushel of Saw-dust; scatter this over the plants infested with these insects, and they will soon be freed, though a second application may possibly be necessary.

To Preserve Eggs.—Apply with a brush a solution of Gum Arabic to the shells, or immerse the Eggs therein—let them dry, and afterwards pack them in dry charcoal dust. This is vastly superior to the plan of putting Eggs up in lime, as the lime makes the shells brittle, and the [illegible] soon worthless, but the Gum process prevents [illegible] effected by changes in the atmosphere.

To make Apple Jelly.—Take of Apple Juice [strained] lbs. Sugar 1 lb. Boil to a Jelly.

Strawberry Jelly.—Take of the Juice of Strawberries 4 lbs., Sugar 1 lb. Boil to a Jelly.

To Avoid Injury from Bees.—A wasp or bee swallowed may be killed before it can do harm, by taking a teaspoonful of common salt dissolved in water. It kills the insect, and cures the sting. Salt at all times is the best cure for external stings; sweet oil, pounded mallows, onions, or powdered chalk made into a paste with water, are also efficacious.

If bees swarm upon the head, smoke tobacco, and hold an empty hive over the head, and they will enter it.

How to Make Rose Water.—Take half an ounce white sugar, and drop into it 2 or 3 drops of Otto of Rose; then grind very fine in a mortar. After it is well ground into fine powder, pour on it half a pint of cold water, grind well for a few moments, and then mix it all with one gallon of cold water. Let it stand for 3 or 4 days, and strain through fine muslin.

Whitewashing.—A pint of Varnish mixed with a bucket of Whitswash, will give it in a great degree, the qualities of paint—and it will withstand all kinds of weather.

Nankin Dye.—Take Arnotto and prepared Kali, equal parts, boiled in water; the proportion of Kali is altered, as the color is required to be deeper or lighter;—used to restore the color of faded nankin clothing, or to dye new goods of a Nankin color.

To make Spice Bitters.—Golden Seal, Poplar Bark, Bayberry, bark of the root, Sassafras, bark of the root, of each one pound; Unicorn Root, Bitter Root, Cloves, Capsicum, of each, four ounces, Loaf Sugar, four pounds. Put to one ounce of this powder, one quart of sweet wine, let it sttnd a week or two before using it. Dose—a wineglassful two or three times a day.

How to make Saur Kraut.—Take a large strong wooden vessel, or cask, resembling a salt beef cask, and capable of containing as much as is sufficient for the winter's consumption of a family. Gradually break down or chop the cabbages (deprived of outside green leaves,) into very small pieces; begin with one or two cabbages at the bottom of the cask, and add others at intervals, pressing them by means of a wooden spade, against the side of the cask, until it is full. Then place a heavy weight on top of it and allow it to stand near to a warm place, for four or f days. By this time it will have undergone fermentation, and be ready for use. Whilst the cabbages are passing through the process of fermentation, a very disagreeable fetid, acid smell is exhaled from them; now remove the cask to a cool situation, and keep it always covered up. Strew Aniseeds among the layers of the cabbage during its preparation, which communicates a peculiar flavor to the Saur Kraut at an after period.

In boiling it for the table, two hours is the period for it to be on the fire. It forms an excellent nutritious and antiscorbutic food for winter use.

How to mend a Stove.—When a crack is discovered in a stove, through which the fire or smoke penetrates, the aperture may be completely closed in a moment with a composition consisting of wood ashes, and common salt, made into paste with a little water, plastered over the crack. The good effect is equally certain, whether the stove, &c., be cold or hot.

Bed Bugs.—A strong decoction of ripe red Pepper is said to be as efficacious an antidote to Bed Bugs as can be selected from the multitudinous recipes for the purpose.

Burning Fluid.—Take four quarts of Alcohol and one quart of spts. of Turpentine—mix well together.

To Extract Paint from Cotton, Silk and Woolen Goods.—Saturate the spots with spirits of Turpentine, and let it remain several hours, then rub it between the hands. It will crumble away, without injuring either the color, or texture of the article.

PHYSIOLOGY OF MARRIAGE,

AND

PHILOSOPHY OF GENERATION.

—o—

LOVE, COURTSHIP AND MARRIAGE.

From all the momentous and lasting consequences which flow from marriage, it becomes the most important connection that can be formed in this world. It is the great era in life, the prominent land mark to which the young look forward with pleasing expectation, and from which the married date the events of after life. The happiness or wretchedness, the peace or discontentment, the prosperity or adversity of the remaining portion of earthly existence, depend very much upon our discharging properly the obligations of husbands and wives.

And to do this properly, we must understand not only human nature, but our human bodies, for we are "fearfully and wonderfully made." We may have every advantage desirable, every necessary qualification, every possible facility for a vigorous and successful outset upon the great arena of business-life—the brightest prospects, the most flattering anticipations, may smile in the future, yet, if we are lacking in knowledge, as regards the mysteries and wonders of our own organization, we cannot properly or pleasantly perform our duties and meet the responsibilities of married life; a cloud will overshadow our domestic happiness, the darkness of which will reach the most remote sources of enjoyment, and the sun of true happiness will sink beneath the horizon to rise no more.

In view of these considerations, how important it is that the young who have taken upon themselves the marriage vows, should possess proper knowledge of all that is calculated to make life happy!

And yet it is conceded that the ideas which most young persons entertain of LOVE are both romantic and foolish, and it is not difficult to account why this is the case.

LOVE is, too often, a proscribed topic either of conversation or advice; all that is known concerning it is, therefore, derived from the fictions of poetry, and the high-wrought descriptions of novels. Education is employed in directing, controlling, or reforming all the other passions and tempers of the human heart; but on this, it is systematically silent. Can we then wonder that a passion so stimulant, so powerful, so influential, shall, unguided, or misdirected, urge on to error and to crime, the weak reason, and the generous, unsuspecting nature of youth? That there is a strong prejudice against the discussion of this subject is confessed; and when the peculiar delicacy attending it is considered, we cannot wonder that such a prejudice should exist. Even the most chaste and correct observations concerning it are apt to give pain: or, at least, to excite alarm in a delicate and pious mind. The delicacy and the difficulty of the subject are confessed: but we ask, is it fit, is it safe, is it not preposterous, is it not ruinous to the best interests of mankind, to leave the whole discussion of it to men of loose and abandoned character?—is it wise to leave young persons to derive their notions and feelings on this subject from the exaggerated, false, and wicked descriptions of it, with which modern literature abounds? Do not these deceptions daily seduce, mislead, and corrupt thousands of the young, thoughtless, and inexperienced? Is it not infinitely better, then, that we should innovate a little on the opinions and feelings and, as we think, prejudices of the world, and break that mysterious and profound silence, which regards the discussion of this topic as either indecorous or mischievous?

Marriage, the author has ever considered as bearing intimately, not only on the happiness of indivi duals, but also on the prosperity and welfare of communities and states, and is the source of all industry, subordination, and government, among men. He, therefore, who shall succeed in rendering marriage a matter of serious consideration, and not blind experiment, will deserve well of society, and cannot offend against delicacy or religious feeling. On this ground, the author feels assured that he need offer no further apology for the humble publication which now solicits the reader's approbation.

In conversing with a Minister on the spiritual and moral condition of his diocese, I learned many things which interested me very much; and there was one thing discussed which especially surprised me. It was said that two-thirds of the misery which came under the immediate notice of a popular clergyman, and to which he was called to minister, arose from the infelicity of the conjugal relations; there was no question here of open immorality and discord, but simply of infelicity and unfitness. The same thing has been brought before me in every country, every society in which I have been a sojourner and an observer.

For a result then so universal, there must be a cause or causes universal, not depending on any particular customs, manners, or religion, or political institutions. And what are these causes? Many things do puzzle me in this strange world of ours—many things in which the new world and the old world are equally incomprehensible. I cannot understand why an evil everywhere acknowledged and felt is not remedied somewhere, or discussed by some one with a view to a remedy; but, no—it is like putting one's hand into the fire, only to touch upon it; it is the universal bruise, the putrefying sore, on which you must not lay a finger, or your patient (that is society) cries out and resists, and, like a sick baby, scratches and kicks its physician.

Strange, and passing strange, that the relation between the two sexes, the passion of love in short should not be taken into deeper consideration by our teachers and our legislators. People educate and legislate as if there was no such thing in the world; but ask the minister, ask the physician, let THEM reveal the amount of moral and physical results from this one cause. Must love be always discussed in blank verse, as if it were a thing to be played in tragedies or sung in songs—a subject for pretty poems and wicked novels, and had nothing to do with the prosaic current of our every day existence, our moral welfare, and eternal salvation. Must love be ever treated with profaneness, as a mere illusion? or with coarseness, as a mere impulse? or with fear, as a mere disease? or with shame, as a mere weakness? or with levity, as a mere accident? Whereas, it is a great mystery and a great necessity, lying at the foundation of human existence, morality, and happiness; mysterious, uni-

-sal, inevitable as death. Love and death, the alpha and omega of human life, the author and finisher of existence, the two points on which God's universe turns; which He, our Father and Creator, has placed beyond our arbitration—beyond the reach of that election and free will which he has left us in all other things! Death must come, and love must come—but the state in which they find us, whether blinded, astonished, and frightened, and ignorant, or, like reasonable creatures, guarded, prepared, and fit to manage our own feelings?—*this*, I suppose, depends on ourselves; and for want of such self-management and self-knowledge, look at the evils that ensue!—hasty, improvident, unsuitable marriages; repining, diseased, of vicious celibacy; irretrievable infamy, cureless insanity.

I also consider that the influence of the genital function on the health of parents, and offspring and morals, is one of the greatest importance; and, under this impression, I have felt justified in discussing it as freely as my predecessors and contemporaries have done.

The present is a reading age, in which novelty, interest, and pleasure, are the principal objects of pursuit; and the diffusion of knowledge of all kinds is unprecedented. In this age, men and women read, think, discuss, inquire, and judge for themselves They now require intelligible information from their medical advisers; and the old system of explanation—a shake of the head, a shrug of the shoulders, is no longer tolerated. A thirst for knowledge and free inquiry has replaced ignorance and mystery.

I offer this explanation to those ignorant persons who are incapable of understanding the bearings of the subject which has given rise to these observations. I feel convinced that the profession to which I have the honor to belong, has more influence on society than any other, and that great good will result both to public health and morals, by the diffusion of correct views on the physiology and pathology of marriage and the sexual function.

It may be necessary to remind those who feel shocked at this species of knowledge, of the present immense circulation of the most erroneous and beastly publications relative to the reproductive function, which are well calculated to demoralize the people, and contaminate the rising and future generations, and which prove the necessity of correct and scientific productions. Are not the most revolting vices now unblushingly recommended as checks to population? and are not the most immoral works circulated and exposed in almost every bye-street through which we pass? Among those vile publications is that falsely ascribed to Aristotle, which is in great circulation, though replete with error and obscenity from beginning to end. Such is the text-book of midwives, and the only guide for their instruction.

We also read in the daily journals of seductions

abortions, murders, infanticides, adulteries, and many other crimes, all the result of perverted opinions on the subjects under consideration. Nevertheless, many consider it wise to withhold a species of knowledge most essential to every man and woman's well-being, and most influential on their future lives, as well as of their offspring. But this course is, in my opinion, productive of great and incalculable injury. I need scarcely observe, that the physiology and pathology of the organs of reproduction are as legitimate objects of study as of those of respiration, circulation, digestion, innervation, &c., and have ever been discussed by the most eminent physiologists of ancient and modern times, as an important branch of medical knowledge. I may also remark in passing, that the references made to the generative function in the Bible, which is in every one's hands, in our church service, in our courts of law, and in the public prints, must convince every person, capable of reflection, that as a function in the animal economy, it is a legitimate object for the consideration of physiologists

The most zealous disciples of Malthus were said to be the Westminster political economists, including Bentham, Ricardo, Place, Mill, Tooke, Brougham, Miss Martineau, and others of minor note. A number of grossly immoral men followed their example, and in 1822 distributed the most infamous handbills throughout the large manufacturing districts in England, which purported to contain "the important information for the working classes, how to regulate the number of a family." Various abominable means were proposed, which few, if any one, would follow, for all were contrary to the dictates of nature, to the precepts of revealed religion, to morals, to the divine and primitive command—"go forth and multiply."

It must be scarcely necessary to observe, that the doctrine of limiting population is based upon a most irreligious doubt in the conservative power of the Divine Creator; which regulates, preserves, and reproduces the illimitable number of organized beings in the animal and vegetable kingdoms.

It was, however, most erroneously contended by the advocates of this cold-hearted and immoral doctrine, that the consequence of controlling the faculty of reproduction would be moral, civilizing, would prevent much crime and unhappiness, that they would improve the manners and moral feelings, alleviate the burdens of the poor, diminish the cares of the rich, and lastly, that they would enable parents more comfortably to provide for, and educate, their offspring. But to these conclusions it may be unanswearably replied, that the limitation of offspring is based upon principles severely condemned and reprobated in the sacred volume, which are subversive of every virtue, and holding out inducements and facilities for the degradation of our daughters, sisters, and wives.

None can deny that, if young women in general, of the lower class of society, were absolved from the fear of consequences, the great majority of them, unless comparatively few who are strictly moral and highly educated, would rarely preserve their chastity from the depravity of licentious men; illicit amours would be common and seldom detected—seduction would be facilitated, and degradation become almost universal, unless among the virtuous and small class already excepted.

The heartless conduct of a seducer has been condemned in all ages, though sanctioned by our poor legislation. No one will deny, that the seducer who, for a momentary and selfish gratification, will deliberately entail misery, shame, and infamy, on a young and hitherto virtuous woman, whose offence was a weakness of judgment, or misplaced confidence or affection, is an unprincipled villain, and the author of the blackest of crimes. It must be admitted by every man who is well acquainted with the natural inclinations of the softer sex, that for one who is seduced or dishonored by inclination, there are a hundred who have been duped or imposed on, or actuated by necessity. This fact has been well observed by many of the most eminent physiologists and writers on medical jurisprudence; and the most ample proof of the sad truth of this position is daily afforded by our public press.

When we consider the mass of crime, of ignorance

and of folly, caused by the abuse of the reproductive function, the natural history, or physiology of this function, is a legitimate object of study for all classes of society. Reason never differed from nature, though certain depraved individuals may advise their disassociation. They have fruitlessly endeavored to recommend checks and preventives to reproduction, which are most severely condemned by society at large.

All Christian moralists maintain that the chief end of marriage is the propagation of the species; that it is sinful in married persons to wish not to have a family, or to use any means of prevention, or to procure abortion at any period from the moment of conception, as the fœtus is a living being according to standard medical authority in all countries, and that to destroy it before or after quickening, is murder. The violation of these precepts is contrary to the law of God and civilized man, and is only recommended by those immoral wretches who set both at defiance.

There are many other causes, which will be noticed hereafter, that excite amorous impulse, and lead to premature illicit sexual unions. So numerous and powerful are these causes, that early marriages would be almost universal, did not reason, physiology, legislative enactments, and prudential considerations, prevent them. But the passions are very strong, modern morals much too lax, and temptations, in all large cities and towns, very great; and hence, libertinism and depravity are the consequences.

It is also to be borne in mind, that persons, in general, must defer marriage until they arrive at a proper age, and until they can support a family, or form mercenary and demoralizing connexions, by unequal unions which too often destroy domestic happiness. It may also be maintained, as a general proposition, that those who marry early in life, after the adult age, and who can support a family, have the best chance of forming their children's character, of watching their progress to the adult age, and providing for them in the world; while those who marry late in life, are generally separated from their offspring while young and inexperienced, and obliged to consign them to the mercy of fortune, and the care of heartless relations and strangers.

These and a great variety of other important considerations relating to the function of reproduction, will be fully considered in the following pages. In fact, the sole object of the medical inquirer is to display nature in her true character, to defend her laws, and to expose the errors and follies of mankind in their violation.

Let us now glance at the extent and importance of the function of reproduction in its moral and physical relations, and we shall readily perceive its great influence on every class of society.

Androgeny, or the power of generation of the human species, in strict physiological language, exists from the period of puberty to old age; it comprises numerous moral and physcal inquiries—as the physiology of puberty; the age proper for marriage; early, premature, ill-assorted, and late marriages; the physiology and pathology of the generative organs; the hygienic and morbid effects of the use and abuse of these organs, on fecundity, health, and longevity; the moral and physical qualifications and disqualifications for reproduction; the influence of monogamy, polygamy, prostitution, and concubinage, on morals and population; legal and clandestine marriages; seduction, adultery, rape, bastardy, criminal abortion; and the influence of age, habit, constitution, temperament, season, climate, plenty, famine, public amusements, war, pestilence, &c.; on fecundity, nativity, and mortality. Such are only a few of the principal medical, legal, civil, political, and social topics, relative to the function of generation. Medical practitioners are generally consulted on all these topics, both by the legislature and every class of society, in civilized countries. Andropogeny, or the production of the human species, is a universal theme of conversation under many different popular terms, and especially with all those capable of begetting offspring. Legislators designate it "the population question," about which so much has been discussed and published; and the different grades of society denominate it " family." Lawyers and divines also discuss numerous questions relating to this subject. The most renowned theologians, philosophers, physiologists, legislators, and jurisconsults, as well as all classes of society in ancient and modern times, have occupied their minds with the study of the various phenomena and anomalies of reproduction, and the numerous questions connected with it.

Institution and Object of Marriage.

Marriage is a natural, religious, civil, and legal contract, wisely instituted for the procreation and conservation of the species.

Man was born for society ; his condition, faculties and propensities, require that he should associate with other men. At every period of his life he stands in need, and wants the assistance of others.

When the human being arrives at the adult age, he possesses the power o generation, and is bound to protect, support, and cherish the individual who co-operates with him, in perpetuating his species ; and hence originates society.

Finally, when senescence, or old age, commences, the same imbecility, the same infirmity recurs as in infancy ; therefore, if society did not exist, the human being would fall to the ground, would be affected with various diseases, unremoved, or unalleviated by remedies, he could have no food. and must be destroyed by hunger. It therefore follows, that the condition of man, at all periods of life, requires the care of his fellow-creatures. His faculties, reason, senses, voice, gestures, and capacity for learning the arts and sciences, require the benefits of civil society. The offices, by which we are bound to all other men, arise from the duties of humanity, or draw their origin from society.

The general principle from which all our social duties are derived, is the golden rule—do unto others as you would they should do unto you—the truth of which precept reason demonstrates to every man; for all men are born equal; the same nature is inherent in all; they enjoy the same faculties, want mutual assistance; they are all formed by the same Deity, and they are destined to the same end; all are born with the same reason, they pass through the same periods of life, and they cease to exist in the same manner. It is, therefore, necessary that they should be united in one common oona of fraternal charity, as if members of the same family; that they should mutually assist each other in their necessities, and that they should live happily together.

Conjugal society, is a perpetual compact, between man and woman, to live together in mutual ove and friendship, for the procreation, conservation, and education of children, and to aid each other by mutual succour for the course of life. The diversity of the sexes was instituted for this purpose; and there is an innate desire implanted in both to perpetuate their species, their names, and to transfer their property to their children.

Marriage was instituted by the Divine Creator in the time of man's primitive innocence, as the means of his happiness, and the perpetuation of his race. The wisdom of its institution has been felt and acknowledged in every age. Man found by experience it was not good for him to be alone, or to lead a life of celibaby or isolated selfishness. Marriage does not, however, restrict its beneficial influence to individuals, but extends to states and kingdoms. "It is," says JEREMY TAYLOR, "the mother of the world, and preserves kingdoms, and fills cities, churches, and even heaven itself."

Of all the social institutions, there is none which exercises so great an influence upon states as marriage. Every state is composed of families, and these are the result of conjugal unions. It was, therefore, wisely ordained that marriage should be a sacred compact, for which those engaging in it should forsake their nearest relations and friends. The parties contracting it forms the strictest union and nearest relation that can be established between two individuals; their temporal concerns are identical, and consequently marriage is universally considered the source of the greatest comfort and most perfect enjoyment on earth, securing all the advantages of sincere friendship, and the reciprocal offices of true and tender affection

Marriage was originally instituted between the first of the human species, as a religious, political, civil, and moral contract of Divine ordinance, the origin of society, the law for the reproduction of the species,—a contract for the transmission of property, a guarantee for obligations the most interesting to mankind. It is, therefore, universally respected.

Man is a rational and social being, deriving his chief of earthly happiness from the delights of society, and the interchange of thought. It is the interchange of the charities and the sympathies of life, which gives to human existence its real and only value. Hence, man in a state of solitude, or even isolated luxury or affluence, would be the most pitiable and miserable of creatures.

Exposed to the corroding cares, sorrows, bitter disappointments, and misfortunes of life, man cannot brave alone, and unbefriended, the ingratitude, envy and malevolence of the world.

The perfection and sincerity of friendship can only be found in the marriage state, where an identity of interest shuts out all petty jealousies and vexations, and a unity of thought, sentiment, feeling, and conduct, exists. The qualities essential to conjugal happiness are chiefly of a mental or moral nature, and not merely of a physical kind, as is unfortunately too generally the case.

It is not enough that children should be procreated by parents; they are also to be nourished, clothed, and educated; they should be nourished by the milk of the mother, and not delivered to other women, unless in certain cases. for nature generally gives to the parent the nourishment required for this purpose; and she never can morally, unless this is withheld, or unless there is dangerous infirmity, or some great cause, omit to afford it: for by the neglec of this sacred duty, the offspring suffers not only great inconvenience, but often loss of health and life and the mother herself becomes liable to diseases, or propogates unhealthy offspring. Nature commands maternal lactation; for the mind and milk of a stranger affect the mind and body of the infant, and render both dissimilar to those of the parents. The injuries and bad effects of strange or mercenary lactation, are universally admitted.

It is well known that when children are committed to the care of mercenary nurses, maternal love and tenderness diminish, or almost cease; whilst infantile affection is naturally bestowed on another individual, and finally it scarcely exists towards the parent.

It is likewise an indispensable obligation on parents, that they inform their children, by word and example, of the existence, culture, and love of the Deity, for in infancy we are most tenacious of perceptions; and the greatest care should be taken that children do not see, hear, or read, unless what is good and right, because their early impressions generally continue to old age.

THE PROPER AGE FOR MARRIAGE—CONSTITUTION—PREDISPOSITION, AND THE IMMEDIATE STATE OF HEATH.—The proper age for marriage, according to the law of this country, is twenty-one for the male, and eighteen for the female; but many physiologists are of opinion that the ages of twenty-five and twenty-one would more accord with the complete development of adults. BUFFON held this position, "the natural state of man after puberty is marriage;" but this is evidently untenable, because the human body is not fully developed at this period of life, the different functions are not perfect, and as the organs are only in the progress of their growth, the offspring would be infirm and delicate; and the sexes totally incompetent to perform the various important duties of parents. It is at, or rather after the adult age, that the mind and body have arrived at perfection; and therefore moralists and legislators have fixed this age as the best for marriage.

It is universally known, that premature or excessive exertion of any part of the body is succeeded by fatigue or decay of such part; and more especially before complete development has taken place. Hence it follows, that the premature exertion of the genital function, or marriage at too early an age, must not only be highly injurious to the parents in most eases, but also to the constitution of the offspring. It is a moral and medical precept, that both male and female should observe the strictest continence until the adult age, so that the great end of marriage, the propagation of healthful infants, may be accomplished.

It is impossible, perhaps, to fix the exact period proper for conjugal union in all cases, because there is so great a difference in the growth of individuals, some being more developed at eighteen or twenty than others at twenty-five. Some girls have been mothers at the twelfth year of their age in this country. It is common in tropical climates to see girls at the age of nine years married, and become mothers at ten; while in the polar regions, menstruation, or the establishment of womanhood, does not occur before the eighteenth or twentieth year. It is, therefore, evident that, taking the whole of mankind, on the face of the globe, into view, it is impossible to fix a certain age for marriage.

The evils resulting from too early marriages are, diminished growth and strength of the male, delicate and bad health of the female, premature old age, or death of either or both, and a feeble, infirm, and diseased offspring.

It has long been observed by physicians, that persons advanced in life, provided they are healthful and vigorous, and have observed continence, procreate much more vigorous infants than the debilitated young, who have injured their constitutions. Professor DEWEES, judiciously remarks, "it is oftentimes better to be old in years than in constitution." This learned physician also observes, that feeble parents may propagate robust children, but these, according to his experience, which is that of more than thirty years, seldom survive beyond the age of manhood, and old age is out of the question. We see the truth of this statement verified every day: we have only to observe the many delicate mothers who daily present their children at our hospitals and dispensaries, emaciated, and often dying, who generally inform us that for some months after birth it was impossible to behold more robust or finer infants.

There is another position maintained by the profession worthy of attention, viz.: that persons who attain extreme old age, often marry and have children. Attestations of this fact are afforded by two remarkable instances.

THOMAS PARR, who died at the age of a hundred and fifty-two, was married at a hundred and twenty, and performed his nuptial duties so well at a hundred and forty as to make him forget his old age. He was compelled to do penance in a white sheet, for an illicit amour in the one hundred and fortieth year of his age; while DE LONGVILLE, a Frenchman, married ten wives, the last when he was in his ninety seventh year, and she bore him a son when he was in his hundred and second. He died at the age of a hundred and ten years. These individuals possessed in some measure, the longevity and vigor of the antediluvians; but, in general, the power of propagation is supposed to cease about the seventieth or eightieth year in a man, and much sooner in a woman. It is said, that the latter becomes sterile at the cessation of menstruation, which, usually, but not invariably, occurs at, or after the fiftieth year, in temperate climates, though, according to M. MAGENDIE, sometimes not before the seventieth year. The universal belief of physiologists is, that while the function of menstruation continues, conception may happen; this seldom occurs after the fiftieth year in this country.

It is true that women in general lose the faculty of conception from the age of forty-five years in this climate; but some attain the function of maturity much later.

Medical practitioners are often consulted by individuals, who are anxious to know whether marriage is, or is not conducive to health and longevity. It is now universally admitted, that an answer in the affirmative ought to be given to all healthful and well-formed individuals of the male sex, from the adult age to the sixty-fifth year, and sometimes even later. Longevity, however, does not depend upon the benefit of proper regimen alone, but on the degree of vitiality which is transmitted by parents. An individual born of healthful and robust parents ought naturally to expect a long life; but one whose parents are delicate, feeble, or aged, or affected with scrofula, syphilis, gout, pulmonary consumption, distorted spine, or calculous diseases, will have a delicate and infirm constitution.

Hufeland lays down the following precepts on the subject of marriage:—

1st. "A person should not marry unless into a family remarkable for longevity," and, he should have added, free from certain hereditary diseases.

2. He should not marry a woman advanced in life, delicate, feeble, or affected with any deformity or disease, more especially those transmissible by generation, as gout, consumption, gravel, herpes, certain diseases of the skin, syphilis, scrofula, mania, or hæmorrhoids.

3d. The age most proper for women is eighteen years, and for men twenty-four or five.

4th. They must not give themselves to the pleasures of reproduction but when the natural impulse is strong, and above all things, avoid propagation during drunkenness or sickness.

5th. Every pregnant woman ought to be considered as a labatory, in which she prepares a new being, to which the slightest physical or moral emotion is injurious.

6th. Women of a nervous temperament, those who are very irritable, nervous, hysterical, subject to convulsions, or epilepsy, ought to avoid matrimo ny, as they will give birth to infants who can live but for a short time.

This last precept is liable to exception, because nervous and hysterical women are often cured by marriage, and may have healthful infants.

Whenever medical practitioners are consulted as to the propriety of marriage, they ought to recollect, that they touch a delicate cord of affections, that man is more than a machine, so that they should combine moral with physical medicine—that science of the heart and mind, with which all the learned and well-informed of the profession are well acquainted.

There are many infirmities which are not sufficient to prevent married persons from affording each other mutual succour, and are no bar to conjugal union; but there are others which totally disqualify persons from engaging in this contract—such as malformations and incurable diseases of the genital organs, of which I shall treat in another chapter.

Every individual who entertains a doubt as to his capabilities for generation, is anxious to obtain medical advice on his condition; and it is much to be regretted that it is too often the practice of the profession to treat the matter with levity or derision. Hence few of the faculty are consulted, an unreserved dis closure of the symptoms is seldom given, and the inquirer is often fearful that his condition may be made known to his acquaintances. Every duly edu cated physician is bound to secrecy, in all delicate matters, and so far from treating his patient with levity or carelessness, should consider his case as attentively as any other that may come before him. Were this line of conduct generally adopted by the medical profession, an immense number of the public would not be driven to seek advice from low, ignorant, and unprincipled empirics, who not only defraud them of immense sums of money, but also destroy, what is far more important, their health.

The period has at length arrived, when sexual dis eases, obtain as much attention as any other class of infirmities, and when the most distinguished medical practitioners devote themselves to their study and treatment.

Physiology and Hygeology of Marriage--Premature and Abusive Exercise of the Congenital Function.

THE consummation of marriage ought to be effected with gentleness and moderation, and not with unrestrained impetuosity, as among brute animals; for, if it is accomplished with violence, more or less severe pain, laceration, effusion of blood, with inflammation of the external and internal genital organs, will be frequently induced. All obstetric authors, and all writers on medical jurisprudence, attest the truth of this statement. SIR CHARLES M. CLARKE, DR. DEWEES, DR. BECK, and many other esteemed authorities, relate examples. Every experienced medical practitioner is aware, that in cases of female violation, more or less contusion, laceration, hemorrhage, and inflammation is produced, more especially in cases of very young persons, and when there is much disproportion between the age and development of the individuals.

When most of these diseases are induced, they are aggravated by the requent repetition of the cause which excited them, it occasions excruciating pains, and generally produces sterility and bad health.

There is nothing more certain than that precipitation and impetuosity in the consummation of marriage often causes, in the very young or aged individuals, exquisite pain, from contusion, laceration, &c.; and these evils result from more sensual passion than the legitimate object, the propagation of the species. In farther support of this opinion I may add, that the Jews and many ancients maintained, that the consummation of marriage ought to be characterized by the effusion of blood; and this is generally the case, but there are many exceptions, as when leucorrhœa or other mucous discharges are present, which relax the external genitals, and destroy the hymen. In these last cases, there may be no effusion of blood, on the consummation of marriage, though the individual is a virgin—a fact well known to every scientific and practical obstetrican and medical practitioner.

It is also well known that pregnancy has occurred and the hymen perfect. Again, a woman may be delivered and such cohesion occur soon after as to totally impede sexual commerce; and in certain cases there will be copious effusion of blood.

I hold it as an axiom, that it is the duty of every author to inform his species as much as possible, and thereby to give information, diffuse knowledge, dissipate ignorance, and familiarise truth and science.

It is also a general conclusion among pysiologists, that repeated conjugal intimacy within a few hours is unprolific, and a mere animal gratification. Abstinence for one or more days, and tolerably good health, are necessary to most individuals for procreation of healthful offspring.

According to most physiologists, morning is the best time for reproduction, that is, after the fatigues of the preceding day are dissipated by repose, and when the majority of healthful individuals possess most virility.

As the hygienic precepts relative to the generative function, are deeply interesting to most individuals, they may be slightly noticed.

1. It should never be indulged in until there is a natural desire and vigorous impulse; and seldom, if ever, before the adult age.

2. It ought to be avoided whenever it produces more than temporary depression of spirits, or the least debility of the moral, intellectual, or physical

states, also during intoxication, mania, and when there is venereal or any other disease of the sexual organs of either party.

3. It ought to be used in moderation, when the individual makes much mental or corporeal exertion, or during recovery from any severe disease, when there is a state of debility, or when restorative aliment, &c., cannot be procured.

4. It ought to be entirely abstained from during the presence of the menses, the child-bed evacuation, which continues for nine, twelve, or more days after delivery, and only used moderately and occasionally during pregnancy and suckling. It ought to be avoided in all painful diseases of the generative organs. It is also particularly injurious immediately after taking food, and until digestion is completed, which is from two to three hours afterwards.

There can be no rule laid down as to the proper exercise of this function, as this will depend on age, habits, occupation, situation, climate, season, aliment and numerous other moral, physical, and external influences, which are capable of modifying their functions.

Women suffer infinitely more harm from abortion than from natural parturition or delivery. Moderate intercourse may be indulged in with caution and gentleness at all times, unless those excepted, but violence is invariably injurious.

Every pregnant woman is the depository of a new

and feeble being, at first imperceptible to the human eye, though the future statesman, philosopher, or emperor, and which is powerfully, though indirectly, influenced by the moral and physical conditions of the mother, or by her state of mind or body.

The motives which influence the majority of the world in contracting matrimonial unions, are generally false, selfish, and most detrimental to the procreation of sound and vigorous offspring; such as ambition, wealth, rank, title, interest, a love of independence, of an establishment, a desire to escape parental restraint, anger, a determination to disinherit relations, disdain for a faithless lover or mistress, necessity, obligation, passion, imitation, and very rarely the proper motive, pure and virtuous affection. It is also generally admitted that parental authority cannot reasonably or morally compel alliances when the inclination of the individual most concerned is opposed; although we see too many forced and unhappy marriages which are to be ascribed to this cause.

It is scarcely necessary to observe, that love is implanted by the Deity in human beings, all grades of mankind have felt the power of this passion—it is the same in all—as the poet has it, "*amor. omnibus idem*"—or, more strictly speaking, in almost all, for it is alleged that some few have never felt its influence. It is equally powerful in the palace and in the cottage; it is universal, or very nearly so; it glows in almost every breast, and it has been sung by the sweetest bards of ancient and modern times. Its power so strongly attaches two individuals, that no human law or intervention can separate them; for though united to others, they never can be happy, nor their offspring vigorous.

As a general rule, it may also be laid down, that parties about to contract matrimonial unions ought to be of the adult age, and in good health.

Man and woman ought naturally to perform the act of marriage when the body has acquired all the development of which it is susceptible. Nature always tends to perfection in all her operations, and assuredly a feeble being and one imperfectly grown, cannot be the source of a sound and vigorous generation; while, at the same time, the premature exercise of certain functions essentially debilitating even to individuals fully developed, cannot but remarkably retard the growth and vigor of persons under the adult age, when carried to excess.

Premature, ill-assorted, and late marriages, are highly injurious to the procreation of vigorous and healthful infants, and to public morals.

It is also a fact, that premature exertion of the generative function is most injurious to the health of the individual and offspring. Agriculturists are so well aware of this fact, that they invariably prevent the premature intercourse of the inferior animals.

It is also right to state, that there ought not to be an extreme disproportion in statue between those who engage in matrimonial unions. A delicate, slightly formed, small woman, whose pelvis is small, ought to hesitate in marrying a large robust individual, as the offspring will be large, produce great suffering in coming into the world, frequently require the use of artificial aid, and sometimes mutilation, while the health and life of the mother may be injured and destroyed. This is the fate of many girls of small stature, who become mothers at the age of twelve or fifteen years, and of those from thirty-five to forty; both of whom generally purchase the pleasures of maternity at a very dear rate. The hip and other bones which form the cavity through which the infant has to pass into the world are not sufficeintly developed in extreme youth; and the ligaments and muscles which cover them are rigid after the age of thirty-five, in most women.

When there is a great disproportion between the reproductive organs, the generative function cannot be performed. Thus, excessive size, thickness, or length of the virile member, may render sexual intimacy excessively painful, or indeed impossible for some time, with very young persons, or those of small stature. These, however, are rare causes of impotence or solid grounds for divorce, because a cure can be effected in most cases.

With respect to the extreme narrowness of the vul

va, if there be the slightest aperture, conception may happen, and the vagina dilate spontaneously during pregnancy, or it may be dilated by instruments or incision.

It is a fact that the genital function is as imperious in the human species, at a certain period of life, as the digestive, but ought to be exerted at all times with moderation, to preserve health, and procreate healthful new beings. It is well known that rigid continence is seldom observed about the age of puberty, and for many years afterwards by the male sex, as the accumulation of the seminal fluid in its receptacles will excite the whole of the genital organs during walking and sleep, and often terminate by spontaneous and involuntary emissions. These, when frequent, as well as all venereal excesses, disorder the mind and body, induce sadness, ennui, disgust at life, extreme lowness of spirits, melancholy, and even loss of reason; whilst natural sexual enjoyment after marriage excites and exhilarates vitality, improves the mental faculties and corporeal functions.

It is also important to state, that the baneful habit of exciting the organs under consideration, often arises from disease or a morbid state of remote tissues, at an age when amorous impulse cannot exist, and this self-abuse is too often continued until the adult age.

Infants at the breast, whose sexual organs are as

imperfectly developed, and who can have no sexual desire whatever, often contract the habit of frequently touching these parts. This apparent phenomenon is explained by physiology. The sexual organs are lined by a mucous membrane, similar to that which covers the lips, throat, intestines, and lungs; and irritation in any part of this membrane may derange every part of the body, which is covered or lined by a continuation of it. There are few infants who do not suffer from irritation in some part of this membrane, induced by numerous causes, as teething, improper food, or cold; and the effect will be irritation or inflammation in the eyes, ears, nostrils, throat, lungs, or stomach and bowels, and also in the genital passages, as every one of these parts is covered by mucous membrane.

Again, we observe children before the age of puberty, and when no sexual desire can exist, instinctvely manipulate certain organs, and some who even make attempts at sexual approach; and hence it is an established custom in all well regulated families and schools, not to allow those of the same or opposite sex, to sleep together.

Sensibility or irritation in the mucous membrane lining the mouth, throat, gullet, stomach, bowels, or genito-urinary organs, is the exciting cause of the vile abuse alluded to, and is induced by too stimulating and improper aliment, as ardent liquors of any kind, spiced meats, &c. The effect of this irritation is manipulation of the generative organs in either sex. Female infants are equally liable to irritation or itching of the external genitals.

It is, however, at puberty, that the genital organs suddenly and astonishingly develop, that touches and manipulations are instinctively practised, and lead to masturbation or self-pollution.

The natural excitement in the organs at this age is succeeded by the secretion of semen, and the menstrual fluid which produce the most extraordinary physical and moral changes, as will be described in the chapter on puberty. All the characters of childhood are lost: there is great amorous impulse, and those who have already experienced it, too often initiate children in the delightful but baneful habit of artificial excitation. This is most prejudicial to children, adolescents, adults, and, in a word, at every period of life. The habit is indulged to excess, and then enfeebles both mind and body. It may be practised almost at all times, both day and night, and produces much more debility than natural enjoyment at the adult age, whilst it induces a host of diseases.

The unmanly vice often excites in young persons the greatest antipathy and disgust to natural enjoyment, until adult age renders reason more mature and perfect. The bad effects of unnatural excitement will be more fully noticed hereafter.

Premature and Late Marriages

MONTESQUIEU affirmed that the fear of military service caused a great number of young men, almost of the age of puberty, to enter into matrimonial connections; that these unions, it is true, were fertile, but that the diseases and misery which they produced greatly diminished the population of France.

Precocious sexual intercourse greatly debilitates the moral, intellectual, and physical power of both sexes, and predisposes the female to abortion and disease.

Premature marriages have been advocated on the grounds of morals, for the prevention of libertinage. but I agree with FRANK, MAHON, MARC, and others, if there be no other means than marriage to restrain youth until it becomes vigorous at manhood, we can only lament the issue of beardless fathers. Moral and religious impressions are more rational means; and seldom does the fear of debauchery lead to early marriages, which generally take place from motives of interest or ambition. LOUIS XI. cohabited before the age of fourteen with his queen, who was not twelve; and, in the opinion of M. MARC, his effeminate and ferocious character depended, in some degree, on the exhaustion of his nascent powers.

It is impossible for a physician to determine, as a general rule, the proper age for marriage, so much depends upon constitution, climate, and other circumstances already noticed, and therefore the age must vary.

Premature marriages are exceedingly injurious to the health of both husband and wife, and the cause of weak and enfeebled off-spring, which seldom arrive at maturity. It is well known to agriculturists, that when cattle breed too early, their young is not worth rearing. The laws of all civilized countries are against early marriages.

Very early marriage is, in our opinion, a serious evil. Acting under the impulse of headstrong passions, or caprice, or dissatisfaction, young persons too often prematurely rush, thoughtlessly and blindly, into engagements which, in after life, become matters of deep and painful regret. The fairy visions of love's paradise now vanish; and the sober realities of life, its cares, its difficulties, and its positive evils soon lead to discontent, heartless repinings, and, worse than all, to a growing mutual indifference. Would that such cases were either rare, or only speculative; but the fact is otherwise. We every day see boys and girls at the head of families, who want discretion to direct themselves. No wonder that families are ill-governed, children ill-managed, and their affairs ill-directed, when the helm is intrusted to unskilful and inexperienced hands. Is it possible, we would ask, that wives of sixteen, or eighteen years of age, should possess that discretion, prudence and wisdom so essential to enable them to govern households, rear children, and form their tempers, and their principles?

From these observations we are unwilling that it should be supposed that we advocate marriages deferred till fortune shall have been acquired, or rank attained. On the contrary, we believe that such marriages seldom realize the anticipations which are formed of them. If an age must be stated below which marriages ought not to be contracted, we would fix it at twenty-five for men, and twenty-one for the female sex. This would find each party in the full vigor of their energies, with some moderate acquaintance with the world; and some experience and discretion in the management and guidance of family affairs. When marriage is unreasonably deferred, the heart, losing the elasticity of youthful ardor and hope, becomes blunted by the vexations and disappointments of life, and is seldom the subject of disinterested love, and genuine affection. The tastes, habits, and feelings then become settled and fixed, are little disposed to accommodate themselves to the peculiarities of others.

The Arminian and Georgian children are married during infancy—a political precaution which preserves them from being sent to the emperor's seraglio or the harems of the grandees; but cohabiting is not allowed until a suitable age. The custom of such marriages is, however, by no means general.

The Brahmins marry their children very young, especially the affluent portion, some at the eighth year, and others at the fifth.

Late Marriages.

LATE marriages are also highly detrimental to the welfare of society, and especially those between persons of a very advanced age. Fecundity cannot follow after the woman has ceased to menstruate; but there is no age at which we can declare man to be absolutely sterile. These facts do not, however, oppose the general rule as to the proper age for marriage, though a man or woman at a very advanced age cannot fulfil the real end of this union, the procreation and physical education of the species. Thus when two aged persons, deprived of the faculties necessary for generation, marry for the purpose of affording mutual cares in old age, and sweetening the last years of life, there is no inconvenience to society, except that of favoring celibacy. But when the woman is not beyond the age of fecundity, the consquences of late marriage are often very serious. She may be barren, which is frequently the case, or she may become pregnant at a period of life when the rigidity of her fibres may not readily yield to the efforts of parturition. Such is often the condition of women between the ages of thirty-five and forty: they suffer severely during a first labor, their lives are endangered and often destroyed. If they become mothers, their offspring is often extremely debilitated, or when the parent is still more advanced in age, her infant is often destroyed at the portal of life, or, if born, it inherits the languor of its progenitors, it becomes an orphan before it is reared, it remains a charge to the public, if there is not a property left to render it independent. When marriages are contracted between persons of a disproportionate age, they are usually followed by great immorality. The power of fecundity ceases with one party, while it is continued with the other. These unions, therefore, give less infants at one time than at another. It is also a matter of observation, that in many instances young women bear no children when united to old men, though they often become mothers on future marriages. Another evil consequence of this class of late and ill-sorted marriages is the physical debility of infants; for the youth of the mother is counterbalanced by the languor of the father.

Conjugal union between a young man and an aged woman causes bad effects upon the social order, for it is a kind of sanction for concubinage. Man can engender to an old age, but woman is sterile after the cessation of the menstrual function. These marriages generally take place on account of pecuniary, or other worldly considerations; they lead the husband to debauchery, and the wife to all the excesses of jealousy. They are, therefore, injurious to society.

Conjugal unions should be entered into with the natural liberty of choice. Young persons form attachments which neither parental authority nor any other consideration can prevent or destroy. But, as a general rule, the consent of parents ought to be obtained; and it never should be withheld when there is mutual love and affection, and an adequate support for the parties and their offspring. Parents often refuse consent on the score of interest, ambition, rank, title, family connexion, and lucre, and compel their offspring to marry against their own inclinations. The most unequal unions take place; the wife might be the daughter of the husband, or the husband the son of the wife; and the usual results are domestic misery, unhappiness, jealousy, infamy, premature or perhaps criminal death.

It has been long remarked, that old men generally beget infirm, delicate infants, as well as those persons who are affected with syphilis, scrofula, gout, phthisis, &c. These, and many other diseases, are transmitted to the offspring. Every one knows that children generally resemble their parents in features, limbs, and dispositions, so that the moral and physical condition of parents are also transmitted to their offspring; although in some cases family resemblances are not always the most striking.

As parents would sin grievously who should not eave marriage to their children's free choice and deliberation, as it is their own personal engagement, so children sin morally against the respect and obedience which they owe to parents, if they marry against their consent, or without their advice, unless the parents' opposition be notoriously unjust.

There never should be a very great difference in the ages of those who are about to form conjugal unions. The authority of parents, guardians, and the conductors of schools, should be exerted over those under their care, more especially when youth have little acquaintance with the world. Inconsiderate and rash unions are often effected while young ladies are in scholastic establishments.

They should discourage visits, private interviews, and all familiarities, unless an honorable intention of marriage is declared in the presence of a competent witness, for otherwise such a line of conduct is contrary to the rules of decency, good manners, and religion, and gives scandal to others.

A continued familiarity between young persons of different sexes necessarily produces attachment and love, or excites amorous impulse, which often leads to female dishonor and ruin. Such familiarities should be prohibited, except where a marriage contract exists.

Marriage in its Moral Relations—Happy and Unhappy Marriages.

It is a generally received opinion among mankind that of all the temporal evils, an unhappy marriage is the greatest. It is the source of confusion, misery and vice, of a bad education of children, of bad citizens, and of a violation of every duty. No one, therefore, ought to engage in this contract without the most mature deliberation and a virtuous intention.

One marries for love, or sensual gratification, which he imagines will be perpetual; but this passion is soon subdued or extinguished, if founded on beauty or other fading qualities. Another embraces this state for fortune, splendor, title, and so on;—and he, too, will, in general, be disappointed.—Most persons expect happiness, pleasure, wealth, &c.; but disappointment is the commonest result. Marriage, unless based on religion, virtue, and nature, is seldom happy.

Unsuitable marriages among persons of different ranks cause dissensions among families, and are generally unfortunate. Persons usually prefer individuals of their own age, disposition, rank and fortune; though, from instinctive feeling and worldly motives, there are exceptions.

Nothing is more dangerous than great contrasts—than, to use the words of the poet, "the union of January and May."

Again, a masculine woman disgusts a man who compares her to himself. In like manner, an effeminate man, in place of being preferred by women, is despised. The best mode of establishing ardent love between the sexes is, that the woman should be feminine and the man masculine. If all conjugal unions were assorted after the dictates of nature, or the secret instinct of sympathy, nothing could, without doubt, be more delightful and lasting than the bonds of hymen. By these well-assorted, natural proportions, both sexes become certainly better and more perfect; the mutual abandonment of one to the other forms one being in two bodies, it doubles the sentiments and life, cares are lessened by participation, and pleasures are rendered more vivid and exquisite.

A husband or wife who is virtuous, prudent, and well-informed, will be the greatest comfort, support, and treasure.

The chief characteristics of a good husband or wife are piety, love, meekness, reasonableness, application to duties, and a love of home, "sweet home."

It is not easy to find such individuals. A philosopher compared a man going to marry to one who was about to put his hand into a sack, in which were ninety-nine serpents and one eel; the moral of which is, that there are ninety-nine chances to one against a fortunate selection.

He might have urged, with much more reason and sense, that a thousand times more chances were against the female sex.

Men have more acquaintance with the world, and are, I am convinced, infinitely more depraved than women.

A good husband or wife is rarely found in highly civilized countries. The reason is apparent, because few strictly follow or adopt the divine precepts of Christianity.

According to these, marriage is a holy and inviolable union, an honorable alliance, a sweet society maintained with constancy, a mutual confidence, a continual chain of good offices and duties mutually paid, a reciprocity of chaste affections, perfect friendship, will, inclinations, interests, and goods. The principal obligations of the powers are love, fidelity, the healthful propagation and proper education of children, and constant care of temporal affairs.

The first duties of the married state are mutual love and affection. This state is the closest alliance and union in hearts, bodies, and concerns.

Mutual fidelity is the second great conjugal duty, which those entering into matrimony vow before their Creator. A marriage, without mutual love, is the most unfortunate; for a perpetual cohabitation with one whose person and conversation are disagreeable, and who is an object of aversion, conjoined with the thought that a divorce only or death can be the deliverance, renders such a union much more uneasy than can be expressed or described.

Every imperfection, capricious temper, vanity, folly, &c., appear in the married state. The demeanor towards the world is agreeable and obliging; but, in domestic life, the mask is thrown off, and an individual appears such as he or she really is. Hence it is incredible how much a wife has to bear from husband who is capricious, haughty, choleric, dyspeptic, and intractable; or, what a sensible husband has to endure from a silly, unreasonable and intractable wife.

It is difficult for married persons to acquire each other's tastes, feelings and opinions. Patience is an indispensable virtue to this state. No one is free from imperfections, both of mind and body: and both husband and wife will have to bear with, and often to forgive, each other.

Unhappy marriages are seldom fruitful.

The chief end of marriage is the propagation and education of children, and bringing them up with piety and virtue, so as to be dutiful to parents, and good citizens. The second end is affording mutual society and comfort in the various transactions of life.

Every prudent individual should endeavor to become well acquainted with the disposition of the woman whom he thinks worthy to be his companion for life, and the mother of his offspring. He should ascertain her temper and peculiarities, and decide whether they are similar or suited to his own.

A captious, peevish spirit; a mind full of suspicions, and easy of offence; a temper sour, fretful, passionate, ever on the watch to find fault and to express dissatisfaction, which no attentions can satisfy, and no efforts please; rude in its language, scornful in its expressions, and unreasonable in its requisitions, treating the old with disrespect, and the young with hauteur;—these are blights and deformities of character, for which no other qualities can adequately atone or compensate.

Nor is it only the *quality*, but the *general similarity* of temper which must be regarded. Where strong affection prevails, a spirit of accommodation will prevail also. But it is not desirable that the spirit of accommodation should be subjected to very frequent, or very rigorous experiments.

Should the wife, unfortunately, be allied to a husband of irreligious character, it is incredible how powerfully his heart may be won over to the love of Christianity by the gentle and peaceful demeanor of his wife; whose virtuous deportment, suavity of manners, and diligence in duty, united with humility and unobtrusivenes, cannot fail to render her both respected and beloved; whilst they forcibly recommend, and beautifully illustrate, the loveliness and the influence of that religion, which produces effects so holy, excellent, and attractive.

A fretful temper is its own tormentor, but it is also a tormentor to every one around, and to none more than to the husband, or the wife, who may be exposed to its influence. No day, no hour is secure. No incident is so trifling, but it may be wrought up into a family disturbance. If it be commanded 'that all bitterness, and wrath, and anger, and clamor, be put away,' surely the injunction has an imcreased obligation on those whose interest as well as duty is to obey it.

The cares of married life are undoubtedly many. The husband and wife are not solitary individuals. In their welfare are bound up the comfort and well-being of many dearer to them than their own individual comfort. In them is centred the hope, and on them rest the confidence, the prosperity and happiness of family and friends. Exposed to the daily mortifications, disappointments and perplexities of the world, it is not marvellous if care clouds their brow, or anxiety wounds their hearts, and therefore their sorrows are numerous. They have their many conflicts with the troubles of this world; they have their corroding cares, sleepless nights, and anxious days; sickness will invade their dwelling. But, it may be asked, is celibacy always "a life of single blessedness?" have the unmarried no cares, no sickness, or no wants? and if they can plead no prescriptive right of exemption from the common lot of man, upon what bosom can they pillow an aching heart, or into what ear whisper their many sorrows? what friend will sympathise, with cordial disinterestedness, in all their varied woes?

The marriage union is the most important of any we are capable of forming in this life, and it is not our own happiness alone, but that of others also, which is affected by our conduct in it. It is a union, not merely constituted with a view to the reciprocal benefit of the two individuals who contract to form it, but exercising likewise a paramount influence on the manners and happiness of society at large. It is, therefore, a matter of the deepest importance that the duties and obligations of our domestic and social relations should be accurately defined, and duly impressed on the hearts and consciences of mankind. It is on a due understanding, and a faithful discharge of these duties, that the happiness of the parties themselves, and the prosperity and welfare of the present and future generations depend.

Mercenary considerations, in many instances, lead to the contracting of this holy union. How often is the decrepitude of age, with a large estate, and a handsome settlement, preferred to the manly vigor of youth, and to virtuous conduct when unconnected with a weighty purse? How frequently is the titled libertine a more favored lover than the virtuous commoner?

Nor can we censure too severely that levity, inconstancy, and duplicity, with which men act in the violation of the most solemn engagements, when, having won the heart and the affections of a deserving and amiable, though portionless female, and disregarding all their vows and protestations, they lead a wealthier, though often a less deserving bride, to the altar. Honor, feeling, and religion, alike proclaim the infamy of the act, and the heartlessness of the wretch who can thus traffic in the most sacred engagements, with all the coolness of mercenary consideration.

If the distinctions of rank, or the adventitious circumstances of fortune, could shut out the oppressive cares of life—if the pride and pomp of worldly distinction could lull the pains of disease—if the splendor of high life could shed one gleam of hope over a dying pillow, or dispel the gloom which broods over "the house appointed for all living;' if, in fact, human calamity and suffering could be averted by the sacrifice of feeling, affection and honor, at the shrine of human vanity and human greatness—then, indeed, but not otherwise, would we extend forgiveness to the guilty trafficker.

There are far more important requisites for marriage than temper and accomplishments, and these are principles and habits. Without attention to these, every promise of happiness will be infallibly blighted.

On what solid ground can a woman anticipate happiness for life, when she confides her person and her property to one on whom the laws of God have no influence? Are the proud, the covetous, the ambitious, the malignant, the censorious, the worldly-minded, the lovers of pleasures more than lovers of God, likely to be the indulgent husband, the fond father, the kind master? Can he who habitually violates the precepts of the gospel, and lives in utter neglect of its authority, be reasonably expected to discharge the duties he owes to man, with more integrity than he manifests to heaven? Let it also be remembered that he who is not under the habitual influence of Christian principles, and consciences, as to its practical duties, is likely to have an unhappy and pernicious influence on the principles, conduct, and happiness of his wife. He who disowns, or neglects the duties of the station he now occupies, has no pledge to offer his bride, that he will more conscientiously respect the obligations of new relations of life into which he is about to enter.

Thus it is in life. An amiable temper, sound judgment, good sense, a well-informed mind, correct taste, religious principles, united with the higher accomplishments of a well-educated mind, and blended with mildness of manner, and gentleness of heart, will be found the substantial qualities which cannot fail to win the affection, and secure the heart

Whilst, however, we condemn, with a just and severe reprobation, the folly and guilt of those who sacrifice honor, and the best affections of the human heart, on the altar of Mammon, we must not be supposed to overlook, or to undervalue, the dictates of prudence. Love marriages, as they are called, usually terminate in bitter disappointment; the claims of a young and increasing family will eventually force themselves on the attention of the parents, and it is to be feared, that the vulgar considerations of discharging bills and meeting family expenses, will prove a fruitful source of those bickerings and disagreements which too plainly show the incautious folly and heedless imprudence with which their union was formed. Love cannot clothe, educate, or maintain a family, nor yet satisfy the importunity of a distressed, or an impatient creditor. We would temper the ardor of passion by the sobriety of reason; and bring the affections of the heart under the control of prudence and discretion.

It is evident from the preceding observations, that judicious and virtuous parents are bound to interpose their authority when there is danger of improvident alliances, and ought to point out the impropriety and inexpediency of marriage. But it is never justifiable that parents should seek to ally their children with those for whom they have no affection, or contemplate only with disgust and repugnance. Paternal authority cannot reasonably compel alliances against which inclination protests; though there are too many forced and unhappy marriages arising from this cause.

The happiness resulting from a well-formed marriage, depends on mental excellence of the parties. This can be only known by long acquaintance. Love at first sight, and ball-room and street matches, are generally the sources of endless misery; they are formed without consideration, and originate in a transient excitement of feeling. True love is founded on esteem, and esteem is the result of intimate acquaintance and confidential intercourse. This is the origin of pure and virtuous love. Marriages based upon this, and on proper religious feelings, are the only happy ones. Never marry without love, but be careful to know well who you love, before your love gets the better of your judgment.

Physiology of the Sexual Organs.

When puberty is established, an indescribable commotion often agitates the individuals of both sexes; all their functions may become deranged: the digestion bad, the action of the heart and arteries irregular, often accompanied by palpitations; the respiration laborious or difficult; the individuals often find comfort only in solitude, their desires and affections are now altered; those whom they heretofore considered dearest friends are often looked upon as objects of indifference, and they now experience feelings to which they were hitherto strangers. The genital organs continue to develop very rapidly; their secretions increase and aggravate the indefinable commotion in the whole body. The prolific fluids of both sexes are elaborated, and fitted for the object which nature intended. There results a superabundance of life, which endeavors to communicate and establish itself; there is a new and imperious want developed, which compels the sexes to approach each other. The influence of this want on the moral state of mankind is thus correctly described by the celebrated CABANIS :—"The new want produces in the young man a mixture of audacity, and timidity ; of audacity, because he knows that all his organs are animated with an unknown vigor ; of timidity, because the nature of his desires astonishes him as defiance to them disconcerts him. In the young girl, this want gives rise to a sentiment of modesty or virgin shame, of which she was heretofore ignorant, which may be regarded as the hidden expression of her desires, or the involuntary signs of her secret impressions."

A complete revolution is effected in the human economy at the age of puberty ; the bones harden, the chest dilates, the voice changes, the constitution becomes strong and vigorous, health is completely established, and many diseases, such as scrofula, rickets, St. Vitus's dance, hysteria, chlorosis, &c., disappear ; though sometimes these diseases supervene at this period. In common with all parts of the body, the brain becomes developed, the intellectual functions are augmented, man is susceptible of the highest conceptions of the mind, the principles of life superabound in his constitution, and he vigorously performs all the noble pursuits assigned him by nature.

Woman, on the contrary, delicate and tender, always preserves some of the infantile constitution The textures of her organs do not lose all their orignal softness, or assume the strength of those of her companion; her eyes become brilliant and expressive, and all the graces and charms of youth illumine her person. Her bosom throbs with tender inquietudes, her character loses i infantile vivacity, her manner and tastes become analagous to those of a full-grown female, her passions become stronger and more constant, her moral and physical sensibility are greater, and she feels a sentiment hitherto unknown to her—the impulse of love—the desire of marriage.

Amid this universal disorder of the economy, the excitement of the reproductive organs predominates, and causes the extraordinary and incomprehensible phenomena already described.

Every effort is now made by parents to suppress voluptuous ideas, but the secret thought of amorous pleasure cannot be extinguished. Nevertheless, an enjoyment purely physical or animal is not the object of research; the heart opens to the most tender sentiments, and guides the first movements of the sexes. Until this time they were actuated either by self-love, parental affection, or esteem for the youth of their own sexes; but now paternal tenderness and mere affection are insufficient for their happiness. Their well-being exists in another individual, and they think that they cannot enjoy real existence, but in the intimate union of their body, soul, and heart, with one of an opposite sex of their own. They meet.

their tastes, ages and sentiments are similar; and now commences the scene of their innocent love. What delightful reflections are offered to the study of a moral and philosophic mind by the innocent love of two young persons, who know no other motives for their actions than the pure inspirations of nature and the heart! The strictest chastity presides at their first interview; a word, a glance, a whisper, the pressure of a trembling hand, is now the enjoyment of happiness. They do not approach each other but with a respectful fear; they dissemble towards each other the nature of the sentiments which agitate them.

In proportion as their visits are more frequent, and their physical love is increased, which it is by the excitement caused by their meetings, their interviews are more numerous, their conversations become longer, more delicate, more intimate; a reciprocal and exclusive confidence is established between them, the trembling hand reposes longer in that of its admirer; their hearts palpitate, and they finally vow eternal fidelity to each other before the altar.

This, however, is the age at which the youth of both sexes should act in that strict accordance with the precepts of religion and morals, as errors committed now are too often irretrievable. The tender sex, which are the objects of the most ardent fire of zealous adoration, and who burn themselves with the same flame, must never yield to the slightest freedom wich is contrary to modesty and honor. They must not countenance for a moment obtrusive familiarity, much less the slightest immodest advances, or their ruin and degradation are inevitable. The usual result of impertinent familiarity, or illicit or anticipated love, is disgust, desertion, and indelible disgrace. A virtuous and firm resolution is the only safeguard, and a fixed determination not to remain alone, or beyond the hearing of others, with him who has captivated the heart. The passion of love is as inherent in mankind as the function of digestion or respiration, and must be gratified as well as all other wants. It is, however, less essential to individual existence than other functions; but when it is established at puberty, as it is in almost all persons, it must be be gratified; and human intervention or laws cannot restrain or extinguish it, except in a very few, if any, instances.

The secretion of the sexual fluids is intended by nature for the conservation of the species. About the fourteenth or fifteen year, in temperate climates, the sexual organs of boys become developed, and a fluid is secreted by the testicles, termed seminal or spermatic, which is destined for the perpetuation of the species. This fluid accumulates in receptacles provided for it (*vescuilæ seminales*), and not only excites the sexual organs, but every part of the body. The functions of the mind are improved, the diges tion becomes more vigorous, the circulation of blood is more rapid in every organ, which is abundantly nourished, and performs its function with much more energy than before this period of life. Hence, we observe the body develops with rapidity, and the individual in a short time loses the characteristics of boyhood, and acquires those of adolescence, or manhood.

Though the sexual organs rapidly develop from the fourteenth to the twentieth year, yet they do not, in general, acquire their complete growth or functions before the twenty-fifth; sometimes not until the thirtieth year; and this is the age the most proper for marriage.

The body of man is not fully developed before the twenty-fifth year of age, the spermatic fluid is less abundant and fitted for reproduction; and persons under this age generally beget delicate, sickly infants, which seldom arrive at maturity. Sexual indulgence, or unnatural excitement, before the age of twenty-one, according to our laws, but before the age of twenty-five, according to the laws of nature, not only retards the development of the genital organs, but of the whole body, impairs the strength, injures the constitution, and shortens life.

The establishment of puberty in woman renders her capable of performing her part in the perpetuation of the species; and this faculty has now to be described.

All researches on the reproduction of plants and animals, from the lowest to the highest, in ancient and modern times, were made with a view of explaining the generation of the human species. But all have hitherto signally failed to explain the mystery of reproduction of man—the transmission of the vital and immortal principles from parents to offspring; and after the investigations of ages, the reference must be for explanation to the Omnipotent Creator of all things. Man is still ignorant of how life begins or ceases. It is all mystery to him. He cannot reason from the analogy afforded by the vegetable and animal kingdoms. This is the most unsatisfactory. As in plants and animals, the propagation of the human species is confided to two *sexes*, male and female. Both are endowed, for this object, with particular organs, called *sexual*, whose united action and reciprocal *contact*, are indispensable to the formation of the new being.

Sexual approach or contact reunites the constituent parts of the future being. These elements are the spermatic fluid of the male, and the ovium or germ of the female. The human female possesses from fifteen to twenty germs, ova, or vesicles in each ovary, but these are never separated during the function of sexual commerce. The process by which these elements are united, is the same as in other mammiferous animals.

The sexual organs having acquired perfect development, are excited by the secretion of the seminal in man, and the development or perhaps secretion of the germ or egg in the ovary of woman; and this excitement leads to sexual union, by which the elements of both sexes are united and the new being is formed.

All the organs or parts which are subservient to generation, are denominated genital or generative organs. The unthinking part of mankind consider the slightest allusions to these organs as indelicate; but the practitioners of the healing art must consider their structure and functions.

The sensations experienced by animals in the act of reproduction, causes them to perform it instinctively. But nobler sentiments preside over the conjugal union of our species; two souls sympathise for each other, and see in common, the wisdom of procreating offspring like themselves; two hearts which condole each other in the troubles of life, and centuple their pleasures by the most intimate union; the delights of a conversation full of tenderness; the affectionate cares bestowed on each other during illness; an assocîotion of talents, qualities, riches, honors, and paternal and maternal love, are the precious advantages which mankind derive from conjugal unions But whatever may be the superiority of man over inferior animals, in respect to generaration, we cannot conceal from ourselves, that, like the brutes, we are seldom influenced by any other motive in our unions than sexual pleasure only. It is useless for us to deny that the majority of marriages which are apparently based on real love, are always the result of our servile and involuntary obedience to the imperious voice of our sexual organs. Every thing that presents to our minds the idea of vigor, of a fine figure, and sufficient ardor, always influences us unconsciously. Woman can never deny that she has a particular predilection for a fine figure, a noble gait and manner, a broad chest, the head elevated, and furnished with a luxuriant growth of hair, the eyes full of fire, the manners amiable, and the gallantry polite. In the same manner, man is always desirous to meet in her whom he selects for his wife, superior mental and corporeal endowments, a fine graceful figure, good eyes, and general development. Many prefer a woman of high moral worth to all other considerations; some allow wealth, titles, and evanescent temporal insignificances to influence their choice; but conjugal unions based on such motives are generally both infertile and unhappy. It will be found, upon reflection, that the superior qualities of mind and physical beauty are the concomitants of great genital vigor. Numerous proofs of this position are adduced in the observations on the morbid and hygenic effects of the use and abuse of the genital function, which will be noticed hereafter.

Causes Which Influence Fecundity.

As a general proposition, it may be maintained, that abundance of aliment increases the number of mankind and of animals; and that years of prosperity are remarkable for a greater number of births, and years of famine or pestilence for the fewest.

"It is necessary for a fruitful marriage," says M. VIREY, "that there should be a certain harmony between the sexes, both moral and physical, and this is manifested in the sympathies of instinct, which, independently of beauty, make us prefer one person to another. The sexes secretly wish their union by a natural impulse which cannot be explained, and which, in a mixed society, renders us more attentive to one person than all the rest; and nature inspires us better in this respect than reason.

"This harmony consists less in similitude of temperament, age, &c., &c., than in diversity; for, usually, we observe a violent, bilious man, prefer a mild and modest companion, while a passionate, impetuous woman finds most charms in a moderate, tranquil man; so that one may be tempered by the other, whether they be too hot or too cold." It is also universally known, that some married persons fail to have a family, who are fruitful after a second union.

When the characters are very different, they cannot entertain the state of harmony, as in a frigid or ardent individual, until age or habit renders them more suited to each other; thus, married persons have passed fifteen or twenty years without offspring, notwithstanding their most anxious desires. ABRAHAM and SARAH, and JACOB and RACHEL, are examples mentioned in sacred writings.

When there is antipathy, disgust, hatred or passion, conception seldom happens; though some of these obstacles may exist as in women who pretend to be forcibly violated, but finally acquiesce in pleasure, and become pregnant; and it is not, as yet, I believe, determined whether impregnation can be effected when a real hatred exists. There are, however, many examples recorded of married and unmarried women who were impregnated when in a profound sleep, as mentioned in the works on Medical Jurisprudence. In such cases there could not be much voluptuousness, though amorous impulse employs the mind during sleep; and there was, at the time, no repugnance for the former, for some degree of it appears indispensable for the generation of a new being.

MARC is of opinion, that the moral causes of sterility in both sexes are, a fear to procreate, too vivid a desire to have children, an antipathy or incompatibility of humor between the sexes, negligence or apathy of the husband to the wife, the diseases and inconveniences of some wives, violent passion and immorality or infidelity.

The fear of procreation often arises from the indigence and inability to support offspring; or, in the upper ranks, from the vanity of women, who imagine that conception and its consequences, will diminish or destroy their charms, or deprive them of devoting that time to frivolous pleasures which the rights of matrimony demand. Reserve and frigidity during the approach of the sexes, is also a cause of sterility.

Comparative Influence of the Sexes, &c., on Reproduction.

THE SEASONS, which are only transient climates, have great influence on fecundity. It is true, however, that man can exercise his genital function at all times, in all latitudes, temperatures and countries. Nevertheless, the physical influences of the atmosphere, of aliments, and modes of life, render certain seasons more fertile than others.

HIPPOCRATES was of opinion that spring was the season most favorable to conception. PLINY termed it the genital season, *geniale tempus*, when all nature possessed ardor, and became pregnant of new creations. At this season, all animals and vegetables reproduce--animated nature is exhilirated—the purity of the air, the freshness of aliments, the infancy of all nature. which renews pleasure the odor of flowers, the melodious singing of birds—all proclaim that this is the season of reproduction. Animals approach each other, the germination of seeds commences, shrubs and trees put forth their blossoms, and there is a universal effort to reproduce in all bodies endowed with life.

In accordance with this law, we have multiplied experience to prove that a much greater number of infants are born in the months of December, January, February, and March, than at any other time of the year, which shows that sexual intercourse is most prolific in the months of March, April, May, or in spring.

In general, the heat of the summer is less favorable to conception than the more temperate seasons; and the equinoxes more than the solstices. The warmth of summer causes perspiration and exhaustion, and though amorous impulse is strong, its enjoyment is followed by greater debility than in spring, and its frequent use is injurious in the former season.

The invariable state of the weather in autumn often induces cholera, diarrhœa, dysenterry, typhus, &c., and this season is generally considered the least favorable for reproduction. Winter, for the reasons already stated, is held to be more congenial to fecundation than the preceding season. The end of winter or commencement of spring is, perhaps, the period in which most conceptions take place.

As the day is a portion of the year, it may be inquired, if there be any period of it more favorable to conception than another—a *hora genitalis*, as supposed by the ancients. It has been remarked that there are more parturitions at night than by day; because, during this time, most impregnations undoubtedly occur. According to M. Virey, the morning is the most proper time for generation:—then the body is repaired by the repose of the night, it enjoys the plenitude of its power: waking is often accompanied by erection, the best sign of vigor;—and it is in the morning sleep that the nocturnal illusions of pleasure most commonly occur. The agitation and labors of the day, repasts, and various objects of distraction, studies and business, render sexual unions less fertile than during the stillness of the night or in the morning.

There is no greater source of reproduction than abundance of aliment. In all countries, the number of consumers increases or diminishes in proportion to aliments. In years of opulence and fertility all increase: men, beasts, and insects, all multiply and fill the earth; but in the sad periods of indigence and misery, and in seasons of calamity, we only observe few individuals born, and these are generally degenerate. So, also, the years of famine are certainly accompanied by a great deficiency in reproduction, as the tables of births very amply attest.

It is very true that Ceres and Bacchus, the mythological deities of aliment and drink, might be fairly considered to influence the rites of Venus. In proof of this position, it is further urged that the most powerful means of mortifying the flesh, according to moralists, is fasting. It is also known that sexual intercourse causes hunger, and needs restorative means, whilst an abundant restoration excites the want of generation.

Experience has also shown, that certain foods excite the genital organs of particular individuals.—The employment of vinous and spirituous liquors produce the same effect on most persons; although their abuse, as also that of warm drinks, such as tea and coffee, are injurious to generation. It is held that inveterate drunkards, or those who engender in drunkenness, produce more daughters than sons, as they are less energetic, their desires less ardent, and the seminal fluid less prolific than in a natural condition. Drunkenness diminishes the powers of the nervous and muscular systems, and often renders the exercise of the generative act impossible or imperfect.

The most unfavorable state for propagation is excessive exertion of the mind or body. It has been long observed, that men of great genius have fewest children. Experience has demonstrated, that the pleasure of love extinguishes the fire of the imagination, abates genius and courage, as innumerable proofs have already attested. Lastly, M. VILLERME is of opinion, that balls, amusements, and public rejoicings at the time of marriage, or at any other period, as also privations, fasting, prosperity, civilization, liberty, misery, and calamity, have different effects upon reproduction; and he arrives at the conclusion, that more infants are born under a clear sun, in countries where the arts, industry and the sciences flourish, and where the atmosphere is pure and the country fertile, than under opposite conditions; and that scarcity and famine produce great changes in the population.

Another question, relative to procreation, which engaged the attention of physiologists and naturalists from the earliest periods, is the comparative enjoyment of the sexes. The majority of authors have awarded it to females. Some have held that pleasure and fecundity are enjoyed in an equal degree by the sexes [Bousquet], and others [Virey, Blundell, &c.], by females. These, it is said, are most tranquil and less agitated than the other sex, as they contribute least to the formation of the embryo;—while the latter are most voluptuous, ardent, excited, and afterwards depressed. The spermatic and ovarian fluids, which effect reproduction, are supplied in very different proportions; that of the male is the most important, as imparting life; and hence, there is more languor on its effusion; while the vaginal and uterine ejaculation, which is alone perceptible in the act of generation, and is not spermatic, but unprolific, scarcely diminishes sensibility, nor is it followed by such great prostration as is the former. The feminine prolific fluid is the germ or ovum, which does not leave the ovary for some days after impregnation, and is only a small drop of liquid.— Hence it is a physiological axiom, that the function of procreation is less debilitating and more delicious with one sex than the other.

If the reason be inquired why one sex is more insatiable than the other, the answer is, because the one dispenses less vitality than the other. It is now universally admitted by physiologists, that there is no supply of a feminine seminal fluid during the act of reproduction, but a germ in the ovary is impregnated, though there may be a more or less abundant secretion of fluid from the membrane and subjacent glands of the vagina and uterus; but the sensibility remains vivid after the effusion of this fluid; while the emission of the male is followed by an immediate abatement of amorous impulse.

It is not to be supposed that when pleasure is most vivid conception takes place more readily, as the contrary is often the fact; for when the uterus is in a state of extreme and too frequent excitement, it often loses its retentive power. We see this exemplified in the lower orders of mammiferous animals over which it is often necessary to pour cold water after copulation, to excite the contraction of the uterus

The same reason explains the infertility of prostitutes and courtesans, who rarely conceive, unless after intercourse with persons whom they prefer. In fact, a uterus incessantly open and stimulated, has a tendency to evacuate itself, and repeated venereal enjoyments induce excessive menstruation, mucous discharges and abortions. In such cases conception rarely occurs, unless the mind be intuitively fixed upon one person, and there is one undivided love. It has been observed that prostitutes who were infertile for years, have become mothers after transportation to Botany Bay, when they became restrained by marriage.

In the same manner, when men abuse the end of marriage, they have no children, because they secrete semen which is not sufficiently elaborated, and which is too feeble. Chastity, on the contrary, augments the vigor of the organs and amorous impulse, and is the surest means of fecundity. Hence, those newly-married persons who have observed a strict chastity before their union, procreate immediately, and their offspring is vigorous; while dissipated or aged persons seldom have children, and if they have, the offspring seldom arrives at the adult age. For this reason, animals which copulate at certain times only, engender by one act. But a rigid chastity enfeebles the passion of love, and may be the cause of infertility.

Abstinence from venereal enjoyment, for a few

days or weeks, favors fecundity, and invigorates both mind and body.

BACON observed that no one of great genius, of antiquity, had been addicted to women; and he stated that among the moderns, the illustrious NEWTON had never enjoyed sexual intercourse. This fact confirms the remark made by ARETÆUS, and since verified by all physiologists, that continence, or the reabsorption of the semen into the animal economy, impressed the whole organism with an extreme tension and vigor, excited the brain, and excited the faculty of thought. From these effects, courage, magnanimity, all the virtues, and corporeal vigor resulted.

The abuse of enjoyment, on the contrary, enervates the body, destroys the memory, extinguishes the imagination, degrades the soul, and renders us stupid. Thus, idiots who abuse this function are excessively lascivious; and eunuchs are remarkably deficient in genius—they want the organs which are destined to secrete the semen, and this plunges the mind as well as the body into a languor and debility almost infantile. It has also been observed that mental exaltation and madness do not manifest themselves before the age of puberty, nor in old age, but in the adult age especially, by the retention of the sperm or ovarian fluid; and hence, castration and pregnancy have radically cured maniacs. Nothing is more certain than this, that animals and plants shorten their existence by multiplied sexual enjoyments.

It was to secure vigor of mind and body that the founders of certain religious sects prescribed chastity and celibacy to their ministers. This rule is in some degree accordant with physiology; for it is well known that our moral and physical powers are diminished by coition, because we impart a portion of our physical and intellectual endowments to our offspring, and diminish them in ourselves

---

Procreation of the Sexes.

THE surest means by which sound and vigorous infants may be engendered, is a good constitution, unenfeebled by excessive intellectual or corporeal exertion, or any chronic disease. It is universally admitted that the moral and physical dispositions are transmitted by generation; and hence we may conclude that healthful and vigorous parents alone produce healthful and vigorous infants.

Is is also generally concluded that diseased or delicate parents procreate diseased or delicate offspring. The same results are observed in plants and animals. Every one knows the truth of these statements. How often do we observe a fine, a beautiful woman of an excellent constitution, united to a small, diminutive, aged, broken-down, or deformed companion, or the reverse; and can it be supposed that the physical powers, the sympathies of such individuals, are favorable to the proper performance of the function of generation?

Love cannot be reciprocal in such cases: and animal or organic impulse will prefer that which is more accordant with itself; even brutes prefer males which are possessed of vigor, power, and beauty; and this instinct is implanted by nature in all animals. Whatever perversion civilization may effect in our hearts, tastes and manners, it cannot extinguish this instinct. Even social or parental authority fails to destroy it; and this often leads to unsuited conjugal unions, to the procreation of feeble offspring, which are doomed to constant sufferings, a miserable existence, unsuppportable to themselves and others of society,—still the rights of nature exist inviolate. Unequal and unsuited alliances are contrary to nature and to sound policy. Ample proof is afforded of the validity of this opinion, by a reference to the physiology of the various ages of life, and the difference in the genital power in each.

One organic law is, that the germ of the infant being must be complete in all its parts, and perfectly sound in its condition, as an indispensable requisite to its vigorous development and full enjoyment of existence. If the corn that is sown is weak, wasted, and damaged, the plants that spring from it will be feeble, and liable to speedy decay. The same law holds in the animal kingdom; and I would ask, has it hitherto been observed by man? It is notorious that it has not; indeed, its existence has been either altogether unknown, or in a very high degree disregarded by human beings. The feeble, the sickly, the exhausted with age, and the incompletely developed, through extreme youth, marry, and, without the least compunction regarding the organization which they shall transmit to their offspring, send into the world miserable beings, the very rudiments of whose existence are tainted with disease. If we trace such conduct to its source, we shall find it to originate either in animal propensity, intellectual ignorance, or more frequently in both.

The inspiring motives are generally mere sensual appetite, avarice, or ambition, operating in the absence of all just conceptions of the impending evils. The punishment of this offence is debility and pain transmitted to the children, and reflected back in anxiety and sorrow on the parents. Still the great point to be kept in view is, that these miseries are not legitimate consequences of *observance* of the organic laws, but the direct chastisement of their *infringement*. These laws are unbending, and admit of no exception; they must be fulfilled, or the penalties of disobedience will follow. On this subject profound ignorance reigns in society.

From such observations as I have been able to make, I am convinced that the union of certain temperaments and combinations of mental organs in the parents, are highly conducive to health, and morality in the offspring, and *vice versa;* and that these conditions may be discovered and taught with far greater certainty, facility and advantage, than is generally imagined. It will be time enough to conclude that men are naturally incapable of obedience to the organic laws, when, after their intellectual faculties and moral sentiments have been trained to observance of the Creator's institution, as at once their interest, and a grand source of their enjoyment, they shall be found to continue to rebel.

In regard to the foregoing propositions, I would observe that a manifest distinction exists between transmission of monstrosities or mutilations, which constitute additions to, or abstractions from, the natural lineaments of the body, and transmission of a mere tendency in particular organs to a greater or less development in point of size, and of energy in their natural functions. This last appears to me to be influenced by the state of the parents at the time when existence is communicated to the offspring. On this point, Dr. PRITCHARD says: "The opinion which formerly prevailed, and which has been entertained by some modern writers, among whom is Dr. DARWIN, that at the period when organization commences in the ovum, that is, at or soon after the time of conception, the structure of the fœtus is capable of undergoing modification from impressions on the mind or senses of the parent, does not appear altogether so improbable. It is contradicted, as least, by no fact in physiology. It is an opion of very ancient prevalence, and may be traced to so remote a period, that its rise cannot be attributed to the speculations of philosophers, and it is difficult to account for the origin of such a persuasion, unless we ascribe it to the facts which happened to be observed."

The degeneracy and even idiocy of some of the noble and royal families of Spain and Portugal, from marrying nieces and other near relations, is well known; and defective brains, in all these cases, are observed.

Many facts illustrate the influence of the state of the parents, particularly of the mother, at the time when the existence of the child commenced, on its mental talents and dispositions.

"The father of Napoleon Bonaparte," says Sir Walter Scott, "is stated to have possessed a very handsome person, a talent for eloquence, and a vivacity of intellect, which he transmitted to his son."

"It was in the middle of civil discord, fights, and skirmishes, that Charles Bonaparte married Lætitia Ramolini, one of the most beautiful young women of the island, and possessed of a great deal of firmness of character. She partook of the dangers of her husband during the years of civil war, and is said to have accompanied him on horseback on some military expeditions, or perhaps hasty flights, short ly before her being delivered of the future emperor.' [Life of Napoleon Bonaparte, vol. iii., p. vi.]

The murder of David Rizzio was perpetrated by armed nobles, with many circumstances of violence and terror, in the presence of Mary, Queen of Scotland, shortly before the birth of her son, afterwards James the First of England. The constitutional liability of this monarch to emotions of fear, is recorded as a characteristic of his mind; and it has been mentioned that he even started involuntarily at the sight of a drawn sword. Queen Mary was not deficient in courage, and the Stuarts, both before and after James the First, were distinguished for this quality; so that his dispositions were an exception to the family character. Napoleon and James form striking contrasts: and it may be remarked that the mind of Napoleon's mother appears to have risen to the danger to which she was exposed, and braved it; while the circumstances in which Queen Mary was placed, were calculated to inspire her with fear alone.

If this be really the law of nature, as there is great reason for believing, then parents, in whom combativeness and destructiveness are in habitual activity, will transmit these organs, in a state of high development and excitement, to their children; and those in whom the moral and intellectual organs exist in supreme vigor, will transmit these in the greatest perfection.

This view is in harmony with the fact, that children generally, though not universally, resemble their parents in their mental qualities; because the largest organs being naturally the most active, the general and habitual state of the parents will be determined by those which predominate in size in their own brains; and on the principle that predominance in activity and energy causes the transmission of similar qualities to the offspring, the children will, in this way, very generally resemble the parents. But they will not always do so; because, even the very inferior characters, in whom the moral and intellectual organs are deficient, may be occasionally exposed to external influences, which, for the time, may excite these organs to unwonted vivacity; and, according to the rule now explained, a child dating its existence from that period, may inherit a higher organization of brain than the parent. Or, a person with an excellent moral development, may, by some particular occurrence, have his animal propensities roused to unwonted vigor, and his moral sentiments thrown, for the time, into the shade; and any offspring connected with this condition would prove inferior to himself in the development of the moral organs, and greatly surpass him in the size of those of the propensities.

I repeat, that I do not present these views as ascertained phrenological science, but as inferences strongly supported by facts, and consistent with known phenomena. If we suppose them to be true, they will greatly strengthen the motives for preserving the *habitual* supremacy of the moral sentiments and intellects, when, by doing so, improved moral and intellectual capacities may be conferred on offspring.

If it be true that this lower world is arranged in harmony with the supremacy of the higher faculties, what a noble prospect would this law open up of the possibility of man ultimately becoming capable of placing himself more fully in accordance with the Divine institutions, than he has hitherto been able to do; and, in consequence, of reaping numberless enjoyments that appear destined for him by his Creator, and avoiding thousands of miseries that now render life too often only a series of calamities.

The views here expounded also harmonise with the second principle of that Essay; namely, that, as activity in the faculties is the fountain of enjoyment, the whole constitution of nature is designedly framed to support them in ceaseless action. What scope for observation, reflection, the exercise of moral sentiments, and the regulation of animal impulse, does not this picture of nature present!

A man and woman about to marry, have, in the generality of cases, the health and happiness of five or more human beings depending on their attention to considerations, essentially the same as the foregoing, and yet how much less scrupulous are they than the mere speculators in money.

There is no moral difficulty in admitting and admiring the wisdom and benevolence of the institution by which good qualities are transmitted from parents to children; but it is frequently held as unjust to the latter, that they should inherit parental deficiencies, and so be made to suffer for sins which they did not commit. In treating of this difficulty, I must again refer to the supremacy of the moral sentiments as the theory of the constitution of the world. The animal propensities are all selfish, and regard only the immediate and apparent interest of the individual; while the higher sentiments delight in that which communicates the greatest quantity of enjoyment to the greatest number.

Now, let us suppose the law of hereditary descent to be abrogated altogether, that it is to say, that each individual of the race was, at birth, endowed with fixed natural qualities, without the slightest reference to what his parents had been or done! this form of constitution would obviously cut off every possibility of improvement *in the race.*

Children of the individuals who have obeyed the organic, the moral and intellectual laws will not start from the highest level of their parents in acquired knowledge, but they will inherit a tendency towards an enlarged development of the moral and intellectual organs, and thereby enjoy an increasing capability of discovering and obeying the Creator' institutions. It will thus be seen that no means hav yet been discovered by which the sexes can be pro created at will.

Theories of Human Generation.

THE theories of generation now maintained are four:—1. The transmission of the spermatic fluid of the male through the uterus, uterine tube, or oviduct to the ovary, a vesicle, ovum, or egg, of which is vivified and passes into the womb to be developed. until the expiration of the ninth month, when it is born, and becomes an independent being. 2. The transmission of a subtle vapor or effluvium from the male semen (*aura seminalis*) through the same parts to the ovary, the impregnated ovum passing into the uterus, to be developed in the manner before stated. 3. The absorption of the seminal fluid of the male from the surface to the vagina. 4. That the ova that is given off from the female once in each month, at each menstrual period, descends the Fallopian tube to the womb, and there meeting the male sperm, or semen, becomes impregnated; and that impregnation cannot take place at any other time, than just *before* or a few days *after* the menstrual flow.

The transmission of the spermatic fluid through the uterus, uterine tube, or oviduct to the ovary, a vesicle, ovum, or egg, is vivified or fecundated, and passes into the womb to be developed until the ex piration of the ninth month or fortieth week, when it is born, and becomes an independent being. This is the general opinion.

But, like every thing else connected with this subject, it is, as yet, ALL A MYSTERY, and, beyond all doubt, ever will remain so; and we think it well for the human race that it should, for it certainly never was intended by the Creator that the wisdom of man should be the means of bring about his own ruin, by attempting to control the destiny of his race, so as to suit his own convenience.

The moment the spermatic fluid arrives at the ovary which is seized by the extremity of the uterine tube, it acts on and vivifies one or more ova or ovules, and forms the new being or beings.

The fecundated ovule is now the seat of a new vitality, it becomes swollen, reddish, and finally bursts its membrane, and detaches itself from the ovary. The fimbriated extremity of the uterine or Fallopian tube is still in contact with the ovary, and favors the passage of the newly-formed being, the embryo, into the uterus to be developed until the expiration of the ninth month, by a series of the most extraordinary changes. When the extremity of the tube loses its hold of the ovary, which may happen according to some writers, from excessive voluptuousness, fear, &c.; the ovule on bursting its covering will fall into the abdomen, there develop itself as an extra-uterine pregnancy, and finally destroy the patient unless relieved by gastrotomy, or the first part of the CÆSAREAN operation. It is, however, a fortunate circumstance that abdominal and tubal preguances are of very rare occurrence.

Almost all physiologists are of opinion that the uterus possesses a power of suction and imbibes the semen after its ejaculation, or a vapour arising from it.

How can we explain the fact, that but one tube only is concerned in conception? What was the object of nature, in forming two tubes, two ovaries, two testes, two seminal receptacles, if one organ in each sex be sufficient for the propagation of the species? Or are the double organs in each sex intended for the formation of distinct sexes?

The same orgasm that affects the ovary and tube is said to render the womb vascular, and lightly congested. Its internal surface, thus irritated, secretes the albuminous concretion, called decidua, which becomes a membrane. These effects are purely sympathetic, because they exist in extra-uterine pregnancies; they are more perfect, however, when produced by the presence of the ovule.

The volume, form, and direction of the uterus are gradually changed after conception; its parieties are enormously thickened; its weight, at the completion of the term of gestation, is two or three pounds, and compared with that of a woman who has been a mother [two ounces], and with that of a virgin [half an ounce], we find it multiplied by nearly twelve and twenty-four.

The illustrious HARVEY made a vast number of dissections of hinds after copulation. and never discovered the male fluid in the womb; hence the opinion was confirmed, that a vapor arose from it—aura seminalis—which passed through the womb and tube to the ovary, one of whose ova or vesicles it impregnated; and that the ovule was conveyed through the tube into the womb to be nourished.

In support of this theory, it is urged that impregnation has happened though the hymen was perfect, and closed up the orifice of the vagina, except at the upper part, when no penetration of the male, further than between the external labia, took place. There are many cases of this kind on record; and a most remarkable one was lately described by Dr. KENNEDY, of Dublin. The penis does not enter the orifice of the womb, which is not much larger, in the unimpregnated state, than that of the male urethra. I have read of several instances in which the application of the male fluid between the external labia caused impregnation; a fact also attested by DR. BLUNDELL, in his lectures in the Lancet: "I know three cases in which the male organ was not suffered to enter the vagina at all, and where, nevertheless,

I suppose, from the mere deposition of the semen upon the labia, impregnation took place. I have known women astonished to find themselves pregnant, being persuaded that impregnation was impossible, until, to their sorrow, the unwelcome truth was unfolded. In a word, from several facts of this kind, too delicate for a fuller disclosure, I am satisfied that very small quantities of the semen introduced into the lower part of the vagina, where there is an aptitude to become pregnant, will give rise to the new structure."

A healthful woman may be impregnated unconsciously, during inebriation, narcotism, catalepsy, and profound sleep. I have also heard of cases in which the greater part of the penis was destroyed by disease, or amputated close to the pubis, and yet persons so mutilated, continued to propagate. In such cases, there can be but very imperfect penetration, but it is to be remembered that the expulsive power of the ejaculatory muscles of the penis remains in its natural condition. These and similar cases prove that perfect or deep penetration is not necessary for procreation, and they also favor the third theory of absorption of the semen from the vagina.

These cases show that it is not necessary that the male semen should be injected into the womb. Dr. Blundell supposes that, when there is a deposition on the vulva, generation depends on the admixture of the male fluid with the secretions of the female: "for dilution does not destroy the fecundating power."

On a careful review of all the theories of human generation, we can only arrive at a conclusion admitted by all, that a *union of the sexes is necessary, that both should be in good or tolerably good health, and that the function ought only to be performed when dictated by nature.*

The primitive fathers and physicians have duly noticed the evils to which I allude; and every experienced medical practitioner can prove their frequent occurrence. It is all well for sentimentalists and the mock-modest to declaim about a notice of them; but nature, justice, morality, and the preservation of the human health, as well as the perpetuation of the human race, demand it. Such, however is the hypocrisy of the day, that even a notice in the dead language is abused and condemned by ignorant intolerant bigots and fools, who are unable to appreciate the importance of the subject.

Fœtus in the Womb

ALL obstetric writers agree that the circulation between the mother and the infant is interrupted by the placenta or after-birth, and also that there is no a direct nervous connection between them. Nerves have never been discovered in the placenta or its continuation, the navel cord, which passes into the infantile abdomen. The mind of the mother, therefore, cannot have a direct influence upon the fœtus, no more than the circulation of her blood. The pulse of the mother is about 70, that of the fœtus in the womb 120—140. Mental and corporeal excitement may derange the function of the brain, nervous system, heart, and digestive apparatus of the mother; but such derangements have only an indirect effect upon the fœtus in utero. It therefore follows that the imagination of the mother cannot mark or deform the offspring, for if it could, no infant would be perfect; because there never, perhaps, was a pregnant woman who was not more or less frightened, or who was free from longings during her condition; and yet how few deformed or disfigured infants are born. The imagination is excited in every case of pregnancy, there is a constant cause, but very rarely an effect. This is bad philosophy; for every obstetrican engaged in practice has repeatedly known pregnant women who had ungratified longings, who had been frightened by dismal objects, or had met with dreadful accidents or misfortunes, and yet their infants were perfect. We see this illustrated every day. Nevertheless, the belief is general among the middle and lower classes, and even among some medical practitioners, that the frights, longings, and imaginations of the mother can mark and deform the offspring; but this opinion is contrary to nature, reason, common observation, and medical science. I have known of instances in which women feared that their infants would be marked; but I never met with one case in which such anticipations was confirmed. The belief in this error is, however, of great antiquity.

Pathology of the Generative Organs.

It is generally admitted, by the most eminent modern writers, that the present mode of female education is highly injurious to health, predisposes to spinal curvature, and, consequently, to deformity of the hip and other bones, thereby often rendering parturition highly dangerous and fatal.

Again, great injury is inflicted on the natural development of children and young females, by the foolish custom of tight lacing, which impedes the functions of the thoracic and abdominal viscera, prevents the development of the breasts and nipples; for these organs are considerably absorbed from pressure—the lactiferous ducts are almost obliterated—the nipples will be undeveloped at the end of pregnancy--lactation will be impeded or absent after delivery—the natural food of the offspring greatly diminished—while the mother will be affected with inflamed breasts, or sore nipples, which may lay the foundation of cancer.

Some complaints are aggravated by marriage, such as inveterate scrofula, epilepsy, confirmed phthisis, caries of the vertebræ, distortion of the spine, diseases of the heart and large vessels, &c.

All disqualifications for matrimonial union may be divided into two classes. First, those caused by defect of mental power; and secondly, those caused by defect of sexual organization. The disqualifications are, therefore, moral and physical, and are usually expressed by the terms impotence and sterility. These terms are often used synonymously, though widely different. *Impotence* consists in the incapacity for copulation, or in the impossibility of exercising the venereal act; *sterility* consists in the aptitude of the organs for procreation, without the power of reproduction. Thus a person may be impotent but not sterile, and *vice versa.* Some writers apply the term impotence to the male; but such a distinction is arbitrary and unscientific. The female may be impotent from malformation, and the male sterile from excessive venery, onanism, self-pollution, and diseases of the testicles. A man who is impotent is necessarily sterile; but a woman may be impotent and not sterile. I need scarcely remark that sterility does not afford a just plea for the [illegible] [illegible]y or marriage. The manifest causes of impote[illegible] [illegible] both sexes, may be divided into physical and mo[illegible]

PHYSICAL, MANIFEST, NATURAL, OR ACCIDENTAL IMPOTENCE OF THE MALE.—The causes of manifest impotence of the male, are absence of the penis or testicles. There must be total loss of the penis, as the slightest penetration into the vagina is sufficient for procreation. There may be congenital want of the penis, or it may be partially lost by accident, as by the bites of animals, burns, wounds, or surgical operations. It may be removed close to the pubes, yet the ejaculatory muscles retain their power, and will propel the semen with sufficient, indeed the natural force, so that it may effect impregnation.

The absence of one or both of the testicles from the scrotum, is no proof of their non-existence in the abdomen ; unless the penis be small, the voice puerile, the beard absent, the form delicate, and the whole physical and moral constitution feminine. It is well known that the testicles may not descend into the scrotum, though they may be fully developed in the abdomen and perform their functions perfectly.

The destruction of one testicle by castration or disease is no impediment to procreation, no more than the loss of one eye is to vision. But when both testicles are completely diseased, their secretion is injured or suppressed, and incurable sterility is the consequence. Frequent seminal emissions, or the sudden secretion of semen during coition, is generally an effectual bar to reproduction. The secreting power of the testes may be very much increased or diminished. The more fluid parts of the spermatic fluid must be absorbed, and the semen must be retained some hours, to effect procreation.

Both testicles may be removed by castration, yet procreation may be accomplished, as the vesiculæ seminales, or seminal receptacles, may contain at the time of the operation a sufficient quantity of semen for one or two prolific emissions, after which the person will be sterile but not impotent.

"It must be admitted, however," M. Fodere observes, "that thickness of the penis, which excites great pain in some women, procures voluptuous sensations in others, and that the vagina is capable of great dilatation, which may be effected by gentle and gradual efforts, and reduced to a state capable of receiving the virile member. Though extreme length of the penis," he continues, "may produce contusion of the os and cervix uteri, it cannot be deemed a just cause of impotence, because, by certain precautions, this danger may be avoided, unless there is a great difference between the age of the parties."

Impotence in men depends on defect of some one or more of these conditions: erection, intromission, and ejaculation of the spermatic fluid. The causes of impotence are more commonly observed in man than in the other sex; and this is easily accounted fo by the greater part the male has to perform in ·· ial congress. This is evident from the phenomena which give the virile member the form and disposition proper for erection, the introduction of the organ, and the ejaculation of the semen, which are effected by a violent and complicated action, which requires a concurrence of many indispensable conditions, as the organs not only contract spasmodically to effect the expulsion of the male fluid, but all the body participates in this convulsion at the moment of emission, as if nature at this instant forgot every other function. The causes of impotence in man arise from two sources, from malformation of the genitals, or from want of action in them; but in females, impotence can only depend on malformation, either natural or acquired.

The causes of want of erection may be divided into physical and moral. The physical causes depend on defects of the body, as paralysis of the penis, curvature of the spine, frigid and apathetic temperament. The moral causes are such as act powerfully on the imagination, and suddenly produce an atony of the genitals, or induce an inactivity in organs properly developed.

Among the causes of want of erection, we must reckon a frigid or apathetic constitution, a total insensibility to sexual desire, and this is said to be of a profound lymphatic temperament.

A habitude of chastity is another opponent to erection, such as characterized the ancient fathers of the desert, and those who, by fasting and other forms of church discipline, generally, but not always, extinguish certain desires implanted by nature, but, in their opinion, contrary to that of chastity. The sexual organs of such persons decay, like all other organs whose functions are not exerted. Long-continued debauchery, whether with women or by masturbation, will also cause impotence. Impotence is often caused by debility of the genital organs, induced by precocious venereal enjoyments, or by the abuse of the sexual function by solitary indulgence or masturbation.

Excessive desire or love may cause impotence Every exciting or depressing passion which operates during the act of reproduction, may be a temporary cause of impotence. All causes of debility, whether temperal or physical, impede the function of generation. Priapism and satyriasis impede seminal emission, and may be causes of impotence and sterility.

It is known to every well-developed adult, that the influence of the mind is very great on the generative function, and may wholly prevent the completion of the act. If the imagination wanders from the real object of desiring species, impregnation is often but not always impeded, and issue seldom follows. STERNE has happily commented on this point, in the first chapter of one of his most popular works; and his views are strictly physiological. When the one party entertains dislike or disgust to the other, or when either allows the mind to be occupied with the image of another individual, the act of generation may be duly performed, and the offspring will bear a strong resemblance to the person who occupied the imagination of the party. Dr. A. T. Thompson gives a remarkable example of this kind in his Lectures on Medical Jurisprudence, published in the London Medical and Surgical Journal.

There are many cases in which impotence is caused by the hatred and disgust of the husband towards his wife, though he is capable of cohabiting with other women.

There are many other causes of impotence besides those already mentioned, which may be briefly noticed. Long watching, great fatigue, mental or corporeal, want of nutriment, excessive evacuations of blood, bile, fæces, saliva, menses, scurvy, malignant fevers, diseases of the brain and spinal marrow, whether from external injuries or poisons, and numerous other diseases, are temporary causes of impotence. Sexual desire is suppressed by acute diseases, and usually returns after convalescence. Zacchias and Beck relate numerous cases in proof of this position We see this further illustrated during the commencement of convalescence after fevers, when erection is frequently observed. Some diseases stimulate the generative organs as calculus in the kidneys or bladder, stricture of the urethra, diseases of the prostrate gland, as well as gout, rheumatism, consumption, piles, mania, itch, leprosy, and other cutaneous affections.

Excessive venery is a frequent cause of want of erection and impotence. I have been consulted in several cases of this description. This is a frequent cause of want of offspring in young married persons, as well as in those who indulge in a solitary vice. In these cases, the semen may escape without the aid of the ejaculatory muscles, is imperfect in quality, and devoid of prolific power until the health is improved. There is generally inflammation of the seminal vesicles in these cases, and seminal debility or spermatorrhœa

The abuses of narcotics, saline refrigerants, acids, acid fruits, &c., are causes of impotence, as they reduce the muscular power below the ordinary state.

Moral Causes.

CHAGRIN, inquietude, and debilitating passions influence the whole economy; jealousy, and profound meditation, impede the faculty of procreation. Thus, at the very moment when enjoyment is abont to be commenced, too eager desire, the excess of love, the fear of not being loved, timidity, respect, doubt of capability, the fear of being surprised, the shame of excessive modesty on being in the presence of witnesses, antipathy, the ecstacy on beholding the attractions of a beloved woman, the continence imposed by real and true love, the sudden knowledge of some physical defect of the female, aversion from filth, odor, and pre-occupations of the mind, are sufficient to oppose erection, and to abate it most suddenly. But who can enumerate all the moral causes capable of impeding or abating erection? A sigh, doubtfully interpreted; a recollection, an equivocal word, are sufficient to destroy the illusion, and congeal the most violent passion. A newly married man has become suddenly impotent, on discovering his wife to be without a hymen, though the absence of this membrane is no proof of unchastity; and a debauchee has as suddenly become impotent, on finding the membrane perfect.—(*Dict. de Sc. Medicales.*)

It is thus with a literary man, a philosopher, or all those who have a ruling idea, which excites the brain more than the sexual organs. Nevertheless uch individuals are often excessively amorous. Great nervousness, frigidity,a defect in the moral or physical condition, render the act of procreation infecund, and often impossible. The fear of being impotent is by far the most frequent and powerful cause of this condition. Many individuals suppose there is no physical power when the moral state destroys their desires, and they are impotent as long as they suppose themselves so. Such is the power of the moral over the physical state of man. Many impotent persons of this class are cured, by quieting the imagination and strengthening the constitution, as I have also observed in numerous instances. Some persons labor under moral or temporary, and not under physical or persistent impotence, and are cured by invigorating the general health and the genital organs.

Impotence, Natural. Manifest, or Incidental in Woman.

The causes of impotence in women are malformations or diseases of the sexual organs. Some of these causes are apparent, others obscure. The apparent causes are, obliteration of the external sexual organs, both soft and bony, absence of the vagina and uterus, and great deformity of the pelvis, with numerous diseases of the external and internal genitals. The vagina and uterus have been found to consist of a dense, fleshy substance; and the vagina has been partially closed by a similar growth. It may be absent, unusually small, impervious from adhesions, tumours, or a frænum passing across above the hymen, or it may be filled with a fleshy production. If too narrow, it may be dilated with a bougie, or a sponge-tent, and when unattended to, must be divided by incision, to admit of coition, or the passage of the infant. The orifice may cohere after conception. There is sometimes a great congenital contrasion of the parts, so much so, that it would be tedious to describe them. In cases of extreme narrowness, impregnation may take place, and the canal be gradually dilated during pregnancy or parturition. The vaginal canal may be totally or partially obliterated, and in such cases an operation is impracticable, and impotence absolute. The vagina has opened into the bladder, into the rectum, on the anterior parietes of the abdomen, and pregnancy has occurred in the two latter cases. The whole of the causes of impotence and sterility in women may be arranged under three classes:

1. Those depending on the organs which receive the male fluid, namely, the external genital fissure, the vagina, and uterus.

2. Malformation, or diseases of the organs that transmit it to the ovaries, and convey the embryo to the uterus, and these are the Fallopian or uterine tubes.

3. The malformation, or diseases of the ovaries, or organs which supply the germs for fecundation.

Inflammation, ulceration, scirrhus, cancer, ossification, calcareous deposit, or tumours in any of these organs, may be the cause of sterility. In fact, any disease of the female genitals, attended with much constitutional disturbance, may be considered a temporary cause of sterility. Tumours of various kinds, adhesions, from disease or mechanical violence, displacement of the uterus, when present in the female organs, are causes of infecundity. Among the temporary causes of female impotence, are excessive dimensions of the clitoris and nymphæ; but these are removable by operation.

The constitution may undergo changes favorable to fecundity. Thus we often see women who bear children, after having been barren for ten or twenty years. Others have a family without experiencing any enjoyment, according to their account, during intercourse; and some who suffer the embraces of their husbands with pain or even disgust.

When persons have no sexual desire, or when there are physical defects of their organs which cannot be remedied by surgical operation, they commit a great moral offence on entering into the marriage state, by depriving another individual of those conjugal rights which nature has established.

To Make Pastes and Pastry.

German Paste.—Three-quarters of a pound of flour; half a pound of butter; half a pound of sugar; peel of a lemon; two eggs; half an eggshell of water. Take three-quarters of a pound of fine flour, put into it half a pound of butter, the same of powdered sugar, and the peel of a lemon grated; make a hole in the middle of the flour, break in the yolks of two eggs, reserving the whites, which are to be well beaten; then mix all well together. If the eggs do not sufficiently moisten the paste, add half an eggshell of water. Mix all thoroughly, but do not handle it too much. Roll it out thin, and you may use it for all sorts of pastry. Before putting it into the oven, wash over the pastry with the white of the beaten eggs, and shake over a little powdered sugar.

Very Rich Short Crust.—Ten ounces of butter; one pound of flour; a pinch of salt; two ounces of loaf sugar, and a little milk. Break ten ounces of butter into a pound of flour dried and sifted, add a pinch of salt and two ounces of loaf sugar, rolled fine. Make it into a very smooth paste as lightly as possible, with two well-beaten eggs, and sufficient milk to moisten the paste.

A Light Puff Paste—American.—One pound of sifted flour; one pound of fresh butter; two teaspoonfuls of cream of tartar; one teaspoonful of soda; a little water. Work one-fourth of the butter into the flour until it is like sand; measure the cream of tartar and the soda, rub it through a sieve, put it to the flour, add enough cold water to bind it, and work it smooth; dredge flour over the paste-slab or board, rub a little flour over the rolling-pin, and roll the paste to about half an inch thickness; spread over the whole surface one-third of the remaining butter, then fold it up; dredge flour over the pasteslab and rolling-pin, and roll it out again; then put another portion of the butter, and fold and roll again, and spread on the remaining butter, and fold and roll for the last time.

Cherry Tart.—Time to bake, thirty-five to forty minutes. About one pound and a half of cherries; half a pound of short crust; moist sugar to taste. Pick the stalks from the cherries, put a tiny cup upside down in the middle of a deep pie-dish, fill round it with the fruit, and add moist sugar to taste. Lay some short crust round the edge of the dish, put on the cover as directed before, ornament the edges, and bake it in a quick oven. When ready to serve, sift some loaf sugar over the top.

Cranberry Tart.—Time to bake, three-quarters of an hour or an hour. One quart of cranberries; one pint of water; one pound of moist sugar; puff paste. Pick a quart of cranberries free from all imperfections, put a pint of water to them, and put them into a stewpan, add a pound of fine brown sugar to them, and set them over the fire to stew gently until they are soft, then mash them with a silver spoon, and turn them into a pie-dish to become cold. Put a puff paste round the edge of the dish, and cover it over with a crust; or make an open tart in a flat dish with paste all over the bottom of it and round the edge; put in the cranberries; lay cross bars of paste over the top, and bake.

Rhubarb Tart.—Time to bake, three-quarters of an hour to one hour. Some stalks of rhubarb; one large teacupful of sugar; some puff paste. Cut the large stalks from the leaves, strip off the outside skin, and cut the sticks into pieces half an inch long. Line a pie-dish with paste rolled rather thicker than a crown piece, put in a layer of rhubarb, stew the sugar over it, then fill it up with the other pieces of stalks, cover it with a rich puff paste, cut a slit in the center, trim off the edge with a knife, and bake it in a quick oven. Glaze the top or strew sugar over it.

PASTE FOR CUSTARDS.—Six ounces of butter; half a pound of flour; yolk of two eggs; three tablespoonfuls of cream. Rub six ounces of butter into half a pound of flour. Mix it well together with two beaten eggs and three tablespoonfuls of cream. Let it stand a quarter of an hour; then work it up; and roll it out very thin for use.

TO ICE OR GLAZE PASTRY, OR SWEET DISHES.—Whites of two eggs to three ounces of loaf sugar. To ice pastry, or any sweet dishes, break the whites of some new-laid eggs into a large soup plate, and beat them with the blade of a knife to a firm froth. When the pastry is nearly done, take it from the oven, brush it well over with the beaten egg, and sift the pounded sugar over it in the above proportion. Put it again into the oven to dry or set, taking care it is not discolored. Or beat the yolks of eggs and a little warm butter well together, brush the pastry over with it when nearly baked, sift pounded sugar thickly over it, and put it into the oven to dry. For raised, or meat pies, the yolks of eggs must be used.

RED CURRANT AND RASPBERRY TART.—Time to bake, three-quarters of an hour. A pint and a half of picked red currants; three-quarters of a pint of raspberries; a quarter of a pound of moist sugar; half a pound of puff paste. Pick the currants and raspberries from their stalks, mix them together in a pie-dish with the moist sugar. Wet the edge of the dish, place a band of puff paste round it; wet that also. Cover the top with puff paste, pressing it round the edge with your thumbs. Cut the overhanging edge off evenly. Then scollop the edge by first chopping it in lines all round, and then giving them a little twist, at regular intervals, with the knife. Take the edges you have cut off, flour them, roll them out, and cut them into leaves to ornament the top. Egg it over and bake it. When done, dredge it with white sugar, and salamander it.

Gooseberry Tart.—Time to bake, about three-quarter of an hour. One quart of gooseberries; rather more than half a pound of short crust; five or six ounces of moist sugar. Cut off the tops and tails from a quart of gooseberries, put them into a deep pie-dish with five or six cunces of good moist sugar, line the edge of the dish with short crust, put on the cover, ornament the edges and top in the usual manner, and bake in a brisk oven. Serve with boiled custard or a jug of good cream.

Plain Apple Tart.—Time to bake, one hour, or, if small, half an hour. Apples; a teacupful of sugar; peel of half a lemon or three or four cloves; half a pound of puff paste. Rub a pie-dish over with butter, line it with short pie-crust rolled thin, pare some cooking apples, cut them in small pieces, fill the pie-dish with them, stew over them a cupful of fine moist sugar, three or four cloves, or a little grated lemon peel, and add a few spoonfuls of water; then cover with puff paste crust, trim off the edges with a sharp knife, and cut a small slit at each end, pass a gigling iron around the pie ha'f an inch inside the edge, and bake in a quick oven.

Open Apple Tart.—Time to bake in a quick oven, until the paste loosens from the dish. One quart of sliced apples; one teacupful of water; one of fine moist sugar; half a nutmeg; yolk of one egg; a little loaf sugar and milk; puff paste. Peel and slice some cooking apples and stew them, putting a small cupful of water and the same of moist sugar to a quart of sliced apples, add half a nutmeg and the peel of a lemon grated, when they are tender set them to cool. Line a shallow tin pie-dish with rich pie paste or light puff paste, put in the stewed apples half an inch deep, roll out some of the paste, wet it slightly over with the yolk of an egg beaten with a little milk, and a teaspoonful of powdered sugar, cut it in very narrow strips, and lay them in crossbars or diamonds across the tart, lay another strip round the edge, trim off the outside neatly with a sharp knife, and bake in a quick oven until the paste loosens from the dish.

DAMSON TART.—Time to bake, three-quarters of an hour. One pint and a half of damsons; five or six ounces of moist sugar; half a pound of puff paste. Pick any stalks from the damsons and pile them high in the dish, stew the sugar well amongst the fruit, and pour in two or three spoonfuls of water. Line the edge of the pie-dish with a good puff paste, cover it with paste, and bake it in a well-heated oven. A short time before the tart is done, brush it over with the white of eggs beaten to a stiff froth, sift powdered sugar over it, and return it to the oven for about ten minutes.

MERINGUE TART.—An open tart of any preserves, jams, or stewed fruit; whites of two eggs; a quarter of a pound of loaf sugar; flavoring of vanilla or lemons. Make any nice rich tart of preserves, jams, or stewed fruit; whisk the whites of two eggs with a quarter of a pound of pounded loaf sugar and a flavoring of vanilla or lemon until it can be molded with a knife, lay it over the tart nearly an inch thick, and put it into the oven for a few minutes until it is slightly colored. erve it hot or cold.

Mince Pies.—Time, twenty-five to thirty minutes. Puff paste; mincemeat. Roll out the puff paste to the thickness of a quarter of an inch; line some good-sized patty-pans with it, fill them with mincemeat, cover with the paste, and cut it close round the edge of the patty-pan. Put them in a brisk oven. Beat the white of an egg to a stiff froth; brush it over them when they are baked; sift a little powdered sugar over them; replace them in the oven for a minute or two to dry the egg. Serve them on a table napkin very hot. Cold mince pies will re-warm, and be as good as fresh.

German Pastry.—Time, fifteen minutes. The weight of two eggs in butter, flour, and sugar; any preserve you like. Take two eggs well beaten, and mix them with their weight in flour and sugar. Beat well together with a fork, lay half the paste on a tin, and put it into a brisk oven. When a little set, spread over it preserve of apricot, or strawberry jam. Then add the remainder of the paste, and bake it again till quite set. When cold, sift a little sugar over it, and cut it into narrow strips.

Tartlets.—Time, fifteen to twenty minutes. Some rich puff paste; any preserve you please, or marmalade. Cut as many rounds of rich puff paste, with a tin cutter, as you require. Then cut an equal number, and press a smaller cutter inside them to remove the center and leave a ring. Moisten the rounds with water, and place the rings on them. Put them into a moderate oven for ten or twelve minutes, and, when done, fill the center with any preserve of apricot, strawberry, or orange marmalade. Stamp out a little of the paste rolled very thin, into stars, &c. Bake them lightly, and place one on the top of each tartlet. Serve them hot or cold.

ORANGE TARTLETS.—Time to bake, fifteen to twenty minutes. Two Seville oranges; a piece of butter the size of a walnut; twice the weight of the oranges in pounded sugar; puff paste. Take out the pulp from two Seville oranges, boil the peels until quite tender, and then beat them to a paste with twice their weight in pounded loaf sugar; then add the pulp and the juice of the oranges with a piece of butter the size of a walnut, beat all these ingredients well together, line some patty-pans with rich puff paste, lay the orange mixture in them, and bake them.

LEMON PUFFS.—Time, six or eight minutes to bake. One pound and a quarter of loaf sugar; peel of two lemons; whites of three eggs. Beat and sift a pound and a quarter of loaf sugar, and mix with it the peel of two lemons grated, whisk the whites of three eggs to a firm froth, add it gradually to the sugar and lemon, and beat it all together for one hour. Make it up into any shape you please, place the puffs on oiled paper on a tin, put them in a moderate oven, and bake.

JERSEY WONDERS.—A quarter of a pound of sugar; ten ounces of butter; one pound of flour; three large or four small eggs; a little nutmeg. Work the sugar and butter together till quite soft, throw in the eggs that have been previously well beaten, and then add the flour and a little nutmeg, knead twenty minutes and let it rise; then roll it between your hands into round balls the size of a small potato, but do not add any more flour; flour your pasteboard lightly and roll out each ball into a thin oval the size of the hand, cut with a knife three slits like bars in the center of the oval, cross the two center ones with your fingers, and draw up the two sides between, put your finger through and drop into it boiling lard, which must be ready in a small stewpan. Turn them as they rise, and, when a nice brown, take them up with a fork, and lay them on a tray with paper underneath them. The lard must be boiling before putting them in; a stewpan wide enough to put three in at once answers best, and, when the lard would froth too much, add a little fresh before putting in any more. When all are done, save the lard in a basin, as it will answer, by adding a little more fresh, to use again.

Mince Meats.

Apple Mince Meat.—One pound of currants; one pound of peeled and chopped apples; one pound of suet chopped fine; one pound of moist sugar; quarter of a pound of raisins stoned and cut in two; the juice of four oranges and two lemons, with the chopped peel of one; add of ground mace and allspice each a spoonful, and a wineglass of brandy. Mix all well together, and keep it closely covered in a cool place.

Egg Mince Meat.—Six hard-boiled eggs shred very fine; double the quantity of beef suet, chopped very fine; one pound of currants, washed and dried; the peel of one large, or two small lemons, minced up; six tablespoonfuls of sweet wine; a little mace, nutmeg, and salt, with sugar to your taste; add a quarter of a pound of candied orange and citron, cut into thin slices. Mix all well together, and press it into a jar for use.

LEMON MINCE MEAT.—One large lemon; three large apples; four ounces of beef suet; half a pound of currants; four ounces of white sugar; one ounce of candied orange and citron. Chop up the apples and beef suet; mix them with the currants and sugar; then squeeze the juice from a large lemon into a cup. Boil the lemon thus squeezed till tender enough to beat to a mash; add it to the mince meat. Pour over it the juice of the lemon, and add the citron chopped fine.

Baked and Boiled Puddings.

For boiled pudding you will require either a mold, a basin, or a pudding-cloth: the former should have a close-fitting cover, and be rubbed over the inside with butter before putting the pudding in it, that it may not stick to the side; the cloth should be dipped in boiling water, and then well floured on the inside. A pudding-cloth must be kept very clean, and in a dry place. Bread puddings should be tied very loosely, as they swell very much in boiling.

The water must be boiling when the pudding is put in, and continue to boil until it is done. If a pudding is boiled in a cloth it must be moved frequently whilst boiling, otherwise it will stick to the saucepan.

There must always be enough water to cover the pudding if it is boiled in a cloth; but if boiled in a tin mold, do not let the water quite reach the top.

To boil a pudding in a basin, dip a cloth in hot water, dredge it with flour, and tie it closely over the basin. When the pudding is done, take it from the water, plunge whatever it is boiling in, whether cloth or basin, suddenly into cold water, then turn it out immediately; this will prevent its sticking. If there is any delay in serving the pudding, cover it with a napkin, or the cloth in which it was boiled; but it is better to serve it as soon as removed from the cloth, basin, or mold.

Always leave a little space in the pudding-basin for the pudding to swell; or tie the pudding-cloth loosely for the same reason.

Baked Puddings.—Bread or rice puddings require a moderate heat for baking; batter or custard require a quick oven. The time needed for baking each particular pudding is given with the recipe.

Eggs for puddings are beaten enough when a spoonful can be taken up clear from strings

Soufflés require a quick oven. These should be made so as to be done the moment for serving, otherwise they will fall in and flatten.

Apple, Gooseberry, Currant, or Other Fruit Puddings.—Time, one hour and a half. One pound of flour; six ounces of suet; water; fruit. Make a paste as for beefsteak pudding, roll it out thin, and line a well-buttered basin with part of it, fill it with the apples pared and cored, a slice or two of lemon peel cut very thin, or a few cloves. Moisten the edges of the paste, cut out a piece and put it over the top, press it well together, and cut it neatly round that it may be of an equal thickness. Put the mold or basin into a floured cloth and tie it closely over. Then put it into a saucepan of boiling water, and boil it. When done, turn it carefully from the basin on a hot dish.

If boiled in a cloth, without a basin, the cloth must be dipped into hot water, dredged with flour, and laid into an empty basin, that the crust may be formed in it.

All fruit puddings are made in the same manner, whether of gooseberries, currants, damson, greengages, &c.

Baked Apple Pudding.—Half a pound of grated apples; half a pound of butter; half a pound of sugar; yolk of six eggs; whites of three; juice of half a lemon; peel of one; a little puff paste. Grate half a pound of apples and add them to the butter beaten to a cream, the sugar pounded, the yolks of six whole eggs, and the whites of three beaten separately, the peel of one lemon grated, and the juice of half a one. Mix all thoroughly together, and put it into a dish, with puff paste round the edge.

Boiled Apple Dumplings.—Time to boil, one hour. Eight apples and some suet crust. Pare and core eight fine apples, and cut them into quarters. Roll a nice suet crust half an inch thick, cut it into round pieces, and lay in the centre of each piece as many pieces of apple as it will contain. Gather the edges up, and pinch them together over the apple. When all the dumplings are made, drop them into a saucepan of boiling water, and let them boil gently for nearly or quite an hour; then take each one carefully out with a skimmer, place them all on a dish, and serve them quickly with butter, sugar, and nutmeg. To be eaten cut open, and the butter and sugar put into them.

Baked Apple Dumplings.—Time, three quarters of an hour. Some baking apples, white of eggs; some pounded sugar; puff paste. Make some puff paste, roll it thin, and cut it into square pieces, roll one apple into each piece, put them into a baking dish, brush them with the white of an egg beaten stiff, and sift pounded sugar over them. Put them in a gentle oven to bake.

THE ART OF
Beautifying & Preserving
THE HAIR.

—o—

There has been less written on this subject, perhaps, than any other in the whole range of medical literature, from what cause I am unable to say. It cannot be, because of the insignificance of the subject, for when we take into consideration the purposes the Hair is intended to subserve in the animal economy, and the expense that is incurred yearly for preparations which are said to invigorate it, and bring it to its original state of healthiness and beauty, we can at once see that it is of vast importance. We will come, then, to the consideration of our task at once, and for want of a better definition, we will say that the hairs are appendages of the skin, contributing to its defence; they traverse the skin like the perspiratory and oil tubes, and extend to the fat beneath the skin.

Within the skin each hair is enclosed in a sheath or tube, closed at its extremity, where it supports the roots of the hair, and constructed of three layers, derived from the skin, namely, a lining of scarf-skin, a middle layer of sensitive skin, and an external and protective layer, the corium. The hair tubes originate on the surface of the skin in the form of little pouches, and grow inwards to the required depth.

Appended to these hair-tubes are oil-tubes and glands, the former are first formed and the latter are productions from their sides, growing as mere pouches, and increasing in length like the tubes from which they originate.

Hairs when left to their natural growth attain a certain length, and are then thrown off by a process similar to the change of the coat in animals, their place being supplied by young hairs, which grow from the same tubes, and this temporary decadence of the hair occurs, also, when it is kept cut of moderate length.

It has been ascertained that the ordinary length of the hair, as shown by measurement in women, ranges between twenty and thirty-six inches, and its weight from six to eight ounces. However, if the hair is kept closely shaven, it becomes persistent, and also increases in bulk and strength. The hair grows at the rate of one line and a half a week, or six and a half inches a year, being twenty-seven feet, if we live to be eighty. The shape of small hairs is cylindrical, and more or less oval for long hairs. The hairs of the head are never perfectly cylindrical, and those of the beard and eyebrows are somewhat oval. When left to their natural growth, the end or tip is always conical and pointed. The surface of the scalp presents about 120 superficial inches, and the number of hairs on the entire head amounts to 90,000 in a thin head of hair, but in a thick head of hair the amount is much greater, for many of the pores give passage to two hairs. At its lower end, the hair tube terminates in a cul-de-sac, and this portion of its cavity is filled by an accumulation of freshly-formed cells and granules, which constitute the root of the hair; above this point, the little mass of cells separates into two parts: a central part of a cylindrical figure, which is the newly-formed hair, and a peripheral layer, which incloses the former and is continuous with, and is the sheath of the scarf-skin which lines the tube. The manner of formation of the hair is the same as that of the scarf-skin on the surface of the sensitive-skin: a fluid filtered from the blood is deposited on the surface of the vescular layer of the tube; this is converted into little granule, (grains,) then into cells, and the cells, by a subsequent modification of their arrangement and form, become the bulb of the hair.

More or less pigmentary matter forms an invariable constituent of the contents of the hair-cells, and upon this depends the color of the hair. The shades of color of the hair seen among mankind are various indeed, but are referable for the most part to some one prevailing type; for instance, when we journey towards the north we find the hair becoming lighter, while if we proceed to the south it deepens in its hues; these differences being generally associated with a greater or less proportion of this pigment in the scarf-skin.

The structure of the hair will be the next consideration, and here we find the curious phenomenon of a three-fold modification of the cells within so limited a circuit as that of the hair-shaft.

At the centre of the bulb, the cells undergo very little alteration from their original spherical form; around them, and comprising the chief thickness of the hair, by a process of lengthening common in the economy of the cells, they are converted into fibres; (a small thread-like substance;) and quite at the outer circumference, a thin circle of cells are flattened into the form of scales, like those of the scarf-skin, or the contiguous layer of cells which constitute the lining membrane of the hair-tube. So that a hair in its pigmy section (where cut into the coloring portion) presents three different textures, a loose cellular or spongy texture in the centre, a strong texture of parallel fibres, becoming more and more dense towards the circumference, externally to this; and a thin varnished-like layer of flattened cells, constituting the polished surface of the hair, as seen more distinctly in a bright light, and more in some persons than others.

We may compare this structure, for the purpose of making ourselves better understood, to the section of a twig or stem o a plant, with its cellular o spongy pith in the centre, its hard, dense wood, en circling the pith, and its smooth and polished bark at the surface. The peculiar structure of the hair in man, as compared with animals of the brute creation, is so characteristic, that the smallest piece might be determined by the microscope, with great precision after the lapse of centuries.

Although the central part of the hair of man is a loose pith, in which the original spherical form of the cells is more or less completely lost, yet in many animals this form is retained with the most exact precision, and such hairs appear to contain in their axes a very beautiful string of beads, showing plainly in dry hairs the emptiness of the cells. In the feather of a bird, which is nothing more nor less than a modification of hair, the white pith, with its dense external covering, is very evident in its shaft, while the quill is an illustration of the outer parts alone, the transparent puckered membrane, which is drawn out of the quill when first cut, being a single row of dried-up cells. In the growing feather, the contents of the quill would be found distinctly cellulated, and containing blood. The fibrous portion of hair is the source of its strength, and the degree of strength possessed by these delicate threads would appear almost fabulous—a single hair from the head of a man having been known to support a weight of 22,222 grains, or over 46 ounces!

The principal seat of the coloring of hair is its fibrous portion; the exterior layer of the hair, composed, as before stated, of flattened cells or scales of an oval form, exhibits a peculiar arrangement of these little pieces. They are so disposed, that each newly formed circle overtops the preceding, like the tiles upon a house top, so that if you will imagine a convex surface coated with oval tiles, disposed, not in measured rows, as upon the roof of a house, but irregularly, you will have as good an idea of the surface of a hair as can be given. Bearing in mind this structure, we have a key to the well-known fact of a hair feeling rough when drawn between the fingers in one direction, and smooth in the other, or to the movement of a hair from its root to its point, when rubbed longitudinally between the fingers. These are the natural consequences of the projection of the edges of the scales. It also explains the circumstance of hairs working their way into wounds when the latter are not properly protected from their contact, or beneath the nails, or between the gums and teeth, as is the case sometimes when proper care is not taken by the hair dresser when cutting hair.

We have before explained that the bulb is the first produced part of the hair, and that, in its earliest state, the bulb is composed of cells distended with fluid like those of the scarf-skin. The fluid, in the next place, is given up from the cells by evaporation, and those latter are converted into fibres and scales. It follows from this process, that the cellulated portion of the hair, namely, that which is in contact with the bottom of the hair tube, must be the most bulky part of the organ, and for this reason is called its bulb ; while the evaporation, which occurs subsequently, explains the lesser thickness of the shaft.

It might be difficult to understand, without some explanation, how a hair could be thicker at its root than in its shaft, unless the root itself were station ery and the producing organ of the part beyond it, which is not the case. The root of a hair, when freshly plucked, has a rounded swollen appearance, well expressed by the word bulb, and presents certain varieties of aspect, being somewhat obtuse, sometimes conical, sometimes perfectly straight and sometimes clubbed or bent. The violence used in its removal is the cause of these appearances, there being more or less of the membranous lining of the hair-tube torn away with it, which latter being drawn across the root, or rolling up on one or the other side, thus produces the irregularity alluded to. However, when this membranous matter is washed away, the fibrous structure may be seen with the microscope to be the chief constituent of the root, and the fibres being different in thickness, color, and length, the root has precisely the same appearance of an old paint-brush, worn away to a single conical stump, a rather uncouth but a very true comparison.

Now, in regard to that portion of the shaft of the hair, which is contained within the hair-tube, it is steadied in its position by contact with the lining scarf-skin of the tube, and as the latter is continually undergoing the process of formation and exfoliation, or a kind of shedding, the superficial scales of the sheath are moved towards the aperture with the growing hair, and are then scattered on the surface in the form of "scurf." The scurf is, therefore, a natural and healthy formation, and though it may be kept from accumulating, it cannot be prevented It is produced on every part of the human body to some extent, where hair is found, although, from the more active growth of hair on the scalp, the facilities for collecting, and the contrast of color, it strikes the eye in that situation most disagreeably.

Sometimes it happens, that instead of obtaining a free escape at the outlet of the tube, it becomes impacted, as known to be the frequent condition of the unctuous substance of the skin. In this case, the hair also is impeded in its onward movement; for, although from the position of its scales, the hair is an agent in the prevention of such an occurrence, and would naturally carry obstacles before it, yet the impaction is sometimes too great for the power which it is capable of exerting.

If a condition of this kind occurs, the hair makes pressure on the sensitive surface of the bottom of the tube, and the impression so produced, transmitted to the nerves, is felt as a sensation of itching, that is, a sensation which, falling far short of pain, is nevertheless disagreeable. A natural remedy for the unpleasant sensation is at hand; the nail of the finger is conveyed to the seat of inconvenience, it disturbs the impacted matter at the aperture of the tube, probably dislodges it, and the hair resumes its accustomed condition.

Persons who are subject to a dry scalp know the suffering which this trifling impaction occasions, for where the unctuous substance is deficient, such a state is most likely to be produced. In the natural condition of the skin, the comb and brush are contrivances to prevent such a circumstance from arising; the regular and efficient use of them, therefore is demanded.

The composition of the hair, as shown by chemical analysis, is a basis of animal matter, (albumen,) of a certain proportion of oily substance of the salts of lime which enter into the composition of bone, flint, sulphur, and two metals, namely, manganese and iron.

The quantity of sulphur is considerable, and it is this substance which is the principal cause of the disagreeable odor evolved by hair when burning. The constituents of hair of various colors also present some differences; for example, red hair contains a reddish-colored oil, a large proportion of sulphur, and a small quantity of iron; fair hair, a white oil, with phosphate of magnesia; and the white hair of the aged, a considerable quantity of bone earth, or phosphate of lime. Fair hair, according to analysis, contains the least carbon and hydrogen, and most oxygen and sulphur; black hair follows next; while brown hair gives the largest proportion of carbon, with less hydrogen than black hair, and the smallest quantity of oxygen and sulphur.

The influence which moisture has on hair is caused by the presence of animal matter in all hair while growing and in a healthy condition. Animal matter, having saline substances entering into its composition, has a great disposition to attract fluids from the atmosphere, and when this occurs, the shaft of the hair becomes swollen and straightened. On the contrary, when the hair contains a larger proportion of oily substance, the influence of the animal matter and salts, in the absorption of aqueous fluid, is checked, and the hair maintains its natural curliness. This is believed to be the explanation of the curling and non-curling quality as it exists in hair. The curling property of hair has given rise to much theoretical speculation on the part of Physiologists One attributes it to flatness of the shaft; another to unequal distribution of the fluids in the substance of the hair; a third to impediment in its escape from the aperture of the hair tube; some to impediment in traversing the deep layer of the scarf-skin; and others to deficiency of gelatine. However, of all these theories, that which describes the curling property to flatness, is most likely right.

The ordinary effect of damp in destroying the curls of the hair is well known, but it is not perhaps so well known that this state of the hair participates in the daily health of the individual. In other words, persons possessing curly hair will find it losing its curly quality very soon when they are not well, giving rise, possibly, to the adage, "a big lick took the kincks out of him."

Climate has a great influence on the curliness or non-curliness of the hair, as shown by the difference in this respect between the natives of the North and of the South—the long lanky hair of the former, as we see for instance in the regular homespun double-and-twisted Jonathan from "down east," and the curly-haired high-strung southerner, from "away down south."

—o—

Uses of the Hair in the Animal Economy.

That the hair effects an important purpose, we have evidence in its almost universal distribution among a large class of animals, and indeed, if we admit the analogy between feathers and hair, among all warm-blooded animals; additional evidence is obtained in the perfection of its structure, and again in its early appearance during the development of the young. As a bad conductor of heat, it tends to preserve the warmth of the body, and in man, it would have that effect upon the head, and serve to equalize the temperature of the brain. It is also an agent of defence against external irritants, as the heat of the sun's rays and the bites of insects; and against injuries inflicted with violence, as we see illustrated in the use of the horse's tail on the helmets of warriors. Of special purposes performed by the hairs, we have instances in the eyebrows and eyelids, which are beautifully adapted for the defence of the organs of vision; in the small hairs which grow in the apertures of the nostrils, and serve as guardians to the delicate membrane of the nose; and in similar hairs in the ear-tubes, which defend these cavities from the intrusion of insects. Among the larger animals, the hair of the tail is used as a whisk to remove flies that pierce the skin to suck blood or deposit eggs; and in those parts of the body which the tail cannot reach, a flowing or bushy mane serves to supply its place. By a power of conduction of outward impressions common to the hair with all rigid bodies, these organs are calculated to perform the office of an apparatus of touch. We feel distinctly the disturbance of the hairs of the head by the movements of a fly, although the little creature is at some distance from the skin; and, on a similar principle, the long and rigid hairs of the upper lip of feline animals are an agent of touch, transmitting whatever impression they receive to the sensitive pulp upon which they are implanted. Indeed, animals of the cat tribe have the power of erecting these hairs, and rendering them fixed, so that the slightest impression of contact is transferred to the nerves of the sensitive pulp.

Nature, by furnishing the head with a thick covering, suggests the propriety of protecting the brain from the effects of intense heat, and there are few points on which she can be disobeyed with impunity.

In considering the special functions of the hair, we should direct attention to the uses of the beard. There can be no doubt, that the mustachio is a natural respirator, defending the lungs against the inhalation of dust and cold; and it is equally in warm climates a protector of those parts against excessive heat. Mr. Chadwick was first led to make these observations by seeing some blacksmiths who wore beards, whose mustachios were discolored by the quantity of iron dust which had accumulated among the hairs; and he justly inferred that, had not the dust been so arrested by a natural respirator, it must have found its way into the lungs, where it could not have done otherwise than be productive of evil consequences. Mr. Chadwick further reminds us of the necessity for the beard in sandy countries, as Syria and Egypt, and mentions the well known fact, that travellers in those countries find it expedient, and even necessary, to wait until their mustachios have grown to a sufficient length to defend their mouths against the admission of the burning sands of the desert. Upon the same principle he conceives that the mustachio would be of service to laborers in all dusty trades, such as millers, bakers, masons, &c.; in workmen employed in grinding iron and steel, and in travellers on dusty roads. In favor of the mustachio as a defence against the inhalation of cold air, it has been stated that persons who wear mustachios are less susceptible of toothache than others equally exposed; and that the teeth are less apt to decay. The use of the mustachio and beard as a means of maintaining the temperature of the parts which it covers is indisputable. Mr. Chadwick also states that the sappers and miners of the French army, who are remarkable for the size and beauty of their beards, enjoy a special immunity against bronchial affections; and in further illustration of the same principle, he has known persons susceptible of taking colds and sore throats rescued from that inconvenience by permitting the growth of hair beneath their chins. The celebrated Egyptian traveller, Mr. St. John, says that Walter Savage Landor was a great sufferer from sore throat, for many years of his life; and that he lost the morbid disposition by following the advice of the surgeon of the Grand Duke of Tuscany to let his beard grow; a certain corrective, as he was assured by that medical authority. There are strong reasons for the opinion advanced by Mr. Chadwick, and others, that the army and navy should wear mustachios and beards. The arguments against mustachios and beard, at least in this country, are founded on the possible neglect of cleanliness. This argument could not apply to the army and navy, where attention is paid to such points.

At the period of birth, the human infant, without reference to sex, is covered with a thick down, and it is then that we have the best opportunity of observing the direction of the hairs; for, during the first year, the greater part of the temporary hairs have fallen, and are succeeded by others which appear upon the surface only in some situations. The first hairs that are developed are those of the eyebrow, then those of the upper lip and around the mouth, and, at a later period, those of the head. The last which push through are the hairs of the fingers and those of the external ear and nose. At the period of adolescence, the hairs acquire a new impulse of growth in co-relation with the more active developement of the frame; and when the powers of the system are on the wane, the hair is among the first of the organs of the body to evince an associated infirmity. It seems to be established that the hairs, at their first formation, do not issue directly from the hair-tubes, but become bent upon themselves, so that they form a loop, whereby the point of the hair is directed towards the root, and the bend of the loop towards the aperture of the hair-tube, or pore. The cause of this position of the hair would appear to be some obstruction at the pore, from the accretion of the unctuous substance of the oil-glands and the cast cells of the hair-tube, for the little scale formed by this accretion is gradually raised by the elasticity of the hair, and when the latter attains sufficient power, is cast off, and the hair bursts from its temporary imprisonment.

In reflecting on the purpose of the hair in the animal economy, we must not pass over its chemical constitution. A large quantity of carbon and hydrogen are by its means separated from the system; and, although several other organs are concerned in the more abundant removal of the same elements, yet it would not be judicious to deny that the comparatively trifling aid of the hair is, under some cir cumstances, of importance in the exact counterpoise of the manifold operations of the animal organism. Vauquelin and Fourcroy have given it as their opinion that the hair, in conjunction with the other products of the skin, is capable of supplying the office of the kidneys.

Again, it has been observed that the growth of the hair is unusually rapid in that disease in which the functions of the lungs are more or less completely abrogated, namely, pulmonary consumption; and we are but too well acquainted with the long silken eyelashes, and long and streaming hair, of the sufferers from that distressing malady.

It is a question, to what extent the hair, after its growth is completed, is susceptible of influence proceeding from its formative element, the skin. In other words, whether it is capable of imbibing fluids derived from the bloodvessels, and, if so, whether this power of imbibition extends to the entire length of the shaft, or is limited to that portion of the hair which is contained within the hair-tube. We have already stated our conviction that a transmission of fluids from the bloodvessels of the skin into the substance of the hair really occurs; the quantity of such fluid and its nature being modified by the peculiarity of the constitution or state of health of the individual. Hence, in a state of perfect health, the hair may be full, glossy, and rich in its hues, in consequence of the absorption from the blood of a nutritive juice, containing its proper proportion of oily and albuminous elements. In persons out of health, it may lose its brilliancy of hue, and become lank and straight from the imbibition of juices imperfect in composition and ill-elaborated; while, in a third group, there may be a total absence of such juices, and the hair, as a consequence, look dry, faded, and, as indeed is the case, dead. That these phenomena do take place in the hair, I have satisfied myself by frequent observations, and I feel also satisfied that the juices penetrate to the extreme point of the hair. That there may be circumstances which may cause a limitation in the distance to which the fluids proceed, is quite obvious; but these must be regarded in the light of modifying conditions.

Now, if it be established that the hair is susceptible of permeation by fluids derived from the blood, it follows that such fluids, being altered in their chemical qualities, may possess the power of impressing new conditions on the structure into which they enter. Thus, if they contain an excess of salts of lime, they may deposit lime in the tissue of the hair, ans so produce a change in its appearance from dark to gray. But the mysteries of vital chemistry are unknown to man, and other and more extraordinary changes may be produced in the juices of the blood by sufficient causes, and then such phenomena may result as the sudden conversion of a part, or, indeed, of the whole of the hair of the head, from a dark color to one of snowy whiteness.

But, besides the sudden or speedy conversion of the entire head of hair from a dark tint to white, the change may be slow and partial, and having taken place, may either continue, or return, on a change of health, to its natural hue.

I am little disposed to speculate on the "modus operandi" of this change of color of the hair, but am content, for the present, to give a fitting place to the fact as it stands. The phenomenon may be the result of electrical action; it may be the consequence of a chemical alteration wrought in the very blood itself; or it may be a conversion for which the tissue of the hair is chiefly responsible.

It is by no means uncommon to find instances of a gradual change of color of the hair referable to a particular period of sickness or suffering.

———o———

Diseases of the Hairs and Hair Tubes.

Augmentation of hair in quaintity can only be regarded in the light of a peculiarity, so long as it is confined to those parts of the body which are properly organized for the production of long hair. It does, however, sometimes happen that hair is produced in places where such a growth is unnatural, and that the unnatural growth is accompanied by an altered state of the entire skin. This is the case in those little patches and spots which sometimes disfigure the face, and are called "moles." Moles are of a dark color, generally covered with hair of a longer or shorter growth, and come under the popular designation of "mother's marks."

Under the circumstances above detailed, and others to which I need not more particularly refer, it comes to be a question: How hairs in improper situations are to be disposed of? They may be removed without difficulty down to the level of the skin either by certain substances called "depilatories" or by the razor, but they speedily grow again, because the root remains behind, and is too deeply implanted to be reached by such means. Occasionally, even the temporary removal of the hairs by the depilatory, and its repetition from time to time, has been embraced as a boon. The ordinary components of depilatories are quicklime, soda, and a combination of sulphur and arsenic; when misapplied or allowed to remain on the skin too long, they are apt to excite inflammation, and therefore require to be used with care. Another mode of disposing of extraneous hairs is by the tweezers, but this process is painful, and, like the preceding, only temporary. It is equally apt with depilatories to cause a stronger growth of the hair, and sometimes gives rise to ugly marks and scars.

Diminution of hair in quantity, from decadence, involves much more serious considerations than the opposite condition. I do not now allude to the fall of the hair dependent on age; this is a natural consequence on man's infirmity, and cannot be regarded as a disorder; but sometimes the fall of the hair takes place in young persons, and then it becomes a serious evil. The degree of evil is necessarily much modified by circumstances; if the subject be a lady, the inconvenience is greater than if it be of the opposite sex. If the fall be limited to parts usually bald in the aged, again, the visitation may be bearable even in a young man. But when the entire scalp is laid bare, and with it the eyebrows, eyelashes, whiskers, and beard are lost, the case is one of no common affliction. A wig but ill supplies the place of Nature's foliage, and burned cork for eyebrows is only passable as a stage effect. But the annoyance is greater than all, when, instead of a total fall, round white patches of scalp become denuded, giving the idea, most unjustly, of some disagreeable or degrading disease. This is one of the numerous family of the ringworms of the public, but, like many other popular notions, wholly incorrect. The grounds of the misnomer are simply these: a disease recognized under the name of ringworm produces a fall of the hair on the part affected, then comes the popular deduction, "ergo," every fall of the hair is occasioned by a ringworm. But in the patches of which I am now speaking, there has been no previous perceptible disease; indeed, the disease is one, not of disorder of the skin, but of the nerves which supply the skin. In partial baldness of the scalp occurring in round patches, the skin is white, as smooth as if polished, and obviously thinner than the surrounding skin. This thinness of the scalp is very remarkable in the baldness of age, the skin is almost transparent, the seams of the bones may be distinguished through it, and it appears to have scarcely any substance whatever. Partial baldness is entitled to the designation "scall;" but I think it better to abstain from the use of this word, as scalled head is the term usually employed to distinguish those cases of baldness of the scalp occurring in patches, resulting from watery or mattery pimples, or from another disease shortly to be described, the true ringworm. Partial baldness may occur in any one, and at any time, and more usually attacks adults than children.

In the preceding paragraph, I have not particularly adverted to the loosening of the hair, which frequently occurs in young persons, or in those of the middle period of life, and which, if neglected, would become real baldness. Such a state as I am now describing is not uncommon in women, and generally terminates, in its mildest form, in excessive loosening of the hair. The case, however, is far from being the hopeless one which is generally imagined; and, if proper treatment be pursued, the hair will grow afresh, and assume all its pristine strength. A useful practice in men, and those of the opposite sex whose hair is short, is to immerse the head in cold water, morning and night, dry the hair thoroughly, and then brush the scalp until a warm glow is produced. In women with long hair, this plan is objectionable; and a better one is to brush the scalp until redness, [one writer says: "Some observe upon the friction or rubbing of the parts with coarse cloths, if redness does not succeed, the case is irremediable; and that the sooner this redness does appear, the more hopeful and speedy the cure,] and a warm glow are produced, and then rub among the hair some stimulating oil or pomatum. This treatment should be practised once or twice a day, or at intervals of a few days, according to the state of the scalp; namely, if tender, less; if insensible, more frequently. When the baldness happens in patches, the skin should be well brushed with a soft toothbrush, dipped in distilled vinegar, morning and evening, and the general plan of brushing, above referred to, followed.

As a general rule, the head cannot be too much brushed, any more than the horse's coat cannot be too much groomed. The groom knows full well that by plenty of combing and brushing he can not only produce a fine coat, but add very considerably to the healthy condition of the animal. And so it is with man; the more the head be brushed, the more healthy will be the skin, the more healthy its function, namely, the production and maintenance of hair, and by a reflected power, the more healthy the individual. I find that hairdressers are divided on the subject of brushing, one party recommending soft brushes and small brushing; the other hard brushes and abundant brushing. As usual, in all these differences, both are right as respects a particular theory; but the brushers have the best of the argument. A hairdresser in the vicinity of Bristol, England, has set the question forever at rest, by the announcement of the following paradox: "You can not brush the head too much, nor the hair too little." He is right; you cannot brush the head too much; but as, by clumsy brushing with hard brushes, you might overstretch or tear the hair, and so destroy its beauty, be gentle in your surface brushing, for here you cannot, in combination with the deep brushing, brush too little. The fact is, there are two purposes to be attained by brushing; firstly, to give health to the skin of the head, and strength and vigor to the hair; for which end you cannot brush too much, or use brushes too penetrating or too hard, such as will produce active friction of the skin; secondly, to smooth the hair, or perhaps go to the length of freeing it from dust, for which object your brushes may be as soft as you please, and your hand as light as agreeable. So that, in truth, each, according to the purpose he has in view, may be perfectly right; but, nevertheless, at perfect variance with his brother.

I apprehend that it was nature's intention in giving us hair as a partial clothing, that we should wear it as it grew; but that circumstances soon arose which rendered it convenient, if not necessary, to cut it in various ways. Thus, hanging before the eyes and impeding the view, the front hair was cut short off across the forehead; then other circumstances following in course of time, made it at last the fashion for the male sex to wear a short crop. Woman still enjoys the privilege of wearing her hair of the length that nature gave it, and so long as it retains its health, she has no need of the process of cutting. But the hair is apt to split at the ends, and such split ends require to be snipped off; that is, such is the present practice, for among our forefathers some attempt seems to have been made to restore this "affect incident to the hairs" by medical means; with this view, "some authors have anointed the ends of them with gall, and after, washed them with a decoction of the capillaries." Another need for cutting is created by the mode in which fashion ordains the wearing of the hair. Some of these modes are very destructive to the hair; it becomes uneven and ragged, and then the scissors are called into use to set them straight. These are the true circumstances which have given origin to, and serve to perpetuate the habit of cutting the hair in women. The operation is, in reality, one of trimming, of co-ordinating, not one either of advantage or necessity to the growth and maintenance of healthy hair. The case is altogether different where the hair is in an unhealthy condition, where much has fallen off, and where a partial and impoverished growth has risen up to represent that which is lost Cutting in this case is indispensable; not, however cutting the long hairs, but cutting the short and impoverished hairs, with the view of giving them bulk and strength, and improving their growth. In such a head as I am now describing, the short hairs offer every variety of thickness, color, and condition, and require the kind of cutting and trimming which a gardener would give to his roses; here, one of weak growth must be cut short off near the surface, that its stem may receive more sap, and the plant may grow up stronger and thicker; there, one requires lopping only at the summit; while, every now and then, shrivelled plants require pruning in a particular way, or even plucking up by the root. There would be enough for haircutters all to do, "if the hair were cut as it should be; but there would be an end of wig-making." Ah! reader, there is philosophy in cutting hair.

Many years back, was pointed out the principle of local treatment of falling hair, weak hair, and baldness; and it was showed that the principle was simply "excitation or stimulation of the skin." I do not mean that mere local stimulation will effect all that is required, without the aid of constitutional treatment, but so far as local treatment alone is concerned, the principle is stimulation; the manner of effecting stimulation, may be, and is, multifarious. An old lady who practises the art of hair-producing in London, gets, as it is stated, her patients between her knees, and then begins a system of pommelling, pinching, rubbing and shampooing the skin of the head, until she stimulates every part of it effectually; another dredges the head with a blistering powder, and a third uses fluid irritants. As far as the end is concerned, the ladies all tend to the same goal; they simply take different paths, and in their want of knowledge of the philosophy of medicine, each believes that her own is the only certain and right road. The same observations apply to nearly all the remedies and specifics for producing and restoring the hair; the greater part of them are stimulants; though some, it must be admitted, rest their claims upon more doubtful attributes.

Alteration of texture of the hair is a phenomenon too frequently occurring to admit of question or dispute. Under the influence of this change, the hair is inelastic and brittle, and breaks across in the operation of combing and brushing. This state obviously depends upon a want of health in the skin, and a deficiency of the proper constituents of natural hair. A similar condition is sometimes seen in the short and stiff hair of the body, as in the whiskers, where, instead of breaking entirely, the hair bends at an acute angle, and its texture is merely bruised. The bruises are detected in the shaft of the hair, by being lighter in color than the rest of the shaft. Oftentimes there are five, six, or even more, bruised points upon a single hair of an inch or two inches in length, and when seen in the mass, the numerous white points suggest the idea of a scurfy or dusty condition of the hair. Under the head of altered texture of the hair, must also be included the bent, twisted, dry, brittle, hemp-like hairs of common ringworm, and the turgid and swollen hairs of the Polish plica.

Altered direction of the hair may be discussed in a few words; the only situation in which the hair is known to give rise to inconvenience by irregularity in the direction of its growth, is upon the margin of the eyelids, where the lashes sometimes grow inwards, and by pressing against the front of the eyeball, occasion irritation, and even inflammation. When such a state as this occurs, the erring hair must be removed by means of a pair of fine tweezers, and the inflammation afterwards subdued by cooling and slightly astringent lotions.

In the chapter upon the structure of the hair, we have narrated some instances of altered color, and given an explanation of the nature of that change. A more frequent change, however, is that in which the coloring pigment ceases to be produced, or in which a calcareous salt is substituted for the natural pigment. This state constitutes "blanching of the hair." It must be a matter of common observation, that in those instances in which the pigment presents the deepest hue, blanching most frequently occurs, and grayness is most common; while in persons with light hair and light complexion, blanching is comparatively rare. There can be no doubt that the production in this climate of a dark pigment is a greater exertion to the economy than one of a lighter kind; and hence, when the power of the ner vous system is reduced, the formation of pigmen is one of the first actions which suffers. It is wisely ordained that it should be so, for color of the hair is one of the conditions of existence most easily spared, and it is one also that may well serve as a monitor of human decay. When grayness shows itself in the hair, it is therefore an indication of the want of tone in the hair-producing organs; and if this tone could be restored, the hair would cease to change, and, at the same time, further change would be prevented. The plan of cutting recommended previously, tends very much to prevent the extension of grayness, and, combined with judicious plucking, may correct the disorder completely. Indeed, it would almost seem that, by proper management, not only might the color of the hair be preserved for many years beyond the natural period of such a change, but also that the hair itself might be retained to the end of life.

Seeing that cessation in the production of pigment is a consequence of deficient tone in the scalp, resulting from weakened energy in the nervous system, we have an explanation at once of blanching of the hair ensuing after fevers or constitutional disease, or of the same state following intense anxiety or alarm. From such a moment, pigment is no longer elaborated, and all the hair produced, subsequently to the shock, is white; even that already formed is not free from the change. These considerations lead us to another kind of remedy for blanched hair, one which acts only on the former tissue, and has no power either of reaching that which is implanted below the level of the skin or the root I allude to "dyeing." I have heard of persons who have been led to adopt this artifice under the supposition that the hair being once dyed will grow for ever after of that color. If they had reflected in time that the dye acts only on the hair above the level of the surface, and that the hair continues to grow of the objectionable color, so as to require a weekly repetition of a disagreeable process, they would, I think, have hesitated before they had offered themselves as willing slaves to a barbarous practice Further, as regards the process of dyeing the hair, one writer very sagely observes: "In the use of coloring, staining, and dyeing of the hairs, and indeed in all the other administrations about them, great care is to be had of the brain, lest, whilst we are busy about adorning those excrementitious parts (as reckoned by some) of the body, we bring some inconvenience or detriment to the more noble residence of the soul, placed underneath." "The gray hairs of the ancients, which give that venerable aspect, and for which, if their deportment correspond with their years, they ought by all sober persons to be had in honor; these, I say, are not to be tampered with, being the natural produce of the cold and phlegmatic juices the pores of those in this declining age are stuffed with, from which these parts are nourished and borrow their tincture: and su ly whoever thinks thus to stave off old age, by coloring his white and hoary hairs, that he may seem young again, only renders himself a byword."—"Yet, if untimely or immature baldness comes on, remedies no doubt may be used; or, if the hair turns gray in youth, there are some who propose by art to change them black; others, especially of the ancients, to strike the golden dye, or make the yellow locks, in former ages held so lovely, and at this time highly esteemed in some countries, though despised by our people."

There are two affections which, in their essential nature, are diseases of the substance of the hairs; one is among the most common of the disorders of the head in this country, namely, common ringworm; the other is a native of Poland and Russia, namely, plica polonica. The relationship of these two diseases to each other has never been suspected hitherto, but the microscopical investigations prosecuted during the last few years render it more than probable that they are closely allied.

In common ringworm, the first symptom that fixes attention to the head of the child is a teasing itching of the skin. When the head is examined, a patch will be perceived, which is slightly raised above the level of the surrounding surface; it is white, and, as it were, dusted over with a fine powdery scurf. Moreover, the skin immediately around the hairs is raised up into little pimples like those of the goose skin. All the hairs arising from the diseased patch are affected in the same way, and if the disorder have been in existence for two or three weeks, the hairs will break off when gently pulled or combed. In another week or two the greater number of the hairs will have been broken off, and the patch will be left comparatively bald. The baldness, however, is not complete, for numerous short stumps of hair remain, and some of larger growth; but these vestiges are bent and twisted, and more like tow than hair. These grizzly remains of hair give one the idea of a plot of grass withered under the conjured influence of blight and drought; and a similar character may sometimes be observed over the entire head; the hair is slender, dry, of various length, and obviously starved and impoverished. In a more advanced stage of the disease, a thick crust, composed of matted hair and scurf, glued together by a watery discharge poured out under the influence of irritation, covers the patch, and spreads more or less extensively over the surface. It rarely happens that only one patch exists on the head; usually there are several, sometimes as many as fifteen or twenty, and often similar spots are found on the face, the neck, the arms, and the trunk of the body. These spots, from their oval shape, have been compared to the scuta or shields, carried by the ancient warriors, and hence have suggested as a specific name for the disease, scutulata. Turner, speaking of this complaint, observes, that the hairs "fall off not altogether from the root, but by piecemeal." He then plunges into the error which gave origin to the term ring-WORM as applied to this disorder. We know full well that there is no worm, or living creature in the case, but that the breaking off of the hair is due to the brittleness occasioned by diseased formation. The appearance of the short stumps of hair is, however, very suggestive of the operation of the moth-grub, and very like the effect produced upon furs by that little agent of destruction. Continuing Turner's remarks upon the broken hair, he speaks of their "being gnawn or eaten asunder by a small worm like that bred in some old wax, decayed fruits, or perhaps the common mite, scarce discoverable by the aid of glasses. Sennertus saith he hath often seen them, although mentioned by very few authors, and been consulted by way of prescription to destroy them. He gives it the name of tinea capillorum, for as the moth called tinea makes holes by gnawing garments, so doth this insect the like by the hairs."

In the domestic treatment of ringworm, the first consideration is cleanliness; to this end the hair should be well brushed and pomatumed, and the head kept clean by these means. It is not sufficient to brush the hair merely; the skin also should be thoroughly brushed with the view of producing friction and exciting the vital action of the scalp. Domestic treatment should be limited to these means, as true ringworm is always associated with some error of the constitution, which the medical men alone can treat efficiently. Shaving the head is unnecessary, if proper attention be paid to cleanliness. It is scarcely necessary to observe, that every precaution should be used which is calculated to prevent contagion. Ringworm carries with it an unpleasant "prestige," and although I am firmly of opinion that the disease is not contagious, I would not recommend the neglect of means adapted to render such an event impossible.

Popular remedies for ringworm are numerous, and comprehend several dangerous applications, that men educated to the study of medicine would hesitate to prescribe. As this is the case, all should be looked upon with suspicion. Ringworm is a disorder most easy of cure when the proper remedies are employed; most obstinate and most serious, both in a physical and a moral sense, when improperly treated or neglected.

One of these remedies, a great favorite, particularly in schools, may be adduced as an instance of the ludicrous rather than of the serious. Common black ink is usually, but by no means always, made of copperas, that is, sulphate of iron, and gall-nuts. Now these substances belong to the class of astringents, and, taken separately, are calculated to form passable, but inferior remedies for ringworm, But we have first of all to determine whether the ink about to be used be really compounded of these substances: proportion is a gordian knot which affords no obstacle to the amateur physician; but then comes another and not unimportant question. Is the eruption, supposed to be the ringworm (there are twenty ringworms,) is it really that kind of ringworm which may be usefully treated by an astringent application? How mischievous it is that these simple reasonings are omitted by the advocates of popular poisons? But even admitting that copperas alone and gall-nuts alone may be remedies of the lowest class, how monstrous to use them in that combination which constitutes an application of a dirty, and often an irritating kind. I have seen serious ulceration of the skin caused by the use of ink to a cutaneous eruption. Another terrible remedy, occasionally employed, is tobacco-water, a poison so rank and powerful as to be banished entirely from medicine on account of its dangerous qualities.

Plica polonica, like ringworm, is distinguished by the swollen condition of the hair, which is distended with a reddish colored fluid. and has the appearance of being converted into flesh. The scalp is much diseased, and bleeds on the slightest touch, and so much pain is occasioned by the trifling movement which accompanies the cutting of the hair, as to give rise to the impression that the diseased hair is really endowed with nerves. A large quantity of fluid weeps from the hair-tube, and agglutinates the hair into a repulsive mass, which is left for nature to remove; a process that requires from ten to twelve months to accomplish.

The hair-tubes are liable to a peculiar state of disorder, in which they have produced around them a yellow, paste-like substance, which collects in such a quantity as to destroy the bulbs of the hair, and by its further increase, to give rise to a most serious form of disease of the scalp, namely, the honeycomb ringworm. The development of this disorder is attended with irritation and itching, and when the skin of the head is examined, a small patch of redness will be detected as the seat of the diseased action. Upon further inspection, a number, and perhaps all the hairs included within the area of this patch, will be found encircled at their base by a minute yellow spot. In a few days, this spot expands; and still later, the yellow matter continuing to increase, forms a small shallow cup around the hair, the concavity of the cup being directed outwards, and its convexity towards the skin, which it deeply depresses. It generally happens that a number of these sulphur yellow cups, produced upon a small circular patch of skin, form a cluster; this arrangement constitutes the clustered variety of the disease in question. At other times, they are distributed singly over the scalp, and constitute the scattered variety. When they exist in the clustered form, they have somewhat the appearance of a piece of honeycomb embedded in the hair, and from this resemblance have received the name "favus," which literally means "honeycomb." The disease obeys the law of extension I have before had occasion to advert to as common in cutaneous disorder, namely, exhausting itself in the part first attacked and ex tending by the circumference, like a fairy ring, carrying devastation as it goes, and destroying the hair completely. If it remain unchecked, it will destroy the whole of the hair of the scalp, and give rise to deep-seated disease, with enlargement and disease of the glands of the neck.

It is not the least curious part of the history of this complaint, that when the yellow paste of the crusts is examined with the microscope, it is found to be composed of numberless cells, connected together in such a way as to suggest the idea of a vegetable formation of the lowest type. Many of the cells are so arranged as to give the idea of stems from which branches pass off; and at the ends of the branches are smaller bodies, that have the character of seeds.

PROPERTIES OF THE HAIR.

Among the most remarkable properties of the hair, we may take notice of the manner in which it is affected by damp air, which, by relaxing its substance, increases its length. It is on that account, that hairs are used for the construction of the best hygrometers. Nor must we omit either the readiness with which they grow and are reproduced, even after being plucked out by the roots, as they may often be seen after the cure of scald-head, by a painful method: nor their insulating property with respect to electricity, of which they are very bad conductors; a remarkable property viewed with reference to the conjectured nature of the nervous principle. The hairs possess no power of spontaneous motion by which they can rise on the head, when the soul shudders with horror or fear; but they do bristle at those times by the contraction of the superficial muscle, which, from its intimate adherence to the scalp, carries it along in all its motions.

The hairs appear totally without sensibility; nevertheless, the passions have over them such influence, that the heads of young people have turned white the night before execution. In this premature hoariness, is the hair, it may be asked, dried up as in old people, when it seems to die for want of moisture and its natural juices?

The following fact seems to show, that they are the excretory organ of some principle, the retention which might be of very injurious consequences A Chartreux, who every month had his head shaved according to the rule of his order, quitting his monastery at its destruction, went into the army, and let his hair grow. After a few months, he was attacked with excruciating head-aches, which nothing relieved. At last, some one advised him to resume his old habit, and to have his head frequently shaved; the head-aches went off and never returned.

We know, says M. Grimaud, that there are nervous head-aches, which give way to frequent cropping the hair:—When it is kept close cut, the more active growth that takes place, sets in motion the stagnating juices. A friend of Malsalva, as Morgagni relates, dispelled a maniacal affection, by having the head of the patient shaved.

The hairs partake of the inalterability, the almost indestructibility, we might say, of the scarf-skin. Like it they burn with a whizzing noise, and give out an abundance of fœtid volatile oil. The ashes that remain from burning them, contain much phosphate of lime. The horns of quadrupeds, and the feathers of birds, give out the same smell in burning, and yield the same products as the hair on the head and other parts, which has led to the saying that these last were a kind of horny substance, drawn out like wire. Acids, but especially alkalies, dissolve the hair; accordingly, all nations that cut the beard, first soften it by rubbing it with alkaline and soapy solutions.

HAIRY MOLES.

We are in a great measure still ignorant of the nature of those brown and tawny marks on the skin, well known by the name of moles, which, though they often serve to set off the complexion by contrast, or by fixing the eye on a particular spot, and withdrawing it, in consequence, from the general view of the features, yet, when they happen, as is frequently the case, to be covered with hair, they are always unsightly and disagreeable; but, in such circumstances, it requires the greatest caution in attempting to remove this hair that grows from moles, for it may lead to consequences full of danger. In more early life there is perhaps less to be feared; but after the age of thirty or thirty-five, at which period cancer is usually developed in the constitution, we should caution you most strongly not to touch a hairy mole with any sort of depilatory. The least fretting or irritation of a mole, indeed, is apt to develope bad sores, if not a confirmed cancer. The reader will agree then with us, that it is better to have a mole, though it be unsightly and covered with hair, than to run the hazard of a foul and probably an incurable sore, or a dangerous and painful cancer. The very idea, we should think, of such an occurrence, would prevent most people from venturing to tamper with depilatory preparations, and particularly those whose composition is kept secret, while their effects are puffed off as little short of miraculous.

COLOUR OF THE HAIR.

In our anatomical sketches of the hair, we have already taken some notice of the natural varieties in the colour of the hair; but, in a work like the present, it will be expected that we should consider these a little more minutely. The colour of the hair varies considerably, according to the different coun tries, latitudes, climates, temperature, &c. This colour even, as well as that of the skin, forms one of the characteristic attributes of the different human races. In our climate, the principal colours of hair are black, light, and red: these are, as it were, three general types, to which are referred an infinitude of other shades. Around the black, the brown, auburn, &c., rally: the light include on the one part the fiery red, and every intermediate shade on the other, down to the light chestnut hair. The fiery red, linked with light-coloured hair by one of its shades, represents, in the reverse one, the colour natural to peculiar plumes.

All authors have laid down the colour of hair as a characteristic mark of the temperament. Black hair is the emblem of strength and vigour. An athletic figure with light hair would appear an object of ridicule. This last shade is the attribute of weakness and indolence. Painters have given it to figures that are not expressive of strong passions, or of great and heroic actions. In voluptuous paintings of the graces, beauty, &c., by adorning the head of youth this ornament, as it were, animates th canvass. The black and light varieties, including their respective shades, are met with in both sexes in nearly equal proportions. But let us only reflect a moment upon the impressions we receive from the fair sex, as far as relates to the shades allotted to the individual, abstractedly from every other consi deration, and we shall find that the female, adorned with light hair, forcibly impresses upon us a sense of beauty, united to weakness,—an irresistible appeal for protection : the very word even by which this subject is described, is expressive of this double attribute. The phrase of "brune piquante," black-eyed maid, on the contrary, forcibly conveys an idea of strength and beauty united. Beauty, then, is an attracting gift, which females enjoy in common, but which, being variously modified by exterior form, entices and attracts either by interesting our feelings, or by exciting them, &c. Languid eyes are frequently associated with light hair; whilst the black is generally the appendage of a sparkling eye, and vivacity ready to break loose from its bounds.

Custom, which influences every thing, changes our taste for the colour of the hair as for that of dress. The black, the light, and their numerous shades, prevail in turn ; and as organization cannot so very readily accommodate our fancy, artificial head-dresses have been resorted to ; an ingenious invention undoubtedly, calculated to bend to our whim the invariable course of nature, and which, by altering at will that expression which physiognomy borrows from the hair, the wearer may, in the course of two minutes, appear in the height of fashion to-day, and perfectly ridiculous to-morrow.

Amidst all those changes, so rapid in respect to hair, the deep red variety, and its different shades, are seldom admitted. Though at one time it was fashionable at Rome, and also for a short time at Paris, a century or two ago, many people express an unequivocal aversion to this colour. We almost consider it a malformation. This opinion is too generally extended not to be supported on some solid ground. The most essential appears to us the common consent existing between this hair and the constitution and consequently the nature of the temper resulting from it. Now the temper associated with that colour of hair, is not commonly the most eligible, in spite of the numerous exceptions recorded by proverbs. Another motive of objecting to this fiery colour, is, that the oily substances with which they are lubricated, often exhale an offensive smell, which the other colours do not possess. What connexion can possibly be between the hair and dispositions of individuals? Is the latter ever influenced by the former? Never. It may be explained as follows:—Every individual is possessed of his own peculiar mode of organization and constitution. From this mode the temper results; but to each mode is attached, on the one part, such and such species of hair; on the other, the predominance of such and such internal viscera, which, though less striking, is still real. The predominance evidently establishes a particular tendency to certain passions, which form the essential attributes of the temper; then the colour of the hair and this are two different results, proceeding from the very same cause, namely, from the constitution; but the one is never influenced by the other.

CAUSES OF THE COLOUR OF THE HAIR.

There can be no doubt that the colouring matter of the hair is of the same nature, though it is doubtful whether it arises from the layer of the skin, which we have called the membrane of colour. Whatever causes, therefore, tend to affect this membrane, must produce a change on the colour of the hair. We have more than once particularly remarked that the colour of the hair corresponds in a remarkable manner with the colour of the eyes, and more particularly, as Mr. John Hunter observed, with the colour of the eye-lashes. In horses, however, though the colour be various, the eyes are always the same; but then the hair is always the same at birth; and the skin does not participate in its subsequent changes, being as dark in white as in black horses. In cream-coloured horses, indeed, there is an exception, the eyes agreeing in colour with the hair, but then the foals are originally cream-coloured, as well as the entire skin.

From this close connection of the colouring principle of the skin, the eyes, and the hair, we almost always find light hair accompanying a white and thin skin, and black hair accompanying a dark thick skin. If again the skin, as is sometimes the case, happens to be variegated, the hair partakes of the same character. Blumenbach gives an example of an entire tribe of Tartars who were thus piebald, and it seems to be no uncommon occurrence among Negroes. When the skin is much marked by reddish freckles also, the hair is red; and, with the milk-white skin of the Albino, the hair is found of a peculiar yellowish tint. When the hair is light, the eyes are generally blue; when dark, they are brownish black; when the hair loses the light shade of infancy, the eyes likewise grow darker; and when the hair turns grey, in advanced life, the eyes lose much of their former colour. The Albino has no more colouring matter in his eyes than in his skin, and hence it is that the blood appears in them and tinges them red.

Animals have a well-known tendency to produce offspring like themselves, and this is remarkably exemplified in what has just been illustrated respecting the natural varieties of the hair. This tendency, however, may frequently be interrupted by accidental circumstances, and peculiarities, unknown to the parent, be produced. By selecting such examples, a breed, peculiar in colour and other circumstances, may be generated. Thus, by killing all the black individuals which appear among our domestic animals, and breeding only from the white, the former will soon be banished. It is thus that hornless cows have been propagated, and a generation of white mice, and, if we may use the expression, of white blackbirds (Turda merula, LINNEUS) have been produced. Sheep are generally white, because white wool is most in demand; but in remote parts, where coloured wool is used for domestic manufacture, black and speckled sheep are not uncommon. A gentleman of Dr. Anderson's acquaintance once propagated a breed of rabbits with only one ear; and Professor Coventry of Edinburgh had a female cat, which, having lost its tail when young, always produced kittens which wanted the tail in whole or in part. Dr. Anderson once procured a tailless cock, which gave origin, on the same principle, to a curious breed of fowls, some of which had no tail, others only a single feather, or perhaps two or three. Another instance, no less singular, is mentioned in the Annals of Philosophy: a ram, accidentally produced on a farm in Connecticut, with elbow-shaped fore-legs, and a great shortness and weakness of the joints, was selected for propagation; and a breed, which is unable to climb over fences, has thus been established! Some breeds of horses are mentioned by authors which have horns like the roe-buck.

In a wild state, however, animals very rarely have any diversity of colour from their species, because no motive exists for propagating any peculiar breed

In this country, the uniformity of colour is so stedfast among the wild bisons, that the Indians look upon every deviation from the usual colour as of Divine origin. We are told in James's Expedition to the Rocky Mountains, that Mr. J. Doherty saw in an Indian hut the head of a bison with a white star on the front. The owner would not part with it at any price; called it his great medicine, and said the herds came annually to seek their companion. If this white-faced bison had been produced in a domestic state, and another been found to pair with it, the race might have been propagated to perpetuity.

From many of the facts already adduced, it is evident that many peculiarities of colour in the hair arise in the various races of men, and even in the same family. We are told, for example, in the Philosophical Transactions, on credible authority, of a black family, which lived where Europeans had never approached, and yet from time to time produced a white child; and the woman, fearing her husband's resentment, endeavoured to conceal it from him. The man, however, insisted upon seeing the infant; and, finding it white, said, "I love it better for that, because my own father was a white man, though my grandfather and grandmother were as black as you and myself; and although we come from a place where no white people are ever seen, yet there was always a white child in every family related to us."

The intensity of light is undoubtedly one cause

that affects the colour, and heat the texture and growth of the hair; but these changes are no more transmitted to the offspring than such as are induced by mechanical means. The child of the most sun-burnt rustic is born equally fair with other children; even all the children among the Moors are born White, and acquire the brown cast of their fathers only if exposed to the sun. The ancients, indeed, believed that all dark-coloured nations are the inhabitants of hot climates; but modern discovery has made us acquainted with light-coloured nations inhabiting the warmest regions, with dark nations inhabiting the coldest countries, and with others of various shades of colour living together in the same climate. Do we not, in fact, behold, says M. Virey, the tawny Hungarian dwelling for ages under the same parallel, and in the same country, with the whitest nations of Europe, and the red Peruvian, the brown Malay, the nearly white Abyssinian, in the very zones which the blackest people in the universe inhabit? The natives of Van Diemen's Land are black, while the Europeans of the corresponding northern latitudes are white; and the Malabars, in the most burning climate, are no browner than the Siberians in the coldest. The Dutch, who have resided more than two centuries at the Cape of Good Hope, have not acquired the sooty colour of the native Hottentots; and the Guebres and Persians, marrying only among themselves, remain white in the midst of the olive-coloured Hindoos.

The effects of civilization are more remarkable and decided than could well be conceived to influence the hair; but as the whole external appearance and system of the constitution is thus changed, it ceases to be a matter of wonder.

The Jews settled in the neighbourhood of Cochin are divided in two classes, called the Jerusalem or white Jews, and the ancient or black Jews. The white Jews look upon the black Jews as an inferior race, and not as a pure cast: the white race appear to have resided there upwards of seventeen hundred years. A race of fair people are described by Mr. Shaw and Mr. Bruce, as residing in the neighbourhood of Mount Aurasius, in Africa. If not so fair as the English, they are a shade lighter than that of any people to the southward of Britain: their hair is red and their eyes blue. They are supposed to be descendants of the ancient Vandals.

The colours of many animals, says Dr. Darwin, seem adapted to their purposes of concealing themselves either to avoid danger or spring upon their prey. Thus the snake, and wild-cat, and leopard, are so coloured as to resemble dark leaves and their lighter interstices. Birds, again, resemble the colour of the brown ground or green hedges which they frequent, and their bellies are light-coloured like the sky, and hence less visible; moth, and butterflies are coloured like the flowers which they rob of their honey; caterpillars, which feed on leaves, are generally green; and earth-worms are of the colo-

of the earth which they inhabit. Those birds which are much among flowers, as the goldfinch and humming-bird, are furnished with vivid colours; while the lark, the partridge, and the hare, are the colour of dry vegetables, or the ground on which they rest. Frogs vary their colours with the mud of the streams which they frequent, and those which live on trees are green. Fish which are generally suspended in water, and swallows which are generally suspended in the air, have their backs the colour of the distant ground, and their bellies the colour of the sky. These colours have, however, in some instances another use, as the black diverging area from the eyes of the swan; which, as his eyes are placed less prominent than those of other birds, for the convenience of putting down his head under water, prevents the rays of light from being reflected into his eye, and thus dazzling his sight both in the air and beneath the water, which must have happened if that surface had been white. There is still a more wonderful thing concerning these colours adapted to the purpose of concealment, which is, that the eggs of birds are so coloured as to resemble the colour of the adjacent objects and their interstices. The eggs of hedge birds are greenish with dark spots; those of crows and magpies, which are seen from beneath through wicker nests, are white with dark spots; and those of larks and partridges are russet or brown, like their nests or situation.

A circumstance more to our point, and still more

astonishing, is, that in countries covered with snow, many animals, such as bears, hares, and partridges, become white in winter, and are said to change their colour again in the warmer months. The cause of all this would seem to be almost beyond conjecture; but Dr. Darwin was too indefatigable in such pursuits to be easily defeated. He accordingly imagines that the colours are derived in some degree from the eye, which is influenced by the colours most constantly painted on it. The Choroid coat of the eye, he remarks, is different in animals. In those which feed on grass, it is green, because the grass is the object most frequently looked at. When the ground, again, is covered, as it is in polar regions, for a long period with snow, this coat of the eye will be similarly affected, and in this way may influence the colour of the skin. Thus, like the Chameleon, all animals may possess a tendency to be coloured somewhat like the colours they most frequently inspect; and, in the same way, colours may be given to the egg-shell by the imagination of the female parent. This effect will not be considered surprising, when it is recollected that a single imaginary idea may, in an instant, colour the whole surface of the body of a bright red, as in the blush of shame. This may be only conjecture; but it is certain there must be some efficient cause, since the uniform production of the same colours, in the instances enumerated, shows that they cannot arise from a fortuitous occurrence of circumstances.

As this theory of Dr. Darwin does appear to be very conjectural, we would rather be disposed to conclude that the causes of the great varieties in colour are but little known; but if we turn our attention to the animal and vegetable world around us, we shall observe it springing before us in a thousand different ways, and giving rise to an infinite diversity of the nicest and most elegant cutaneous tapestry. It is indeed, as Dr. Good has remarked, to the partial secretion or distribution of this natural pigment that we are indebted for all the variegated and beautiful hues evinced by different kinds of plants and animals. It is this which gives the fine red or violet that tinges the nose and hind-quarters of some baboons, and the exquisite silver that whitens the belly of the dolphin and other cetaceous fishes. In the toes and tarsal membrane of ravens and turkeys, it is frequently black; in common hens and peacocks, gray; blue, in the titmouse; green, in the water-hen; yellow, in the eagle; orange, in the stork; and red, in the flamingo. It affords that sprightly intermixture of colours which besprinkle the skin of the frog and salamander. But it is for the gay and glittering scales of fishes, the splendid metallic shells of beetles, the gaudy eye-spots that bedrop the wings of the butterfly, and the infinitely diversified hues of the flower-garden, that Nature reserves the utmost force of this ever-varying pigment, and sports with it in her happiest caprices.

GLOSS AND CURLING OF THE HAIR.

The fine silky gloss of the hair depends on the internal pulp of it being in a healthy and abundant state, and on the natural oil being freely produced and given out. When this is unhealthy, the oil is either too abundant, in which case its superfluity produces greasy hair ; or too scanty, in which case the hair is dry and harsh, or thin and lank.

On being exposed to the heat, the hairs are but slightly contracted ; they twist in divers ways ; but this proceeds from quite a different cause of contraction in other organs. The moisture which the hair naturally contains is evaporated by heat, and the particles drawn nearer together : hence, when the hair is damped again by a fog, the bath, atmosperic air, &c., it uncurls, and becomes lank. The greasy substances these organs are imbued with on dressing the hair, provides them with a coating impermeable to water, maintains the head-dress, and prevents it from imbibing this fluid ; after it is washed the hair will sooner curl, as it has often been observed since it was the fashion to wear it short. This at first sight seems a paradox : it is not so, however. In fact, by carefully rubbing the hair the unctuous fluid it was covered with is removed or it combines with the soap suds used for that purpose : by this means it easily penetrates the hair when the pores are left free ; and afterwards by evaporating, together with the fluid it already contained, an effect that was prevented by the unctuous substance, it is drier, and therefore more disposed to curl.

A further proof that it is the external sheath of the hair that imbibes the humidity which it loses after being curled, and droops, is, that a detached portion of the scarf-skin will also curl, on being twisted with curling-tongs, and is restored again to its natural state if it be immersed in water. The extensibility and contractibility of the tissue are very obscure in hair; it is its resisting quality that prevents fracture; it hardly admits of extension.

The gloss and polish of all bodies depends, as must be obvious, on the smoothness and continuity of their surface. The nails are consequently more polished and glossy than the skin, because they are more hard and compact, and also more smooth and uniform. The hair is in the same way more glossy than the skin, from being of a harder consistence; but as there are inequalities, as we have seen, these must be either filled up, or the gloss and polish will be very much impaired. Think for a moment what causes the polish of a rose-wood or mahogany table, and you will see that the gloss of the hair must follow the same law. If you use varnish for the table, it fills up and smooths the most minute inequality of the surface. If you use oil, it does the same, provided a sufficient quantity be left unrubbed off. Water will also produce a similar effect; but as it dries up almost instantaneously, it cannot be used with advantage.

In order, therefore, to preserve the hair glossy, a substance must be found that will not evaporate readily, like water, and which will fill up all the overlappings of the imbrications described above. If the hair, then, is dry, and without gloss or lustre, substances of an oily quality must be selected to preserve it in a due state of moisture; and for this purpose a countless variety of oils and pomatums have been at different periods fashionable. Many of these are so equal in properties, as to render it a matter of indifference which of them is employed. Others contain ingredients which improve or deteriorate their qualities. These every individual can best prove by trial, as every different sort of hair will require different proportions to bring it to a gloss, and not overdo it, and make it look greasy. The greatest numbers of the hair oils are prepared by perfumers, from receipts, which are kept a secret, are vended under specious names, each trying to outvie and outsell the rest by the advertising praises lavished on the article. With these we have little to do, and shall not even mention any of them individually. All of the articles so advertised, however, it may be remarked, are very expensive; and those who have tried them will agree with us, that their qualities are most extravagantly overrated, and the promises held out are seldom fulfilled.. Instead of spending our time and space upon these advertised articles, we shall give here a few receipts for hair oils, which will be found more than a half cheaper, and no less efficient.

HUILE ANTIQUE A L'ORANGE.

With one pound of oil of behn, mix three ounces of essential oil of orange, and put it into small bottles, well corked, with wax over them, to preserve it from the air, and prevent the perfume of the orange oil from evaporating.

In the same manner you may make Huiles Antiques au Citron, a la Bergamotte, au Cedrat, au Girofle, au Thym, a la Lavande, au Rosmarin, &c. Take care, as a general rule, to proportion the quantity of the perfumed essence which you employ, to its strength.

HUILE ANTIQUE A LA ROSE.

Procure a tin or white-iron box, about a foot square, opening by a grating on one side, and divided in the middle by a portion of white iron, drilled full of small holes close to each other. Fold in four a cotton towel, soak it in oil of behn, and place it on the grating so as exactly to fit the box. Upon this cloth place your rose leaves, fresh gathered; leave them for about twenty-four hours, and then replace them with fresh rose leaves. The cloth may then be removed, and the oil, now charged with the perfume, carefully expressed. This may be mixed with fresh oil of behn, and bottled for use.

In the same manner you may make Huiles Antiques, a la Fleur d'Orange, a la Violette, a la Jonquille, au Jasmin, &c., and by means of various mixtures, a l'Heliotrope, aux Mille Fleurs, au Pot pourri, &c.

MACASSAR OIL.

Take a pound of olive oil, coloured with alkanet root, and add to it one drachm of the oil of origanum. It may be remarked that olive oil is an excellent basis for hair oil, and it is also the most economical; for a thin, stale, olive oil, will do equally well as a superior oil, because the powerful odour of the perfume takes off or destroys any disagreeable smell peculiar to stale and thin olive oil. When you have mixed your perfume with it, you must shake the bottle in which it is contained, twice a day, for at least one week.

Another way of giving the hair a beautiful gloss, is, by means of soap, which, in the case of hair that is apt to be greasy, is better than any sort of oil, as it moistens without matting it, as oil in those cases usually does; that is, if it is not put on in too great quantity.

WASHING THE HAIR.

When the hair becomes greasy and dirty, it ought to be washed with warm (not too warm) soft water and soap; an operation which is very requisite when pomatums and hair oils are much used, as they are apt to combine with the scales which are always coming off from the skin, and form a thick crust very detrimental to the gloss and beauty of the hair.

Some authors, however, strongly disapprove of washing the hair at all, and muster up, we know not how many, evil consequences as likely to follow the practice. One would imagine, from the tone of some of these philippics, that all the disorders incident to the head were more or less caused by washing the hair.

M. Arago, in his late voyage round the world, remarks that the South Sea Islanders, who have fine long hair with a silky gloss, promote its beauty by frequently washing it. We may also add, in favour of the practice of washing the hair, the testimony of the author of the "Hygiene des Dames," who recommends this every time that a bath is taken. "My Ladies," says he, "will, perhaps, make the length of their hair an objection. I answer, that as the most beautiful hair is the most difficult to keep clean, it is precisely this sort which requires to be washed often and carefully, and the bath is the most convenient means of doing this. Besides, the finest gloss is imparted by water, provided the hair be quickly dried and immediately combed and brushed, in summer in the sun, and before the fire in winter. As to the inconveniences which might be supposed to result from leaving the head to dry, it is far from being improbable that the frequent megrim complained of by women, may be traced to a deficiency of moisture in the hair, which prevents the comb or the brush from completely detaching the scales that form there and shut up the pores of the skin through which the perspiration ought to pass."

CURLING OF THE HAIR.

If you hold a piece of paper near the fire, you will see it bend and curl up as soon as it is brought un der the influence of the heat. Why, it may be asked, does this happen? Because the moisture contained in the side nearest the fire is evaporated and passes off, leaving the parts destitute of support, and they will hence mutually approach nearer to each other, than when they were previously separated by the presence of moisture. That this is the true explanation, you may satisfy yourself by feeling the paper which has been heated, and you will always find it more compact, hard, and "dry," than before it was exposed to the heat. In a word, it has lost moisture, though no moisture may have been previously perceptible in it.

In the very same way do the curling irons act on the hair, abstracting more moisture from one side of it than from the other, and consequently causing it to bend, as we have seen in the instance of the paper. Or, independent of moisture, if the hair be weakened on one side and strengthened on another, it will certainly bend and curl; and this inequality of strength is the usual cause of the natural curling of the hair.

The stronger hair is, the more easy it is to be brought into curl, and the longer also it will remain curled; because when it is weak and lank, it appears to be more elastic than when it is stronger. Hair also which is weak and dry at the same time, which frequently happens to be the case, as well as hair which has a tendency to be greasy, will not take nor keep curling well

CURLING FLUIDS.

The liquids which are sold for the professed purpose of assisting in the curling of the hair, are chiefly composed of either oily or alkaline substances; and perhaps you will find that the essence of soap, for which we have given the receipt above, is as good as any other. Any combination of potash or hartshorn with some of the aromatic oils, will answer every purpose of the most expensive curling fluid.

Oils, if not put on too copiously, for this will destroy the effect intended, are the best preparations for keeping in the curls during moist or damp weather, or in ball-rooms or theatres, where they are exposed to moisture from perspiration and from the breath; because oil, when spread over the hair prevents it from imbibing moisture, which will infallibly cause it to lose curl.

CURLING IRONS.

The employment of hot irons to aid in curling the hair, is said to be very injurious to its growth, and Madame Voiart says, she has seen the finest hair become thin and fall off from this destructive practice "Whether it hinders the young hairs from growing,' she continues, "or dwarfs the roots of the larger hairs, it is certain that nothing has a more speedy effect in thinning them." We cannot, however, see that the irons can have any effect beyond the part of the hair which they touch; and if care be taken that they are not applied too hot, so as actually to destroy the hair, we see no material objection to their occasional use. Their daily application, we confess, notwithstanding the greatest care, will in a short time prove injurious; but the evil can only extend to the hair, which may be destroyed, and cannot in any way prevent its future growth.

PAPILLOTTES.

Madame Voiart is extremely hostile to the use of this most common means of curling the hair, as the imprisonment of the hair in papers is hurtful, she thinks, to the proper vegetation of the ringlets, which ought to decorate the forehead and temples. Nothing besides is so unseemly as the head of a young lady hedge-hogged—herissee—(we must coin a word) over with papillottes. The greater number, however, of those to whom nature has given fine silky hair are condemned, particularly on gala days, to wear this ridiculous coronal a great part of the day. When these papers shackles, which take away half the natural ornament, are of a tint harmonizing with the shade of the hair, it is a little less ungraceful; but paper of this kind is not always at hand; and, even if it were, what disagreeable marks papillottes always leave on the forehead by the pressure of the "fichu de nuit."

NATURAL GROWTH OF THE HAIR.

The luxuriance or thinness of the hair must, where there is no disease, depend on the supply of the materials which compose it, and the capability of the agents destined for their appropriation. It is plain also, from what was amply stated under the head of Anatomy of the Hair, that though many bulbs exist below the skin, which never shoot out any hairs, yet in some individuals, owing to peculiarity of constitution, or hereditary affections, these roots may be occasionally less numerous or less productive. In the case of deficiency in the number of roots, it is obvious that art can do nothing; and any pretensions or promises to make the hair thicker, when this is the cause, can only be made by designing and fraudulent empirics. It is in the power of art, however, to do much for developing and promoting the growth of these bulbs, and the hairs produced from them. Where we speak of baldness and its causes, we enter fully into all the methods of increasing the thickness of the hair by means of what may either stimulate or relax.

INJURIOUS METHODS OF DRESSING THE HAIR.

Whatever deprives the hair of its free and natural flow, and of its natural moisture, must have a tendency to check its growth, and render it thin and short. Whatever also may draw or twist it from its natural direction, will also prove injurious. For these reasons we think we are fully justified, on the clearest principles, to say, that the usual methods of curling the hair, of twisting it or plaiting it, an also of loading it with [illegible] powder, are all extremely injurious to its natural growth.

EFFECTS OF CURLING, TWISTING, AND PLAITING THE HAIR.

The hairs, on emerging from the skin, assume such a direction, that those on the anterior part of the head, almost without variation, pass obliquely forward, and tend to drop over the forehead; those of the middle, and to some extent of the posterior part, follow a perpendicular direction; and, finally, those of the remainder of the posterior and inferior part, cross obliquely, so as to produce a natural fall along the posterior part of the neck. The same remark applies to the side of the head, in which, as much from direction as from its weight, they fall over and cover the ear. When a hair is drawn out accordingly, no pain is felt except that which proceeds from the skin, which it crosses; hence, by drawing a hair in a direction opposite to its natural one, pain is more severe than by drawing it in the direction of the pores. It is not pretended to be denied that the extension by which the roots of the hairs are fixed to the adjacent parts, may not be also partly the cause of this pain; but to the effects of this we request attention.

We have seen, by Mr. Chevalier's description, that the hairs pass outwards in a very oblique direction; of course it follows, that if violently pulled out of this direction, the current of the fluid which rises in their tubes, and on which their fine color and glos depend, will be obstructed or prevented. Now, thi is what we complain of in the case of curling particularly when papillotes are used, and still more when the hair is twisted, as it often is, into a hard knot or bow on the top of the head, or plaited in a fanciful manner, or even when parted and bound with a ribbon or fillet. We do not mean, by these remarks, to say that the hair ought never to be so dressed. We have no wish to oppose our authority to that of taste or fashion; but we feel it to be our duty to mention the probable effects, that, when any thinning of the hair is observed to occur, it may be the better accounted for, and its progress checked Where it is not drawn tight from the skin, but left rather loose and easy, no injury can follow: it is only when it is prevented from allowing a free current to the juices which nourish it, that we can blame the modes of dressing under review.

ADVANTAGEOUS MODES OF DRESSING THE HAIR.

Having thus shown the principles which influence the growth of the hair, and the injurious methods that are frequently employed for the purposes of dress or decoration, we must next advert, as parti cularly as our space will allow, to the modes of dressing which are favorable to its growth, and which tend to promote its luxuriance. As in the former case, we shall limit our observations to a few of the more common and simple operations on the hair, such as combing, brushing, and cutting.

EFFECTS OF COMBING AND BRUSHING THE HAIR

You will at once perceive the utility of combing and brushing the hair, if you reflect for a moment on its structure; for, as curling or twisting it prevents the nourishing fluids from getting a free passage from the bulb through the tube, so must every operation which makes the hair straight promote this passage. Unless, therefore, the hair is frequently combed or brushed, its growth, particularly if it is long, will be much retarded. When the hair is very long, and twisted up into a hard knot on the top of the head, as it is frequently the fashion to wear it, the current of the fluids along the tubes must be obstructed; and the obvious remedy for this, as it cannot, in opposition to fashion, be given up, is frequent combing and brushing it out in its whole length. Not only, indeed, is the fluid obstructed in its ascent from the bulb, by the twisting or curling, but, in consequence of its imbricated structure, it is apt to get entangled and matted, so as very much to increase this injurious effect, and frequent combing becomes indispensible. A little of any of the oils already recommended, used at the time of combing and brushing, will generally be useful.

The practice of dipping the comb in water in which a few drops of Eau de Cologne have been put, is very beneficial, particularly if care be taken not to moisten the roots of the hair, as this has been found not to agree with certain individuals.

The hair must be brushed, with a rather hard brush, dipped by the surface only in a mixture of water and some mild spirit, such es Eau de Portugal or Cologne. It is to be afterwards combed with a comb rather fine, but not so fine as to injure the skin of the head. The brush, again dipped in the Eau de Cologne, is to be used, if the hair be naturally greasy; but if dry, then some pommade will be preferable.

EFFECTS OF CUTTING THE HAIR.

It must be obvious, from what we have already said, that if the hair is kept short, the fluid will not be so liable to be prevented from rising in the tubes, as in long hair, which cannot well be kept always straight. Fine flowing tresses, though, are the most attractive ornament of female beauty, and we cannot too strongly deprecate any fashion which would proscribe them.

The hair of children should be kept short till after eight or nine years old; as the cooler the head can be kept, the less danger there is of many maladies belonging to that part, especially water on the brain. When the production of the four double teeth is attended with much inflammation, (as sometimes happens,) it is not improbable that this may occasion the developement of that fatal disease; and whatever diminishes the heat of the head is likely to be advantageous. Besides, there is reason to suppose that children who have a great quantity of hair, are those most liable to eruptions on the head, and certainly in them these eruptions are the most difficult to cure. The trouble, also, of keeping long hair sufficiently clean, and the length of time neces sary for this purpose, is often a cause of much ill humour, and many cross words, which would be better avoided, between children and their attendants

Mothers, whose vanity may be alarmed, lest constantly cutting the hair for so many years should make that of their daughters coarse, may be assured they have no cause for this apprehension, if the hair be kept constantly brushed. I have never seen softer, finer hair, than on girls who have had it short (like that of school-boys) until they were in their tenth year. When there is any inclination to "break out" in the head, fine combs are very likely to promote it; and there is no doubt that the heads of children, which are never touched by them, are much cleaner than those which are scratched and scraped every day. If any dirt appear on a child's head, which a brush will not take away, that particular part should be rubbed with a towel, and soap and water; but in general the brush will be found quite sufficient to keep it perfectly clean. The more the head is combed, the more it will require to be combed, as one will find it who tries the experiment. It must be allowed, however, that there are many exceptions to this as to every other rule.

It is an imprudent act of cleanliness to remove all at once the scurf which sometimes gathers on the head, and even spreads over the foreheads of young infants; and this is, probably, one of the reasons why we often see the children of persons in easy circumstances tormented just after their birth with that troublesome stuffing in the head, which is, in some places, vulgarly called the snuffles. When the infant is somewhat inured to the external air, at two months old or later, (according to the season of the year,) whatever scurf adheres so firmly to the head as not to come off in washing, may be safely and effectually removed, by rubbing a little butter on a small part of the head one day, and cleaning it with a box comb the next, before it is washed; then a little more butter should be rubbed on another part of the head, which should be cleansed in the same manner the day after; and in thus removing the scurf by degrees, the head becomes clean in a very short time, without any danger of cold. In many places, the lower class have a prejudice against removing the scurf from children's heads at all, waiting till it comes off of itself; but this is also an error, and leads to many of the bad consequences of dirt, as they neglect to wash the head, which should be done every day, as long as the scurf is suffered to remain. When the head is once perfectly clean, the best means of preserving it in that state is by a brush, which should be changed from time to time for one harder. The seldomer a fine comb is applied to the head of an infant the better; and on no account should those of ivory, tortoise-shell, or bone, be ever used; for, even when they do not wound the skin and produce a sore, (as frequently happens,) they are very likely to augment the production of that substance they are intended to remove.

In some rare cases, cutting the hair has very singular effects upon the head. In certain individuals it does harm, in others it is advantageous. When the hair is profuse and thick, thinning it or cutting it short, has been known to cure obstinate head-aches; and, strange to say, the same thing has been strongly suspected to be one cause of head-aches.

DECAY OF THE HAIR.

The hair, as we have seen, is composed of a root and a hollow joint stem, into which a colouring oil rises. From these facts we can deduce a very rational account of the causes of grey hair; and it is a medical maxim, to which there are few exceptions, that a disease seldom can be cured without knowing its cause. If, therefore, we can give you a satisfactory account of the causes of grey hairs and baldness, we put you in half possession of their remedies, even though we go no farther, or, at the very least, show why no remedy need be tried.

CAUSES OF GREY HAIR.

It is supposed by Dr. Darwin and others, that the bright white reflected from the winter snow, is the cause of the animals in the high northern latitudes, becoming white in winter. His opinion on the subject seems to have been derived from the chameleon, which is said to take the color of every thing at which it looks. If it looks on a grass field, it becomes green.

if at the sky, it becomes blue ; if it look at snow, it becomes white. He maintained accordingly, that it was the action of the white snow upon their eyes which turned all the polar animals white in winter ; and for a similar reason he would infer that the larks are grey, because they frequent sandy fields ; and canaries yellow, because they are reared in brass-wire cages. He forgets to inform us how our cattle and our sheep escape being green, or how a painter escapes having his face variegated with all the colours of the rainbow.

On the contrary, we are strongly inclined to believe that the winter white colour of the polar animals is mainly to be attributed to the cold. For if you can so contract, by any means, the skin at the root of the hair, as to compress the tube and prevent the coloured oil from rising, there will only remain the dry body of the hair, and it will of course be white.

Such a contraction of the skin may be produced by cold, by grief or fear, and by fever and other diseases ; and the skin, independent of the hair, will assume a similar appearance to a fowl stript of his feathers. Every body has heard instances of the hair, by grief or fear, being turned white ; for

> Deadly fear can time out-go,
> And blanch at once the hair.
>
> MARMION.

Our principle gives a clear explanation why the hair becomes grey in old age, as at this period the skin, like the bones, shrinks and contracts for want of moisture; and the same effect will follow in the young, from any cause that will make the skin shrink and contract so as to strangle the hair at its roots, and prevent the coloured oil from rising in its tube. The same principle will show you the utter inefficiency of most of the advertised remedies and preventives of this; as, unless they be directed to the removal or prevention of the cause, it is quite impossible that they can be successful.

Grey hair is, therefore, usually a mark of shrunk or contracted skin, whether it be the effect of external causes, such as cold; or internal causes, such as grief, fever, head-ache, or too much business; and whether it occur in manhood or in old age.

There is another cause of grey hair, worthy of mentioning, as of extensive influence, namely the superabundance of lime in the body. The bones are known to be chiefly composed of lime, jelly, and oil, but the lime often predominates so much that the bones are rendered extremely brittle; and often, also, bones are formed in the heart, the brain, &c., where they produce serious trouble. The brittleness of the bones is sometimes so great, that a fit of coughing will break them.

Now this superabundance of lime in the body is caused by every sort of intemperance and external indulgence, in a word, by whatever robs the body of its juices. It is consequently the usual attendant of old age, when the juices fail. When it does ocear, the tubes of the hair at the roots seem to be obstructed by this lime; the colouring oil cannot of course get into the stem of the hair, and it becomes grey, dry. The same thing has been known to follow small-pox or scrofula, which may therefore be also a cause of grey hair.

There is another cause of gray hair, which is worth explaining. The hair in a healthy state is semi-transparent, and partly varies its colour according to the light in which it is viewed. It may also be observed, that the darker the hair is, it will be the more thick, strong, and transparent. On the same principle, a very thick transparent piece of ice, or a thick piece of glass, appears almost black. A diamond, when finely polished, always appears in the centre of a deep black, because all the rays of light pass through it, and none can therefore be returned to the eye. All these substances, however, become white whenever you destroy their transparency; as you can prove, by scraping the piece of ice on the surface, or preparing the glass as it is done for sinumbra lamps. In the same way you will find that all white hair is opaque, and does not permit the light to penetrate it; because, we say, the colouring matter, which also makes it transparent, is prevented from rising, in consequence of the strangling of the root by the shrunk skin.

PREVENTIVES OF GREY HAIR..

If you would avoid this prominent mark of approaching old age, you must avoid all the causes of it which we have now pointed out, as constricting the skin, and strangling the hair at its roots, as well as whatever may throw into the blood an undue portion of lime. We say an "undue" portion, for a certain quantity of lime is indispensible in our system for repairing the wear and tear of the bones, the teeth, &c. The lime necessary for the repair of bone is manufactured by the stomach and liver, along with the blood, from various articles of our diet which contain it. The greatest supply is usually from the water which we drink, or which is employed in the various processes of cooking and preparing of liquors. All animal food, also, contains some portion of lime, as well as some of the sorts of vegetable food. Ascertain then by chemical trial, whether the WATER used for your tea, coffee, soups, &c., contains a large proportion of lime, and, if it does, you must either have it chemically purified, or remove to some other place where the water is more free from lime. If the water is hard, you may be certain, without farther trial, that it contains too much lime to be safely used by the gouty; nor is it safe indeed for the most healthy to use much hard water. Every grey hair will be the least of the evils which it has every chance to occasion. Pump water is, therefore, always bad, except in rarer instances, when it is soft. Rain water which has not come in contact with lime during its fall, is the safest for tea and other liquids.

Bread will always contain a portion of lime, derived both from the wheat, which naturally contains it, and also from the water used to mix the flour, but it is also well known, that both the millers and the bakers are in the habit of improving the colour and increasing the weight of flour by mixing it with whiting, which is a preparation of lime. Nothing can be worse than bread of this description; and it will be advisable to ascertain carefully, whether your bread or your flour is so adulterated. It is of more importance to have the flour examined, because it is the common popular opinion that all the bread adulterations are made by the bakers; and when bread is made at home, all suspicions of fraudulent mixture are lulled. The truth is, however, that the miller is much oftener culpable of such frauds than the baker: and therefore, even home-made bread is not safe unless you are certain what sort of flour you employ. Lime is also much employed in the refining of wines, the manufacture of sugar and other articles of diet, and it is scarcely possible that no portion of it should remain in the goods when brought to market.

REMEDIES FOR GREY HAIR.

We are not aware that it has ever been attempted to cure grey hair, by restoring the functions of the skin to youthful freshness and pliancy; though, from what we have already stated, it would appear that such a cure may be within the limits of possibillity. But it can only be tried under skilful medical direction, and few perhaps would willingly subject themselves to any regimen that might be point ed out for the mere purpose of giving their hair a more youthful shade of colour, as this can be more expeditiously done by some of the advertised hair dyes. It is worthy of remark, however, that by the regimen to which we allude, not only the hair would be benefited, but the whole body would, in some degree, experience renovation and improvement. It would lead us too far from our subject, and take up too much room, to detail this plan so as to make it practically useful.

CAUSES OF BALDNESS.

The more remote causes of baldness are as numerous as those which influence bodily health, and tend to accelerate the advance of old age; but the more immediate causes, or rather the consequences of the remote causes, may be reduced to three, which we shall now consider in their order.

1.—CONTRACTION OF THE SKIN.

Since the superabundance of lime in the body is one main cause of grey hair, as we have just seen, of which the reader may convince himself by observing the early grey hair of people who live in a limestone or chalk district, or where the water is peculiarly hard, so is the constriction of the pores of the skin one of the chief causes of baldness. What the surgeons call "cutis anserina," which means 'goose skin,' from its resembling the skin of a lucked goose, may be produced, as we have seen above, by cold, by grief, by fear, or by fever; and in this way the hairs may be partially strangled, preventing the rise of their colouring matter and of course turning them grey; or they may be cut off or snapt short on their exit from the skin, and the roots only left behind, but wholly confined and kept out of view below the skin, the consequence of which will be baldness. As, from various causes, the skin strangles or destroys the hair, the remedies which can remove this state of the skin will be the most likely to succeed in effecting a cure.

2.—RELAXATION OF THE SKIN.

We have just said that one of the chief causes of baldness is the contraction of the pores of the skin which cuts off or snaps short the hairs at their exit, and leaves only the roots behind, but wholly confined and kept out of view below the skin. It will also be necessary to remind you of the fact, that the hairs do not rise perpendicularly from their roots, but pass very obliquely, and at an acute angle, through the two outer coats of the skin, serving to bind these down to the inner coat, as if Nature had used the hairs for sewing thread, and hence the difficulty of pulling them out. On these facts, taken in conjunction with the structure of the roots of the hair, we have already shown how baldness may arise from causes which produce an unnatural contraction of the skin; and we now take up the converse of the position.

People are often heard to complain of their hair not falling off—but "coming out" in great quantities whenever it has been combed or brushed. By observing them narrowly or inquiring farther, it will be found that the complainants are of a weak or relaxed constitution, affected with indigestion, consumptive, nervous, or bilious; or that they have been weakened by intemperance or long illness. It frequently, for example, occurs among women who have had a tedious confinement in child-bed, or to robust men who have been long confined with fractured bones or other injuries. It is still more common in the weakness remaining after a severe fever, for the whole hair to fall off, or come out; and even in women, with whom baldness, if not altogether unknown, is rare, this temporary loss of the hair is common.

The cause in all those cases is very clear, though we are not aware that it has hitherto been mentioned in books. The skin, being under the influence of the whole system, is weakened in consequence of the general disorder, and, instead of maintaining its natural healthy tone and firmness, becomes relaxed and loose. The pores also become enlarged, and perspiration much more abundant; for it is almost a uniform circumstance, that those whose hair is coming out, or has come out from relaxation are prone to sweat on the least exertion or exposure to heat.

The skin, accordingly, having become relaxed

from the causes we have just mentioned, the firm interlacement of the hairs with it is partly destroyed, and they have consequently little to hold them except their own roots. Now, by pulling out a hair with the root, and examining it, you will at once see that the root can have extremely little power of retaining it, as the root is soft and pulpy, and, besides, it is naturally fixed in the softer portion of the skin, or, as some anatomists say, in the fat immediately underneath it. The firmness and tone of the outer skin being therefore relaxed and the hairs owing their chief stability to this, it is not wonderful that they should be loosened and come out.

From these plain principles, it will at once appear, that, as remedies for baldness or thin hair, arising from debility and relaxation, nothing can be more improper than the hair oil usually applied, as oil of any kind cannot fail to increase the relaxation of the skin. We wonder, indeed, how the proprietors of the expensive nostrums, puffed off with this view, have so long been able to gull the public with so barefaced a hoax, as a few trials must demonstate the truth of what we have now said. If the patient, then, is prone to perspire, particularly on the head; if there be general weakness, indigestion, nervous or bilious ailments, or other symptoms of infirm health and shattered constitution, avoid, we advise you most earnestly, all oils and greasy applications, however much lauded and puffed by those who are interested in their sale.

3.—DECAY OF THE ROOT OR BULBS.

Towards the decline of life, the hair feels the influence of the general obliteration that occurs in almost all the exterior vessels. It first ceases to be supplied with colouring matter; the internal pulp dies, the external part only remains, and the hair of the head turns gray or white; that of the beard and other parts follows. This decay, however, admits of innumerable varieties, according to the freshness or falling off in individual constitutions. In some men it is observable at the age of thirty, and in rare cases even ten years earlier; in others at forty, fifty, or sixty. A multiplicity of causes, originating from the passions and affections of the mind, diseases, food, &c., will produce this premature old age of the system, indicated by decay of the hair.

At an uncertain period, after the hair has become white, it falls off; then the small bag, which contained the root, is obliterated by degrees, and finally disappears. I have examined, says M. Bichat, several bald heads minutely after death. The skin of the scalp was remarkably smooth on the internal surface, although it had been cleared of all fat and cellular substance; not one of the numerous prolongations formed by the ducts can possibly be traced, after the hair they contained has been removed. I have also, continues M. Bichat, dissected a subject who had become completely bald in consequence of a putrid fever. In this subject, all the bulbs were left perfectly unimpaired; and in the bottom of the bulbs, even the rudiments of new hair were already observable. There is a difference therefore between the fall of the hair in old age, and that proceeding from disease. In the former case every thing dies, because the vessels which produce the root cease to supply it with fluids; whilst in the latter case, the hair only falls, and the bulb or root remains healthy.

The different changes which the hair, the skin, and all the exterior organs of the body undergo by age, proceed entirely from the laws that overrule nourishment, and not from the action of exterior bodies upon these organs. This forms an important distinction between organic bodies and those that are inorganic. The latter have two different ways of wasting, by the contact of exterior things: one mechanical, by rubbing, tearing, &c.; and another chemical, by combining with substances, such, for instance, as air, the divers principles of which admit of being combined in a thousand different ways, whence both its nature, and that of the different forms it comes in contact with, are changed. All inorganic bodies grow old, in this sense of the word. After a certain time they lose their former appearance. Let us only observe our public buildings stuffs of every description, paintings, engravings, grounds, metals, stones, &c., every thing, in short, which in the arts, manufactures, commerce, sciences, and necessaries of life, are composed of inert substances, whether these substances have never been animated, or, having enjoyed life, could not exist without it, as the solid parts of the vegetable creation, the bones, horns, as well as the hair of animals, &c.; every thing in nature, in short, must ultimately bear the marks of the rude hand of time. Every thing grows superannuated—is stripped of its original lively appearance. Every thing outwardly decays as well as inert organized bodies; but, as the surrounding forms only have acted in respect to the former, the inward part has still retained its youth, when the interior is already old, if we may be allowed such expressions. Thus, we find that the massy rock, the exterior of which, blackened by time, still retains inwardly the appearance it was possessed of in the very early days of the creation: internal organs, on the contrary, both in animals and vegetables, will decay in the progress of time. Age stamps the internal as well as the external organs with marks of decay. Surrounding bodies act effectually upon us: they actually impair life, as it were; but they act as stimulants, by exhausting sensibility and contractibility, and not by combining from mechanical contact and friction. The tongue is sufficient to make this distinction obvious. At the sight of a new building, a new dress, of a landscape newly painted, the expression of youth is never used. Why then do we say, an old building an old stuff, &c.? These expressions may pass as metaphors, but they cannot possibly express a state similar by its nature to that of an old animal, or an old plant.

MARK OF CURABLE BALDNESS.

One of the most usual causes of baldness being as we have seen, a hardening or acquired insensibility and thickening of the skin, whatever can be found to remove this affection will most certainly make the hair grow again even on a bald part, so long as the bulbs remain vigorous and undecayed. As a mark, by which it may be ascertained whether the skin has not entirely lost its tone, we give you the following, which has been confirmed by considerable experience :—Rub the bald part smartly with the hand for a minute or so, and if it becomes easily red, there is hope for a cure ; but if it remains obstinately white and unaffected by the friction, it may be pronounced incurable. This is founded on the principle, that the more irritable the skin is, it possesses the more life, and has the greater chance to be brought back to the freshness of boyhood ; while on the other hand, the less irritable and the more dead it is, the hopes of rendering it soft, and permeable to the hair again springing from its roots, must be less sanguine.

PREVENTIVES AND REMEDIES FOR BALDNESS.

When the hair is observed to be growing thin and losing its former luxuriance, it will be proper to ascertain the cause, before any measure is resorted to, by way of prevention or remedy : for it may be perceived, from the statement which we have just given of these causes, there may be some danger of injuring, rather than benefiting the growth of the hair—the loss of which is threatened. For example, in a relaxed state of the skin, indicated by copious perspiration, or a tendency to corpulence in the system, or by nervous weakness, what could be more preposterous than oil, bear's grease, or any other relaxing application ; and yet these are the very things which are resorted to, though the only effect they can possibly have, will be to hasten the fall of the hair, by increasing the relaxation of the skin. Should the hair, therefore, be observed to come out much in combing and brushing it, then it is the time to apply for medical advice, and as I have devoted so much time to the subject, I think you can with safety entrust it to my care.

On the other hand, when there is a harsh, dry, contracted skin, and when the bulbs are beginning to decay for want of a supply of nourishment, because the small blood-vessels which carry it are, for the same reason, cramped and obstructed in their course, and the current of blood is impeded, oils may tend to relax the skin ; but there is something more required than this.

PATCAED OR PARTIAL BALDNESS.

Besides the general baldness just described, it often occurs in patches both on the scalp and beard the skin being left very white, smooth, and shining, and the rest of the hair suffering no change in colour or thickness. Sometimes this partial baldnes commences at the back part of the head, and winds in a line not exceeding the breadth of two fingers towards each ear, and occasionally towards the forehead. It is sometimes cured spontaneously, and sometimes by medicine; in which cases, when the hair begins to grow again, it is of softer texture and lighter colour than the rest. Dr. Bateman is of opinion that it has some connexion with ringworm, as it has been observed among children exposed to this infection; but as no eruption, even according to his own account, can be traced, we think his doctrine must be rejected as conjectural and unfounded.

"If the scalp," says Bateman, "is cleared by constant shaving, and at the same time some stimulant liniment be perseveringly applied to it, the bald patches may at length be remedied, and the hair be brought to its usual strength and colour. Some of the more active ointments may be employed with friction; but liniments containing an essential oil dissolved in spirit—two drachms, for example, of oil of mace in three or four ounces of spirit of wine, or prepared oil of tar, camphor, turpentine, &c., are more efficacious." We should prefer pouring cold water over the head every morning to most other things, though all applications in many cases are equally unavailable.

MISCCLOURED HAIR.

As the hair receives its colour from the same source as the colouring membrane of the skin, whatever varies from the character or colour of the one will in the same way influence the other. From this source, as may be inferred from what we have said above, the hair obtains iron and sulphur, as also the blood-red oil, which is procured by digestion from red hair, and forms a third constituent, since it does seem, from the experiments of Vauquelin, that this is a result of the iron. The greyish green oil, which this excellent chemist has been also able to extract from dark and other black kinds of hair, is another distinct principle; and, from an excess or deficiency, or a peculiar combination of the colorific constituents, we are able to account for some of the extraordinary hues which the hair is occasionally found to exhibit, though others seem to elude all explanation. The chief varieties they display are the following: hair of a blue colour, or changed from another colour to a black; or of a green colour, of which we have had very numerous examples; or spotted, like the hair of a leopard,—of this the examples are more common than of any of the preceding varieties.

Many of these singular hues are said to have followed upon some natural colour of the hair, and in some instances suddenly. This is particularly the case with the second variety; or that in which the hair has abruptly become black, which seems to have occurred as a result of fever, of exsiccation, and of terror. Schurring gives a case in which the beard, as well as the hair, was transformed from a white to a black.

We have observed above, that one of the causes of white or rather hoary hair, is a dry, shrivelled, or obstructed state of its bulbs, by which the colorific matter is no longer communicated. And it is possible that as both terror and fevers, and many other violent commotions, have sometimes proved a cure for palsy, they may occasionally produce a like sudden effect upon the minute vessels of the bulbs of the hair, remove their obstructions, or arm them with new power, and thus re-enable them to throw up into the tubes of the colourless hair the proper pigment of colour.

ON BEARDS, MUSTACHIOS, AND WHISKERS.

In most classes of animals, the male is distinguished from the female by some exterior production or other. The comb of the cock, the mane of the lion, the horns of deer, &c. are examples of these distinctive characters. In man the beard is the attribute of the male; it covers the chin, the sides of the face, the lips, and the upper part of the neck, leaving the cheeks and the surrounding parts of the eyes bare; hence those parts which serve to express passions, would be concealed by the hair if it were allowed to cover the lower part of the face. Although the hairs of the beard are generally shorter than those of the head, yet they are longer than similar productions on the body. They are usually of the same colour as the former, but somewhat darker, and have more of the red cast, which is frequently conjoined to light hair. They curl, are stronger, and are more resistant, and invariably less oily than those of the head. The fullness of the beard varies very considerably in different individuals. Strength and power, in general, are the properties of those in whom it abounds, and assumes a deep black. It may also be remarked, that, in different species of animals, the strongest males are those in which the exterior production, by which they are distinguished from the females, is most perfect. This characteristic may be said to indicate the energy or weakness of the constitution. A small lion is never seen with a large mane: large horns always belong to a fine deer; long and strongly twisted ones to a well built ram. The same observation is not applicable to the other hairs common to both sexes: those of the arms, &c. are often quite as large, and even more numerous, in a weak than muscular person.

The habit of shaving, as in most parts of Europe and America: of wearing the beard long, as in Asia; of plaiting it as in China, gives to the face various expressions, by which each nation is characterised. A manly and characteristic physiognomy, expressive of powers and energy, cannot be deprived of this exterior covering without losing a part of that character. That of the eastern nations coincides with their natural vigour, and forms a contrast with the effeminacy of their habits. We are rather inclined to think, that, on perusing the history of the people of different nations that suffer their beard to grow, and of those who are in the habit of shaving it off, we should be induced to believe that the muscular power is in some degree connected with it, and that part of the power is in some measure lost by the habit of shaving. Every body knows how very powerful the ancients were; how strong were the nations that wore long beards; how very strong, again, were an order of monks, who, by some monastic law, were compelled to wear long beards. A multiplicity of causes may certainly connect weakness with the beard; but, in a general point of view, we believe that some connections may be admitted between the powers and the beard. Deprive the cock of its comb, which, in respect to this part of the feathered creation, is the attribute of the male, as the beard is that of man, and he becomes in some degree more languid. We are convinced that the lion would lose part of his strength if he were deprived of his mane. The results of the experiments tried by Russell on the castration of deer are sufficiently known; after this operation, their horns either grow in an irregular manner, or cease to shoot forth. This exterior attribute of the male in this species manifests itself towards the period of virility, when the powers increase. The same observation applies to the human beard. This single coincidence would be sufficient to prove that the latter was intended as an exterior character of the masculine sex. Eunuchs remarkable for a weakness of powers, frequently lose part of their beard.

PRINCIPLES OF SHAVING.

The first thing necessary to be done, in order to render the hair of the beard easy to be cut, is to make it hard, crisp, and brittle; for you may as well think of cutting moist paper smoothly with a pair of scissors, as of shaving your beard while the hair is soft and oily. But it is the chemical nature of all hair to be more or less oily, as oil forms one of its main ingredients, which is readily seen on burning it, and this is farther augmented by the greasy secretions from the skin. Were you to shave dry, or with plain water, therefore, the razor would either slip over the soft, oily hair, without cutting it it at all, or would only enter it about half way, and, instead of cutting directly through it, would bend the hair and slice it in the length, and in this manner, dragging it outwards from the root, would cause a similar pain to that of pulling off the skin. When the razor is thus employed in slicing and pulling two or three hundred hairs at once, the operation must have all the characters of literally flaying alive. The longer the beard has been suffered to grow, the longer, of course, will be the slice of the hair, and the greater the pain. It is upon this principle, indeed, that the whole science of easy shaving is founded.

The best means hitherto discovered for rendering

the beard crisp and brittle, without injury to the skin, is the application of an alkali, which combines with the oil of the hair, and leaves only its hard fibre. Alkalies, however, in order to be fitted for shaving, must first be combined with some sort of oil, such as olive oil, otherwise they would be too strong, and would injure the skin. About 60 parts of soda, 60 of olive oil, and 30 of water, is the composition of the best spanish soap.

INCONVENIENCES FROM SHAVING.

It requires some care, when the face is irritable, to shave without inconvenience.—A patient of Mr. Earle's of St. Bartholomew's Hospital, cut himself while shaving, and probably he had divided obliquely some of the hairs near the roots, which continued to grow : but not finding a proper passage through the skin, they coiled up beneath it, and formed several very painful pimples, that put on a very angry ulcerated appearance, and, unless Mr. Earle had carefully extracted tne roots of the hairs, they might have ended in a fatal cancer. He says that many such cases arise from the irritation of shaving, and the patients usually refer to a slight cut, or scratch, from a blunt or a foul razor. A wound thus made, is irritated and aggravated every time the patient shaves ; or, if not, the hair being allowed to grow, gets matted together, and prevents the application of proper remedies. He properly directs the hair to be cut close by small cornea scissors ; and if the wound does not improve, but continues foul and spreading, to cut out all the diseased parts with the knife, or burn it out with caustic, as a little pain at first is better than running the danger of an incurable cancer. The older the patient is, the more is the danger, as cancer seldom attacks the young. There is greater chance of danger if a wart or a mole has been cut or scratched. We request our readers not to treat such as if it were a light or trifling matter; for it may end in a loathsome disease, and a painful death.

ON THE EYE-BROWS AND EYE-LASHES.

THE EYEBROWS.

Part of the soul, if we believe the elder Pliny, resides in the eyebrows; but though we may be sceptical in this, we must agree with Lavater that they always give the tone of the expression of the face, and are the least equivocal interpreters of the feelings: though pride have its birth in the heart, it always takes its seat on the eye-brows. In women, the eye-brows, from being more soft and delicate, are more easily moved than in men; and hence they have for the most part a stronger expression, and, according to the German poet Herder, may become the seat of serenity and chagrin; of intelligence or stupidity; of sweetness or discord: the iris of peace, or the bended bow of war; the test of dislike, or the sign of affection. Since the eye-brows, therefore form so important a feature of the countenance, they will require careful attention to improve and preserve their beauty.

The reader may have remarked that the eye-brows are commonly of a darker shade than the hair of the head, a circumstance more remarkable in those who have light-coloured hair. A good hint may thence be derived for improving both their beauty and usefulness without betraying the artificial means employed. We mean, that as it is natural for the eye-brows to be a shade darker than the hair, a slight additional artificial tinge will not be readily detected, while it will give a tone of character to the forehead that must be deficient where the eye-brows are light. Very light eye-brows indeed impart to the countenance a sort of babyish vacany and simpletonism, which must always detract from the influence of the most beautiful features or the finest eyes. In light eye-brows also the hair is usually less in quantity than in the dark, which is another reason for adding to their colour by artificial means. For this purpose we recommend the following wash for darkening the eyebrows: Dissolve in one ounce of distilled water, one drachm of sulphate of iron, add one ounce of gum-water, a tea-spoonful of Eau de Cologne. Mix, and after having wetted the eye-brows with the tincture of galls, apply the wash with a camel hair pencil.

Though, however, it is indispensable to beauty t have the eye-brows of a dark colour, and also a protection to the sight, as they are the natural shade of the eye; yet, when they become larger and shaggy, it gives a look of vulgarity, and is also a mark of old age; we must request you to attend to this, and, if the hair grow too long and thick, to keep it down with the scissors. If this be not sufficient, some of the longest hairs may be removed by the tweezers. The same means may be tried, and are much better and safer than any depilatory, to diminish the extent of the eye-brows and prevent them from spreading. We have a very different taste in this respect from the ancient Romans, who considered it indispensable in a beauty to have her eye-brows meet, what is in Scotland called LUCKEN BROWED, from a notion that the person whose eye-brows are so formed is or should be LUCKY. Instead therefore of painting the space between the eye-brows to imitate hair, we consider it more handsome to have all the hair removed, and the eye-brows well separated. The Roman fashion, it must be confessed, formed a better outwork to prevent the perspiration of the forehead from falling into the eyes; and this, besides forming a shade for the light, is their chief office, according to Socrates, who instances the form and place of the eye-brows as a strong argument for Providence.

INDEX.

Appendix to Index.

Miscellaneous Recipes:

www.ingramcontent.com/pod-product-compliance
Lightning Source LLC
Chambersburg PA
CBHW021113270326
41929CB00009B/856

* 9 7 8 3 3 3 7 2 4 8 7 0 3 *